THE
AMERICAN
CHURCH
EXPERIENCE

THE
AMERICAN
CHURCH
EXPERIENCE

A CONCISE HISTORY

THOMAS A. ASKEW

AND RICHARD V. PIERARD

Baker Academic
A Division of Baker Book House Co
Grand Rapids, Michigan 49516

Published by Baker Academic
a division of Baker Book House Company
P.O. Box 6287, Grand Rapids, MI 49516-6287
www.bakeracademic.com

Printed in the United States of America

Library of Congress Cataloging-in-Publication Data

Askew, Thomas A.
   The American church experience : a concise history / Thomas A. Askew and Richard V. Pierard.
    p. cm.
   Includes bibliographical references and index.
   ISBN 0-8010-2722-5 (pbk.)
   1. United States—Church history. I. Pierard, Richard V., 1934– II. Title.
BR515.A845 2004
277.3—dc22   2003062916

To
Jean Mary Askew
and
Charlene Pierard
with appreciation, admiration, and affection

Contents

Preface

The tragic events of September 11, 2001, impressed on Americans how interdependent we are as a people and the role religious faith plays in contemporary society. Yet many in the pews have only the faintest awareness of the way Christianity, in all its expressions, has over the years shaped our national experience.

We wrote this overview to encourage thoughtful reflection on American church history, specifically, and the history of Christianity rather than the broader history of religion in America. The book examines a number of denominational strains and emphasizes the commonalities and interactions among the various groups rather than exploring internal denominational histories. To keep the narrative within reasonable bounds, we do not delve into many of the interpretive controversies in American church history. An extensive, up-to-date bibliography, however, can assist readers who wish to pursue specific matters in more depth.

As we trace the broad outlines of American Christianity, we pay particular attention to the evangelical tradition. The current resurgence in evangelical religion has given new visibility to what has been a vital current in American Christianity, especially in the nineteenth century and beyond. This dynamic continues to influence contemporary church life, even that of post–Vatican II Catholicism.

The word *evangelical* is ambiguous and has many doctrinal and behavioral nuances. In its broadest sense, *evangelical* is derived from the New Testament Gospels and refers to proclaiming the gospel of Christ's triumphant resurrection and sharing this "good news" with others. The Protestant Reformation churches in Germany, both Lutheran and Reformed, adopted the word *evangelical* to emphasize their primary mission of proclaiming the gospel. Elsewhere, especially in Britain and North America, people generally apply the term to that strand of the Christian tradition whose basic elements include: (1) a stress on the Bible as *the* authority for belief and practice; (2) a turning to or acceptance of Christ in faith as pivotal for the Christian life; (3) nurture as an ongoing process of cultivation of spirituality in the church and home; and (4) witnessing to one's faith in both its evangelistic and social expressions.

The words *conservative* and *liberal* as used throughout the book merit definition as well. *Conservative* appears in contexts dealing with theology and is applied to those who subscribe to the orthodox beliefs of Christianity: the divine inspiration and authority of Scripture, the Trinity, Christ's deity and atoning death, the bodily resurrection and judgment to come, the necessity of grace, and the church as the body of Christ. For stylistic variety, the word *conservative* is sometimes used in place of *evangelical,* even though we recognize that evangelical priorities reflect a mood or a perspective as much as a theology and that they have often led to actions hardly conservative in nature. The terms *liberal* and *modernist* refer to theological formulations that place less emphasis on scriptural authority, regard reason and human intuition as equally valid sources for religious truth, often give new meanings to traditional doctrines, and are this-world oriented. The designation *mainline denominations* identifies those denominational traditions whose origins lay in the colonial and pre–Civil War periods and which were the preeminent Protestant communions throughout the twentieth century. The term *secular* describes an outlook that excludes transcendence, emphasizes natural causation, and affirms modern culture in human experience.

We acknowledge the contribution of others to the making of this book. The dedication page records appreciation for our wives, Jean Mary Askew and Charlene Pierard, whose literary insights always proved instructive. Over the years, a coterie of historian colleagues have contributed more than they realize to our understanding of church history; thus, we express special gratitude to Earle Cairns, Augustus Cerillo, Robert G. Clouse, Mark Hutchinson, Robert D. Linder, Martin Marty, Mark Noll, Deborah van Broekhoven, Andrew Walls, Charles Weber, David F. Wells, and Ronald A. Wells. The same holds true of Peter W. Spellman, who two decades ago coauthored with Thomas Askew a historical survey that greatly influenced the writing of this one. Historians Russell Bishop, Nicholas Rowe, and especially Garth Rosell read all or parts of the text and offered significant suggestions. Also, thanks go to Professor Thomas R. Askew, Kalamazoo College, who shared perspectives and hard-to-locate materials. The authors are indebted to Gordon College, which offered context and climate for the writing of this book, particularly the facilities of the college's East-West Institute of International Studies, directed by Thomas A. Askew. Administrative assistants Janet Brice and Shirley Houston helpfully prepared manuscript drafts. President R. Judson Carlberg, Provost Mark Sargent, and former Dean of Chapel and East-West Institute founder Reverend Raymond C. Lee, now of Hong Kong, added encouragement along the way, as did colleagues in the college's department of history. Gordon librarian and archivist John Beauregard all along aided our research efforts, while Amy Marsella and her coworkers in the Gordon Printing Service provided needed assistance. Martha Lund Smalley, curator of the Day Missions Library at the Yale Divinity School, has rendered invaluable aid to our research over the years. Also helpful were archivists Christian Sawyer, Paul Ericksen, Robert Shuster, Wayne Weber, and Doreen Fast at the Billy Graham Center, Wheaton College. Further, we would like to thank the following individuals who helped us secure photographs: Margaret Gonsalves, Archdiocese of Boston; Betty Layton, American Baptist Historical Society; Roger Green, Gordon College; Diana Yount, Andover-Newton Theological Seminary library; David Malone, Wheaton College library; Seth Kasten, Union Theological Seminary library; Martin Noland, Concordia Historical Institute; and Edie Jeter, International Mission Board, Southern Baptist Convention. Finally, Robert N. Hosack, Melinda Van Engen, and their Baker Book House associates supported this work from the outset; without such exacting editorship the project could not have appeared in its present form. Of course, for any errors of fact or interpretation, the authors alone are responsible.

History, like memory, is essential for Christian communities. Memory reminds us of experiences we may have forgotten, and history provides insights we might otherwise have overlooked. As the saying goes, When we stand on the shoulders of those who preceded us, we can see farther. It is our hope that this book will contribute to such an enlargement of vision.

PART 1

THE
OLD WORLD
HERITAGE

1

Christianity as a World Faith

Nearly two centuries have passed since the astute French traveler Alexis de Tocqueville penned the observation, "There is no country in the whole world, in which the Christian religion retains a greater influence over the souls of men than in America."[1] Today his words ring as true as ever. In no industrialized nation is the level of commitment to the various forms of Christianity any higher than in the United States. In spite of the inroads of secularization, which have virtually de-Christianized Europe, and the legal separation of church and state that characterizes the nation's constitutional system, Americans continue to be deeply religious people, and churches play a vital role in their private as well as public lives.

Although on the surface Christianity in America appears to be a unique phenomenon, it is in fact the natural outgrowth of over a millennium of Christian development. It did not spring out of nowhere, nor was it merely an extension of the already existing churches in Europe. The faith that the early settlers brought to the New World was shaped by its physical and cultural environments, just as Christianity always reflected the character of the cultures in which the gospel message took root. Historian Andrew Walls states in his many works that while the message of Christ is for all humankind in every time and place, Jesus became flesh in a particular time and place, thus providing for the sanctification of the cultural traditions and institutions of individual peoples. The deep devotion of Americans to the

1. Alexis de Tocqueville, *Democracy in America,* vol. 1 (New York: Schocken Books, 1961), 359–60.

Christian faith and the diverse forms in which it exists today are products of its European backgrounds, the impact of widespread frontier communities inhabiting great geographic expanses, the encounter with diverse peoples, the emerging democratic values of the new republic, and the continuing waves of immigrants that swept up on the American shores. However, it is at the same time rooted in a heritage that goes back to the founding of the church.

The Origin and Expansion of Christianity

Christianity originated as an obscure Jewish sect in a distant corner of the most multicultural empire the world had ever seen. It surely would have passed away with the demise of its founder, Jesus Christ, had it not been for the vision of the disciples, who witnessed not only his tragic death but also his triumphant resurrection. These historical events inspired them to proclaim the "good news," the *evangelium*—or, in English, the "gospel"—of Christ's saving acts and the hope of eternal life. Thus, missionary expansion was the hallmark of this faith, beginning with the Great Commission, which Jesus gave to his disciples before he returned to heaven (Matt. 28:18–20). The Acts of the apostles, the fifth book of the New Testament, details the earliest outreach of that small band, beginning first in Jerusalem. They spread the message throughout Palestine and Syria, then into the Hellenistic (Greek) portion of the Roman Empire, and finally to the capital of the empire itself. There are tantalizing indications in the Bible about missionary efforts by other early Christians, and we know from contemporary sources that the faith penetrated much if not most of the Mediterranean world within two generations.

This process continued unabated, in spite of periodic persecutions.[2] The gospel was carried across the Alps into Gaul and Britain, across coastal North Africa, up the Nile River into Nubia and Ethiopia, and eastward into Mesopotamia, Armenia, Persia, and even India. In subsequent centuries, Christian missionaries traveled the Silk Road into central Asia and western China, and Christian sailors were found on the ships that plied the Indian Ocean. However, ebb and flow was to mark the progress of Christianity over the next centuries.

Constantine legalized Christianity in the Roman Empire in the fourth century, and Theodosius made it the official faith a few decades later. The imperial structure eventually disintegrated, however, under the stresses of the Barbarian (Germanic) invasions. The Roman tradition continued at the far end of the Mediterranean basin in the Byzantine East, while Islam, which arose in Arabia in the seventh century and was rapidly spread by aggressive

---

2. This process of becoming a world faith is excellently described in Dale Irwin and Scott Sunquist, *History of the World Christian Movement*, 2 vols. (Maryknoll, N.Y.: Orbis, 2001, 2005).

Arab forces, supplanted Christianity in North Africa and greatly curtailed its influence in western and central Asia.

In the West, following the Germanic migrations, only Ireland remained as an unshaken outpost of Christianity, while the papacy in Rome languished in a region dominated largely by non-Christians. From this small Celtic island began a new missionary movement that brought Christianity to the Germanic peoples who held sway in western Europe and Britain. The Germanic Christians then evangelized Scandinavia and those parts of central and eastern Europe that had not yet come under Christian influence.

Meanwhile, in the Byzantine Empire centered in Constantinople, the largely Greek-speaking Eastern or Orthodox Church took on an identity of its own that increasingly differentiated it from the Latin or Western Church. The ability of the Roman popes to exercise authority in the East declined, and in the eleventh century, the two wings of the "catholic" church separated. Meanwhile, the Orthodox Church evangelized the Slavic peoples of eastern Europe, resulting finally in the conversion of Kievan Rus and soon the more distant duchy of Moscow. Following the interlude of Mongol rule, the Muscovite Russians began their own missionary work by sending settlers eastward into Siberia.

The Byzantines came under assault from a new Islamic force, the Turks, in the eleventh century. At the same time, in the West, Latin Christianity underwent renewal, and large numbers of "crusading" knights swarmed to the East, ostensibly to rescue the Holy Land from Turkish rule. The crusaders, however, ultimately failed to achieve their objective, and two hundred years of brutal warfare contributed to a legacy of Muslim distrust of Christianity that persists to this day. The crusaders also undermined the Byzantine Empire with their attack on Constantinople in 1204, and the Byzantine state declined rapidly and fell to the Ottoman Turks in 1453. However, Eastern Orthodox Christians were allowed to survive as a tolerated minority in the vast new Ottoman Empire.

Roman Catholic Christianity Faces Increasing Difficulties

Although Roman Catholicism had established religious and cultural hegemony over western and central Europe, it faced new challenges. The Crusades resulted in the expansion of trade ties with the East, which in turn unleashed commercial impulses and a new spirit of acquisitiveness that began to displace religious fervor. The new wealth even found its way into the Roman church. The popes spent much of the fourteenth century living in luxury in Avignon, France, while the lavish lifestyles and lax behavior of popes and bishops alike invited criticism. To meet its insatiable need for money, the papacy engaged in such dubious practices as requiring holders of church offices to purchase them and selling indulgences (a reduction of time spent in purgatory). In the fifteenth century, the pope functioned largely as a Renaissance prince in Italy, living in luxury, patronizing the arts, and engaging in warfare with other princes.

Figures such as John Wyclif (c. 1320–84) in England and the Bohemian cleric John Hus (1369–1415) not only criticized the immoral behavior of the popes and bishops but also called into question a number of basic Catholic doctrines, including the role of the priest as a mediator between people and God. They supported the priesthood of *all* believers and the innate ability of common persons to read and understand Scripture. The church responded to these criticisms with persecution and even execution.

An important by-product of the establishment of commercial ties with the East was the introduction of classical texts from antiquity that had been lost to the West. This contributed to the rising spirit of intellectual inquiry that was central to the Renaissance and an emphasis on textual study. Such study led scholars to question documents the Roman church used to buttress its claims to supremacy in economic and political matters. The most famous revelation was that the Donation of Constantine, in which the great emperor gave the pope the right to rule over Rome after he moved his capital to Constantinople, was actually a forgery. The news of this cast a dark cloud over the integrity of the church. The publication of the original Hebrew and Greek texts of the Scriptures furthered the tendency to question church doctrine. The mystical devotional writings of Thomas à Kempis (1379–1471) and others and the works of the Christian humanists, above all Erasmus of Rotterdam (1466–1536), added to the spiritual ferment.

Still, when Christopher Columbus embarked on his Atlantic voyage in search of a direct trade route to Asia, the dominance of the Roman Catholic Church in a unitary Western Christendom seemed unassailable. Although financed by the Spanish throne as an economic enterprise, the expedition was seen by Columbus and his royal sponsors as a new thrust for spreading the Christian religion. Thus, Roman Catholicism arrived in the Western Hemisphere in the train of Spanish and Portuguese conquest. From the 1500s through the 1700s, Roman Catholic priest-missionaries established mission parishes as far north as the area that would later become the southwestern United States. Among the many Catholic missionaries to America, the Franciscan Junipero Serra (1713–84) remains the best known.

Priest-missionaries also engaged in extensive mission work in Asia. Jesuit leaders such as Francis Xavier established a church presence in India and Southeast Asia. Thousands became Christians in Japan through Catholic missionary effort, but persecution drove the faith underground in the 1630s and all but wiped it out. Jesuit missionaries entered China and became advisors to the emperor, while workers from various orders brought Christianity to the Philippine Islands and other areas of China.

During the 500th anniversary of the Columbian voyage in 1992, many took advantage of the opportunity to reflect on the mixed legacy of the Iberian European encounter with the peoples of the Americas. Historians freely condemned the pillage and exploitation of Native Americans, the epidemic spread of European diseases, the introduction of African slaves, and the melding of the church with Spanish imperial policy. At the same time, they had to acknowledge that some Catholic clergy worked tirelessly to champion the plight of the original inhabitants of America. For example, Bartolomé de Las Casas (1474–1566) carried his arguments all the way to the king in Madrid and the pope in Rome, but little permanent reform resulted. The indigenous peoples were forced to accept the new circumstances of life.

To serve its constituents in the Americas, the Roman Catholic Church established the first permanent Christian transatlantic institutions, including schools, universities, and publishing houses. Its attempts to minister to diverse ethnic and social populations reveal the pluralistic nature of the American experience from the beginning. Meanwhile, ecclesiastical and theological tensions were rapidly growing in Europe.

The Magisterial Reformation

In 1517, the German monk Martin Luther (1483–1546), who had discovered the concept of justification by faith through his study of Scripture, launched a

Martin Luther (1483–1546)

reform of Roman practices. At that time, Germany was divided into a number of large and small political units over which the central governments of both pope and emperor had little more than nominal control. Like England and other European countries, Germany was groping toward national unity. The emergence of a middle class and a regional army fed this embryonic nationalism. Such a context and the personal support of certain German princes enhanced Luther's influence as he moved farther and farther from Rome. Eventually, territorial churches were formed under the sponsorship and control of the rulers of various independent German states.

Others fanned into flame the spark Luther had ignited. Ulrich Zwingli (1484–1531) in Zurich and John Calvin (1509–64) in Geneva both carried out reform programs. Calvin, through the wide dissemination of his *Institutes of the Christian Religion* and his strong emphasis on divine sovereignty and representative church government, had a far-reaching influence, particularly in England, Scotland, and ultimately America. With uncontrollable rapidity, through pamphlet, sermon, and conversation, the protest against Rome spread into nearly every corner of Europe within twenty years of Luther's initial challenge.

These three figures, Luther, Zwingli, and Calvin, are often called the "magisterial" Reformers because of their willingness to link the church to the political authorities of a region. This cooperation between civic and religious authority seemed desirable for both protection and mutual support. The notion of religious freedom in the modern sense was unthinkable to them. The church and the state were to work together—the one to foster righteousness, the other to bring about external peace and punish evil deeds.

The magisterial Reformers taught that Scripture alone is the final authority in a Christian's life. The pulpit took primacy over the altar, and the sermon replaced the mass as they endeavored to introduce Bible preaching. This directly opposed the Catholic doctrine that truth is found through a combination of Scripture, tradition, and papal interpretation. A second major difference between the Reformers and the Catholic Church centered around the doctrine of salvation: How does one become a Christian? The Roman answer was again a combination. A person is saved through faith *supplemented by* good works, particularly partaking of the sacraments. The Reformers proclaimed that one attains salvation by faith alone, that is, faith in the finished work of Christ. In his *Commentary on Galatians,* Luther wrote, "By this means we are delivered from sin and justified, and eternal life is granted to us, not for our own merits and works but for our faith, by which we take hold of Christ."

The magisterial Reformers also emphasized the careful professional training of ministers, as well as general education for the laity; a view that *all* work, not just the clerical ministry, is a divine calling; and a backward-looking orientation. This last feature is often forgotten. These leaders were attempting to return the church to its roots, and they scanned the early centuries of church history for principles and models to follow. They did not limit their inquiry to the first-century apostolic church. Luther, in particular, felt that the church had retained its pristine integrity until the tenth century. Lutherans thus retained a church polity led by bishops and acknowledged that one received divine grace through participation in the sacraments. The sorry spectacle of the Crusades and papal corruption had caused the church to drift. Thus, a respect for church tradition was found in the Lutheran and Reformed groups, which constituted the so-called right wing of the Reformation.

The Radical Reformation

The left-wing groups, those of the "radical" Reformation, were quite different. Two early representatives of radical reform stand out: the German extremist Thomas Müntzer (c. 1490–1525), a former follower of Luther who led the ill-fated peasant's revolt, and the Swiss Anabaptists, who began as a dissident group of Zwingli's followers led by Conrad Grebel (1498–1526). Dissatisfied with the slow and seemingly compromising actions of their mentors, these groups insisted on returning to New Testament patterns and seeking to restore what they considered to be the apostolic church. This is why they represented a more extreme departure from the Roman inheritance. Whereas Luther and Calvin saw the church as territorial, encompassing all those in a certain region, the radicals viewed it as a voluntary body called out from society. Entrance into membership came through a new birth wrought by the Holy Spirit, registered by an individual's acceptance of God's grace, and attested to by believer's baptism. While the magisterial Reformers viewed baptism as a "sign" of membership in the Christian society that could be bestowed on all, including infants, the radicals considered baptism the visible token of the inward regeneration that had taken place. Their foes derisively called them *Ana*baptists—those who baptize *again*.

The Anabaptists were the largest and most aggressive segment of the dissident Protestants. Since they rejected the concept of a Christian state and refused to participate in its activities, they were seen as revolutionaries. If their views of nonresistance were allowed to become the norm, Protestants would not be able to defend themselves against the Catholics or the Turks, who were invading central Europe. As a result, the Anabaptists suffered martyrdom by the thousands. They stood for strict moral and ethical standards and, in general, excluded any from their fellowship who departed from these ideals.

Under the pressure of persecution, the Anabaptists, who often attracted the lower classes, divided into several groups, which made them appear all the more dangerous to the established order, especially since they had no geographic center or single formulation of the faith.

Menno Simons (1496–1561).
Courtesy of the Billy Graham
Center Museum, Wheaton, Illinois.

The Mennonites, taking their name from the influential Menno Simons (1496–1561) of Holland, were the largest of these groups. From homelands in Germany and the Low Countries, many eventually found asylum in Pennsylvania. A number of Anabaptists founded religious communities in Poland, Prussia, and Moravia, and in the late eighteenth century, many migrated to southern Russia. Other radicals chose the path of individualistic Christian mysticism and clustered into small inconspicuous groups.

Keeping aloof from middle-class culture, commercial life, and political involvement, large numbers of Anabaptists moved to the frontiers of European society where social and religious conformity were less prevalent, and the community of saints could live unmolested. Numerous Anabaptists succeeded in maintaining a community lifestyle peculiar to themselves, one that warded off the corruptions of the world. The most famous group was the Amish, a group that resulted from a schism within the Swiss Mennonites. This faction, led by Jacob Ammann, migrated to Pennsylvania in the early 1700s and maintained a traditionalist lifestyle that rejected modern dress and conveniences. Another Mennonite group, the Hutterites, founded in Moravia in 1528, practiced communitarian living. Heavily persecuted in Europe, they moved to the Ukraine and finally went to North America in the 1870s.

The tendencies and principles planted by both the magisterial and radical Reformers found fertile soil in Britain. Unique combinations from both wings emerged there and spread throughout the world. American Protestant Christianity would be conditioned in the struggles surrounding the Reformation in England.

Roman Catholic Reformation

Concurrent with the Protestant revitalization movements was a new burst of life in the Roman Catholic communion itself. Mystical writers, such as the Carmelite nun Teresa of Avila (1515–82), one of the outstanding women of Spanish history, advocated a deeper life of spirituality. The monk John of the Cross (1542–1605) wrote devotional works such as *Living Flame of Love,* which is still read today.

The Council of Trent, meeting sporadically between 1545 and 1563, sought to firm up the doctrinal foundations of the church, stem the tide of Protestant advance, and prevent the breakup of the mother church into national churches. Some have labeled this endeavor the Counter Reformation, but that term overlooks the fact that the council addressed both theological and practical issues that would strengthen the church. Salvation was declared to be obtained by faith but enhanced by human cooperation and good works. The seven sacraments were reconfirmed, but such abuses as simony (sale of church offices) and nepotism were banned. This council enforced the supreme teaching authority of the pope and bishops and specified that the Latin Vulgate was the only Bible version acceptable for use in the churches. All translations had to be based on it. Priority was also placed on the education of the priesthood and the promotion of overseas missions in newly encountered lands.

The foremost religious order that carried out the new orientation in the church was the Jesuits (Society of Jesus), founded by Ignatius Loyola (1491–1556). This order, which was directly responsible to the pope, exercised a worldwide influence through its educational work to strengthen the Catholic faith and its missionary outreach in Asia and the Americas. The greatest legacy of Jesuit work in North America were the many schools and colleges the order founded that exist to this day as beacons of Catholic learning and intellectual life.

2

The English Reformation

The English Reformation, replete with high intrigue, clashing ideals, dramatic shifts, and human frailties, is as colorful a period as any in history. This is the turbulent milieu out of which emerged the various English-speaking congregations in North America.

The Character of the English Reformation

Serious trouble erupted between England and the Roman church in the later 1520s as a result of the marital difficulties of Henry VIII. But distinct rumblings had been heard a century and a half earlier when the Oxford scholar John Wyclif openly challenged the authority of both the pope and the church by appealing directly to the New Testament. He gave the English the Scriptures in their native tongue and organized lay preachers, Lollards, to proclaim reforming ideas across the land, a message especially appealing to the lower classes.

As was the custom among royalty, the youthful Henry entered into a politically advantageous marriage to Catherine of Aragon, who had been married to his late elder brother. In 1527, after eighteen years of wedlock, during which his desperate desire for a male heir had been frustrated (only one daughter had survived infancy), Henry appealed to Pope Clement VII for an annulment of his marriage, an act forbidden by church law on the basis of Leviticus 20:21. Clement refused, as he was under pressure from Catherine's nephew, Charles V, the Holy Roman Emperor and king of Spain. But Henry would have his way. In 1533, he secretly married Anne Boleyn and had the Archbishop of Canterbury, Thomas Cranmer, annul his marriage to Catherine. The pope responded by excommunicating the king, who in turn had Parliament declare him to be "the only supreme head on earth of the Church of England." This action in 1534 made the break with Rome official.

The fact that Henry perceived his "reform" as political and ecclesiastical rather than theological was demonstrated by his official reaffirmation of Roman dogma in 1539. He did, however, make two concessions to the Protestant spirit: He issued the Great Bible in 1539, built on the translations of William Tyndale and Miles Coverdale, and he closed all the monasteries and confiscated their properties. This replenished the crown's depleted treasury, and by sharing his acquisitions with the gentry, Henry secured their loyalty and gave them an economic interest in the changes. His successors would establish Protestantism in England, but not without a hard struggle.

At his death in 1547, Henry was succeeded by his ten-year-old son, Edward VI, born of his third queen, Jane Seymour. Although he was dead by age sixteen, the deeply religious and anti-Roman Edward, who had Cranmer as his mentor, rapidly moved England in the direction of Protestantism. Images were removed from churches, English replaced Latin in worship services, priestly marriage was legalized, and the laity were allowed to receive the communion cup. To replace the Catholic order of worship, Cranmer authorized a new Book of Common Prayer, and a moderately Calvinistic creed was drawn up. Parliament officially imposed these changes on the nation, although many were still committed to the old ways.

When Edward died in 1553, his half sister, Mary Tudor, the daughter of Catherine of Aragon and an ardent Catholic, took the throne. Changes were inevitable. Mary set out to restore Catholicism by forcing Parliament to repeal the religious legislation enacted during Edward's reign. She and her cousin Reginald Cardinal Pole (the Archbishop of Canterbury) reestablished old statutes against heresy and ordered the execution of three hundred Protestants, among them five bishops, including Cranmer, Nicholas Ridley, and Hugh Latimer. Many other Protestants left England to find safety among their brethren on the Continent.

Mary's efforts were doomed to failure. Although married to Philip II of Spain, she could not produce an heir, and her half sister Elizabeth, the daughter of Henry and Anne Boleyn, waited in the wings to rule. After only five years, the sickly Mary died in 1558, having earned for herself the inglorious title Bloody Mary.

Determined to end the religious strife, Elizabeth I (1558–1603) moved to establish a national state religion—the Anglican Church—that all people were obligated to follow. Through the Elizabethan Settlement, the Church of England was given its Protestant form, which continues to this day. The

Elizabeth I (1558–1603). *Elizabetha,*
courtesy of the San Diego Museum of
Art (gift of Mr. Mifflin Ward).

1559 Act of Supremacy passed by Parliament severed all ties with Rome and
declared the monarch the "supreme governor" both politically and ecclesi-
astically. An Act of Uniformity reestablished the Book of Common Prayer,
and the Thirty-nine Articles, an outgrowth of Cranmer's creed, became the
formal doctrinal statement. Its moderation satisfied everyone except hard-line
Catholics. The church retained the pre-Reformation hierarchical structure of
bishops and parish priests.

To the north, an alliance of Scottish nobles and middle-class townsmen
moved Scotland toward a Calvinistic church, in spite of the existence of a
Catholic monarch, Mary Stuart (Queen of Scots). Led by the fearless John
Knox (1505–72), a former priest who had studied in Geneva with John
Calvin, the Scottish Parliament in 1560 severed ties with the Roman church.
A presbyterian form of church government was instituted with ruling elders
in the congregations, elected presbyteries of laypeople and clergy that would
oversee several congregations, synods encompassing a larger geographical
area, and a national assembly. Mary's tempestuous personal life as well as
the struggle with Knox led to her abdication, exile in England, and eventual
execution by Elizabeth. When Mary's son, James VI of Scotland, succeeded
to the English throne as James I, he unified the two Protestant nations under
one ruler, although each nation possessed its own style of established religion:
episcopacy in England and presbyterianism in Scotland. Presbyterianism in
America descended from the Scottish Reformation, as many Scots migrated
to Northern Ireland in the early 1600s, and a century later their descendants
crossed the Atlantic to find new homes in the colonies.

Meanwhile, a division occurred within Calvinism on the Continent that would influence the development of Christianity in England and in America. The Dutch theologian Jacobus Arminius (1560–1609) called into question some basic tenets of Calvinism, and his followers quickly spread the new ideas in the Dutch church. In short, the Arminians rejected Calvinist predestination and the limitation of Christ's atonement to those who are "elect." Because people have free will, it was possible to reject the promptings of the Holy Spirit and spurn the offer of salvation. Believers who turn away from Christ can fall from grace. The Arminians were condemned at the Synod of Dort (1618–19), thus ensuring that the Dutch and German Calvinists, as well as their American descendants, would adhere to Calvinist orthodoxy. In England, however, the anti-Calvinist movement identified with Archbishop William Laud (1573–1645) and the later Methodist movement of John Wesley were influenced by Arminianism.

The Emergence of a Puritan Faction

Some individuals in England wanted to push reform farther than their political superiors would allow. Strongly influenced by Calvin's teaching, these Protestants were uncomfortable with practices too Roman for their liking and called for purification of the English church, thus earning the derisive nickname Puritan. They actually were divided. Some wanted the state church in England reorganized on the pattern of Calvinistic churches with a presbyterian form of government. Others desired a national church that allowed each local congregation to regulate its own affairs. A small, more radical Calvinist group, usually labeled Separatists, rejected the state church entirely and, like the Anabaptists, held to the idea of a "gathered" body of believers who were united in a voluntary church covenant. They were persecuted for their views.

Both of the main Puritan factions gained adherents during the long reign of Elizabeth and waited anxiously for the chance to gain superiority. There was excitement in Puritan circles when James Stuart of Scotland inherited the English throne in 1603, but hopes quickly evaporated when James stoutly affirmed the episcopal model of bishops and king. His one concession to the Puritans was the authorization of a new translation of Scripture. It was completed in 1611 and is known to this day as the Authorized or King James Version of the Bible. Puritanism, meanwhile, gained support in Parliament, and its influence spread among the populace.

When Charles I (ruled 1625–49) came to the throne, he felt threatened by the democratizing influence of Puritanism. He strongly asserted his "divine right" to rule, supported the episcopal structure of the Church of England, and insisted on liturgical unity, which alienated the Puritans. Parliament resisted

Oliver Cromwell (1599–1658)

the king's attempts to impose monarchical absolutism in England, and tensions finally erupted in civil war in 1642. The Puritan opponents of the king gained the support of the Scots by agreeing to adopt the presbyterian form of church government in the Church of England.

A Puritan member of Parliament, Oliver Cromwell (1599–1658), created his own regiment and soon became leader of the parliamentary forces. The conflict became more complicated as various radicals, such as Baptists and millenarians (those looking for the coming kingdom of Christ), rose to positions of influence in Cromwell's forces. Within five years, the parliamentary forces were essentially victorious, but the king saw divisions within the ranks of the Puritans and resumed the conflict. His army was quickly defeated, and the extremists in Parliament secured his execution in 1649. The monarchy was abolished, and Cromwell led the Commonwealth, as the new republic was called, until his death in 1658.

Meanwhile, Parliament had abolished episcopacy in 1643 and had authorized a body composed of Puritans and Scottish Presbyterians, known as the Westminster Assembly, to draft a new Calvinistic system of worship, theology, and church polity. In 1647, the Westminster Confession of Faith was adopted, making the Anglican Church both Calvinistic and presbyterian. It remained in effect until the restoration of the monarchy under Charles II in 1660, when episcopacy was again reinstated. However, the Westminster Confession would remain the cornerstone of both British and American Presbyterianism.

Under Cromwell a degree of religious tolerance for non-Anglicans was practiced, and new Christian sects appeared. One such sect was the Quakers, founded by George Fox around 1650 as the Friends of Truth. They taught that Christians should be guided by the "Inner Light," that is, God's voice speaking directly to the soul. By 1670, Fox's Friends had become a significant group, one that emphasized the indwelling light; worship in plain meeting houses without ministers, sacraments, or liturgy; commitment to nonviolence; and the equality of men and women.

In 1660, Charles II took control of the throne. At once he began flirting with Catholicism, and Parliament passed several measures to restrain its influence, most notably the Test Act of 1673, which permitted only members of the Church of England to hold public office. Thus, the Dissenting or Nonconformist Protestant bodies lost the freedom they had enjoyed during the Cromwell era. Then Charles's brother, who reigned as James II (1685–88), openly professed the Catholic faith and resisted parliamentary claims to authority. In 1688, he was overthrown and replaced by his Protestant cousins from Holland, William and Mary, and Parliament affirmed its rights vis-à-vis the king in the famous Bill of Rights of 1689. This Glorious Revolution marked the decisive end of royal absolutism in England. As part of the revolution settlement, the Nonconformists were allowed freedom of worship through the Toleration Act of 1689, but they continued to be barred from participation in public life.

A New World Beckons

Queen Elizabeth's policies did not fully resolve the problem of religious differences in England. Yet in spite of the dissenters, Elizabeth was satisfied that internal religious strife had abated. In England's bitter struggle with Spain, whose ruler Philip II wanted to depose Elizabeth and restore Catholicism in England, Elizabeth had emerged victorious, and a modicum of stability had returned to the nation. The regime could now consider expansion in America, but the English failed to establish a permanent foothold there before her death in 1603. With the accession of James I, who possessed little personal wealth of his own, prospects for successful English colonization of America seemed dim. The only way to push forward British expansion was through the help of private investors.

Joint-stock companies such as the London Company and the Plymouth Company were granted the rights to engage in commerce and to exercise limited political powers, enabling them to become overseas arms of British authority. When the London Company placed a settlement on the banks of the James River in 1607, the stage was set for the development of a British colonial system and with it the establishment of English-speaking churches.

PART 2

COLONIAL FOUNDATIONS (1607–1783)

3

Church Planting
on the Atlantic Seaboard

Although English seamen had scouted the North American coastline during much of the sixteenth century, and several had even set up temporary fishing stations, lasting colonization did not begin until May 24, 1607, when three ships with a handful of men landed on the shore of a place called Virginia, after the "Virgin Queen," Elizabeth I.

Established-Church Beginnings in America: Anglicanism

The instructions of James I in the first charter of Virginia were explicit: "The true word and service of God" was to be "preached, planted, and used" in the new colony "according to the doctrine, rights, and religion now professed and established within our realm of England." On the surface, the basis of the first permanent English colony in America was religious. However, religious motives were anything but primary for the London merchants who financed the venture. The Virginians, like most early settlers, sought commercial profits. They expected treasure, such as Spain had been extracting from their American territories. But whether an individual was nominal or fervent in his beliefs, the Christian religion deeply influenced these early Americans. It was part and parcel of the spiritual environment in their native land, and it formed the ideological basis for law, family life, and government in the New World.

The first decades of Virginia's history were fraught with difficulties. After the harsh winter of 1609–10, only sixty of the five hundred settlers were still alive. The colonists came close to abandoning the site, but the able leadership of the governor, Lord De La Warr, restored their determination to continue. What early hopes there were of Christianizing the Native Americans came to naught, and warfare with the aboriginal inhabitants decimated the population of Jamestown in 1622 and 1644.

Despite its grave troubles, the colony retained its religious base. Between 1607 and 1619, the Virginia Company guided the colony's religious affairs from London by determining church policies and sending ministers. The Virginia House of Burgesses, a local representative body of colonists created in 1619, had the responsibility of ecclesiastical legislation. Only when a royal governor was appointed in 1624 was Anglicanism "established" in Virginia. With establishment the church became an official tax-supported church. It was authorized to hold public worship, it could expel those who dissented from the orthodox doctrinal position, and its members alone were eligible to vote and hold public office. This establishment persisted in Virginia until the American Revolution, although by 1700 Quakers and Baptists were present in the colony, and other denominations soon arrived.

In 1720, there were forty-four unevenly sized parishes in Virginia, each with a church and possibly an auxiliary chapel, placing the total number of places of worship at roughly seventy. Unlike New England, Virginia lacked a college for pastoral training, and able ministers were in short supply. Even after the College of William and Mary opened in 1693, young men who desired ordination to the Anglican ministry were compelled to travel to England, as only a bishop could ordain new clergy. Sustaining vital parishes was always problematic, given the wide geographic area involved. American spaciousness presented a challenge and an opportunity for the many varieties of Christianity that would eventually flourish in North America.

Church life in early Virginia was also affected by the dramatic rise of tobacco culture and the accompanying dependence on African slave labor. Importation of Africans to supplement the handful of white indentured servants in the labor force began in 1619 and reached its zenith in the next century when chattel slavery was fully defined in law. Slavery became a fundamental feature of Virginian culture, as it would in the other southern colonies, where agricultural needs made the institution profitable. The tragic reality is that, with the exception of a few Protestant radicals, slavery was universally accepted in the seventeenth century.

As the Africans adjusted to their new existence, they were not receptive to the religion of the Europeans, who displayed little commitment to Christianizing the slaves. Several colonies even passed legislation stating that baptism of a slave did not confer on him or her the right to freedom. Gradually, however, the gospel found its way into the slave community, and many blacks adapted it in creative ways, both to their particular plight and to the style of religious celebration indigenous to their African homeland. The founding of black churches, however, was still a long way off.

The lands south of Virginia, colonized as the Carolinas and Georgia, also maintained a nominal Anglican establishment, although it was less organized than in Virginia. Most of the inland inhabitants were Quakers and, later, Scotch-Irish Presbyterians. Anglicanism, however, was officially established in South Carolina in 1706, in North Carolina in 1715, and in Georgia in 1758. Designed to assist the Anglican establishment were two new bodies, the Society for Promoting Christian Knowledge (1698), which began as a venture to provide Christian books for ministers in the colonies, and the Society for the Propagation of the Gospel in Foreign Parts (1701), which sent missionaries to work among the Indians.

Roman Catholic New France

In 1608, the year following the settlement of Jamestown, Quebec was founded by Samuel de Champlain. Though French Protestant Huguenots participated in the early years of Quebec's development, the colony soon withdrew the Protestants' rights, resulting in a society dominated by Roman Catholicism, a reality that continues to the present.

The French explorations in the North American interior and their mission efforts among the native peoples were extensive. Women were active in the mission in New France, the best known being the Ursuline nun Marie Guijart (1599–1672), who prepared grammars, catechisms, and liturgies in the Huron and Algonquin languages. Jesuit Jean de Brébeuf (1593–1649) adapted to Huron culture, and his Georgian Bay mission was quite advanced for the times in that the Native American converts were not forced to give up their traditional ways of life. The Iroquois, however, attacked the mission in 1619 and killed Brébeuf, the other missionaries, and their Huron converts.

Jesuit missionary Jacques Marquette (1637–75) and Franciscan Louis Hennepin (1626–c. 1705) assisted French explorers in the interior. French trading posts and missions were founded throughout the Great Lakes and Mississippi Valley regions. Vincennes, on the Wabash River, was a strategic center and religious outpost. These areas came under British colonial control after 1763, and the influence of French Catholic missions declined thereafter. The territory south of the Great Lakes and east of the Mississippi River was ceded to the newly formed United States in 1783. The legacy of Roman Catholic mission efforts in the heartland of the continent is reflected today in the scattered French place names.

The Plymouth Colony in New England

In 1609, a group of Calvinistic English Separatists who had formed a dissenting congregation at Scrooby in Nottinghamshire wearied of persecution in England and took refuge in Holland. After a decade in Leiden, a number of them arranged with the Plymouth Company to sail aboard the *Mayflower* bound for Virginia, where they hoped to form a new English community. In September 1620, thirty-five Separatist "Pilgrims" on their way to a "New Jerusalem" set sail with sixty-six other passengers ("Saints" and "Strangers," as they were classified on the passenger list) on their historic voyage to America.

Strong winds and storms drove the *Mayflower* off course, bringing it to the forbidding shores of Cape Cod. Outside the authority of their charter, the group adopted its famous self-governing compact on board the tiny ship and spent the long winter suffering the effects of inadequate food and disease. Still, in the spring, not a single Pilgrim returned to England. Their view of God's sovereignty and providence gave them the inner strength they needed to confront the harsh conditions and maintain their independence from the Church of England. In a few weeks, a settlement named Plymouth was organized. It maintained a separate identity until 1691, when it was absorbed into Massachusetts by a new royal charter. Though politically weak and economically limited, the Pilgrims had a strong faith, a heartfelt gratitude, and a sense of calling not unlike that of ancient Israel, as was so well expressed in the writings of their governor William Bradford. They became the enduring symbol of American religious identity.

Religious Diversity in the Middle Colonies

Located between Virginia and Connecticut, New Netherland (later New York) was originally settled by the Dutch West India Company in the 1620s. Crippled by mismanagement, internal dissension, and extremely slow growth, it was an inviting target for expansionist-minded England. In 1664, James, Duke of York and brother of Charles II, sponsored the naval operation that secured New Netherland's peaceful surrender. At the time of the takeover, the colony was the most religiously heterogeneous in America and a portrait of the later religious makeup of the other colonies. Dutch Reformed, French Calvinists (Huguenots), German Lutherans, New England Congregationalists, Quakers, Mennonites, Baptists, Roman Catholics, and a few Jews encountered one another on Manhattan Island and in the surrounding area. After repeated rebuffs by the Dutch population, the royal governor in 1693 finally induced the New York Assembly to adopt a vague establishment law under which Anglicanism became the official faith in four of the counties.

The Roman Catholic George Calvert Lord Baltimore (c. 1580–1632) set out to found the first colony in America that embodied the principle of religious toleration. He received a land grant from Charles I in 1632 but died before he could make use of it. His son, Cecil Calvert (1605–75), founded Maryland, where Catholics were in the minority. The assembly passed the Act of Toleration in 1649, granting freedom to all Christians. Though the law is frequently hailed as a great advance toward religious liberty, it was also economically and politically motivated. It was rescinded five years later by the Puritan-controlled Commonwealth in England. After decades of religious and political animosity, Anglicans gained control of the assembly and made the Church of England the official church in 1702. There would not be another noteworthy influx of Roman Catholics into America until the Irish migrations of the nineteenth century and the annexation of Mexican lands in 1848.

Although the Dutch Reformed Church had been "established" in New Netherland by the Dutch West India Company, the original settlers lacked religious fervor. They had not emigrated to escape religious persecution, for Holland was the chief European sanctuary for the persecuted. Trading, especially in furs, was their interest, and only roughly seven thousand Dutch ever came to the colony in spite of incentives to stimulate growth. Under English rule, the Dutch Reformed Church, consisting of only a dozen or so struggling congregations, continued to worship in freedom. The most serious obstacle was not the English government but disinterest and complacency. Not until the preaching of one of its ministers, Theodore Frelinghuysen, put into motion the forces of the Great Awakening were the Dutch churches—especially those in New Jersey—roused out of lethargy. Still, the Dutch Reformed were the principal practitioners of Calvinistic Presbyterianism in seventeenth-century America.

Following George Fox's ministry in England, Quakers appeared in every British colony during the last half of the seventeenth century. The center of Quaker activity in America was New Jersey and the Delaware Valley. By 1681, more than one thousand immigrants, mostly Quakers, had arrived in New Jersey.

In that year, the crown gave William Penn (1644–1718) a large grant of land in consideration of a debt due his late father, and it was named Pennsylvania. He called his colonial enterprise "an Holy Experiment," one in which all Christians could worship God in peace and love. He even recognized the rights of the aboriginal inhabitants in his newly acquired territory.

The population grew rapidly, numbering twelve thousand by 1689. By this time, most colonial laws against Quakers had been abolished. As wealth increased and a new generation arose, spiritual life seemed to decline. Traveling Friends (Quakers) in the early eighteenth century spoke of "a dry lifeless state" in many of their meetings and "excessive drinking" among a number of their members. Still, their number continued to increase, and these Christians outpaced all others in the American colonies in their concern for Indian rights, the plight of slaves, and nonviolence.

Late in the seventeenth century, many Germans began leaving their homeland for America. Religious intolerance, wars, and economic uncertainty drove thousands to seek a new life abroad. The first German settlement in America was Germantown, near Philadelphia, where a group of Mennonites arrived in 1683 from the Palatinate. Many of them eventually made their way west to Lancaster County. They eschewed outward ritualism and elaborate scholastic theology in favor of a religion of the heart. Maintaining a sharp division between church and state, they were pacifistic, refused to swear oaths in court, and opposed government control of private matters. Old Order Mennonites, particularly the Amish, were part of the immigration and adopted a distinctive lifestyle. Later German groups included the Dunkers or Brethren (1719), the Schwenkfelders (1734), and the Moravians (1735). Such groups first settled in eastern Pennsylvania, which became a haven for religious minorities, and quickly spread westward.

German Lutherans were found as early as 1649 in New Amsterdam. After the turn of the century, the Lutheran church in America began to grow, especially in Pennsylvania. The German Reformed, who came from Switzerland and the Rhineland, planted their first church in Germantown in 1719. Marked by a Presbyterian polity and a rich devotional tradition, they had perhaps fifteen thousand adherents in Pennsylvania by 1730. In doctrine and worship, they were much like the Lutherans, and the two groups lived in reasonable harmony. With the exception of the Mennonites, most German groups had been affected by Pietism, a major revitalization movement that stressed a new birth, holy living, emotional experiential religion, devotional Bible study, domestic and foreign missions, and ecumenical contacts among awakened Christians.

Thus, within its first century, American religious life took on the diverse quality that would characterize its entire history. Some settlers came for commercial gain, while others sought a place to worship God in their own way. The geographic expansiveness, rigorous frontier environment, separation from European restraints, and presence of many Christian groups created a climate that nurtured religious diversity and advanced social and personal freedom. The precedent set in the middle colonies, an area often given short shrift in accounts of the religious history of early America, actually became normative in the later development of American religious identity and is deserving of scholarly attention.

The Puritan Commonwealth in New England

The most complete attempt to erect a Protestant commonwealth in the New World was that of the Puritans. Their migrations to Massachusetts and other places in what came to be known as New England swelled after Charles I insisted on adherence to the doctrines and principles of episcopal Anglicanism. Between 1630 and 1640, some twenty thousand people left England in search of more supportive surroundings. Most of these migrants settled in the Puritan colony on Massachusetts Bay north of Plymouth. Their enterprise began in 1629 as a chartered joint-stock company and rapidly transformed the region into a large and influential colony. These settlers were inspired by the Calvinistic ideal of living in covenant relationship with God, and their vision was to erect a cultural and social order under God's sovereignty that would be "a city on a hill" for all Christians to emulate.

The oldest remaining Puritan meeting house in New England, Hingham, Massachusetts, built in 1680

These Puritans claimed to be members of the Church of England, but once they crossed the Atlantic, bringing their charter with them, they became functionally independent of the Anglican Church, as were the Separatists at Plymouth. They instituted in Massachusetts the type of church they had wanted in England—a church with a congregational polity, without bishops or hierarchical structure, with authority residing in the individual congregations, and whose ministers met in synods to provide coordination of their efforts. Thus, Congregationalism took root in America.

Stripped of all the outward signs and symbols of Anglicanism, their churches were simple meetinghouses where congregations gathered both to worship and to conduct the political business of the community. Services consisted of psalms, hymns, prayers, a sermon, and communion. However, as Harry S. Stout shows in *The New England Soul* (1986), preaching was paramount in the Puritan worship experience. There were also weekday lectures to supplement the Sabbath worship. Although no central authority existed to enforce uniformity among the congregations, those who lived in the Puritan towns were clearly expected to conform to certain basic moral and religious beliefs.

Next to religion, the Puritan settlers of New England valued education. In 1636, in the midst of their struggles with poverty, they established a college at Cambridge that was later named Harvard. Publicly supported common schools soon appeared in their settlements in Massachusetts and Connecticut, and another college, Yale, was founded in New Haven in 1701.

With Governor John Winthrop (1588–1649) overseeing the political welfare of the community and John Cotton (1584–1652) and other preachers presiding over its spiritual destiny, church and state moved hand in hand in the Massachusetts Bay Colony. Only Congregationalists were permitted to hold the title of freeman and to participate in the colony's political life. Those who did not practice Congregationalism, such as Baptists, were permitted to reside in the colony as long as they did not cause disturbances. They were excluded from politics, however, and were obligated to support the established church.

Another center of Puritan life was the Connecticut River valley. In 1635, Thomas Hooker (1586?–1647) and his Newtown congregation were granted permission to migrate westward to this region and found a new colony. Others followed, establishing settlements at Windsor, Hartford, and Wethersfield. Hooker had a less restrictive view of church membership. The Fundamental Orders of Connecticut, adopted in 1639, did not require freemen to be church members. In 1662, the Connecticut settlements were joined into a united colony, including the stricter "Bible Commonwealth" founded by the Reverend John Davenport at New Haven in 1638.

From the outset, the English settlers lived in proximity to and traded with the Native Americans, whom some Puritan ministers sought to evangelize. Most successful were John Eliot (1604–90), who organized "praying towns" of Christianized Indians in eastern Massachusetts, and Thomas Mayhew Jr. (1621–57), who did likewise on Martha's Vineyard and in Nantucket. To assist mission efforts, Eliot translated the New Testament into Algonquin, the first Bible published in America. The Europeans expected the "praying Indians" to abandon their traditional ways and to adopt a lifestyle similar to that of the English farmers, an expectation that was not welcomed by most native peoples. King Phillip's War (1675–76), named after a chief, was an attempt by Native Americans to halt white settlement and severely tested the faith of the Indian converts. The warring tribes mistrusted the Indian Christians, and the Massachusetts authorities were suspicious of them as well. As a result, many of the Indian believers were imprisoned on an island in Boston Harbor and eventually sent into slavery in the West Indies. The conflict severely damaged the appeal of the gospel to New England's original inhabitants.

John Eliot (1604–90). Courtesy of the Billy Graham Center Museum, Wheaton, Illinois.

The tight-knit religious community could function only as long as the population was of a manageable size. As the seventeenth century progressed, the first signs of the religious diversity that would characterize later American life appeared in the New England colonies. Neither the Puritan saint nor the Anglican divine was intellectually or socially prepared to tolerate the dissent that began to weaken the foundations of their ideal social order.

The first to rebel openly was Roger Williams (1604?–84), an eloquent young pastor from Salem. He challenged the validity of the royal charter on the grounds that it allowed settlers to take Indian lands without adequate payment. He also publicly assailed the union of church and state, questioned the right of civil authorities to legislate in matters of conscience, and urged the Salem congregation to separate from the rest. The majority of his church seemed ready to follow him.

Such outspoken views were considered dangerous by the Puritan leaders, who feared that such dissension would tear apart the entire social fabric. They also feared intervention by England, which was growing suspicious of the young colony. In 1635, the elected assembly, the General Court, banished Williams from Massachusetts Bay. He fled and founded a settlement in Rhode Island that in gratitude he named Providence. Here there were no religious requirements for political involvement, no taxes to support an official church, and no compulsory church attendance. The religious toleration of the territory quickly drew other dissidents, especially Baptists, who founded churches in Providence and Newport by the late 1630s.

Anne Hutchinson (1591–1643), a formidable woman who challenged customary gender roles by leading independent theological discussions, was also seen as a threat to the social order and was found guilty of sedition at an ecclesiastical trial in Boston in 1638. Stressing grace rather than works and emphasizing personal revelation (her accusers labeled this antinomianism), she antagonized the orthodox leadership, who ordered her banishment even though she was pregnant. In 1638, she and her followers founded Pocasset (Portsmouth) only a short distance from Providence. A few years later, the Baptist Obadiah Holmes was publicly flogged in Boston for unauthorized preaching.

The arrival in Boston in 1656 of two female Quaker missionaries provoked an immediate retribution by the civil authorities, who imprisoned and swiftly deported them. The Massachusetts General Court then enacted a law imposing harsh punishments on Quakers, who were viewed as heretics because they claimed direct revelation from God. A similar law was passed in Virginia in 1660. Ultimately, three Quaker men and one woman, Mary Dyer (1605–60), were hanged in Boston after they ignored warnings to stay away. The colony's leaders soon realized that such extreme measures were as ineffectual as they were cruel, and they were abandoned.

Religious dissent was only one factor in the erosion of Puritan hegemony. While Oliver Cromwell ruled in England (1649–58), New England Puritanism thrived, and the mother country exerted little influence on the political affairs of the colonies. After the restoration of the Stuart monarchy in 1660, however, both New England's autonomy and Puritanism's control over the populace declined. Charles II ordered that liberty of worship be granted to Anglicans, that they be permitted to partake of the Lord's Supper in Congregational churches, and that baptism be extended to their children. The Puritans refused, and the king responded by revoking the Massachusetts Bay charter in 1684. In 1691, Massachusetts was forced to accept a royal governor and a new charter that was highly distasteful to the Puritans because it banned all religious tests for suffrage. From that time on, the established social order was seriously weakened, although Congregationalism itself was not fully disestablished until 1833.

Further evidence of religious tension were the infamous witch trials held in Salem in 1692. Based on "spectral evidence," twenty people accused of being witches were found guilty and were put to death before the mass hysteria subsided. The incident reduced respect for the colony's clergy and in the long run dealt a severe blow to the credibility of Puritanism itself.

Along with religious dissent and political changes came significant revisions of church policy, the most important being the Halfway Covenant. This was essentially an attempt to accommodate the new generation of Puritans who had been baptized as infants and did not profess a conversion experience. The Massachusetts Synod of 1662 ruled that baptized adults who lived uprightly could be accepted as church members, an important matter because voting rights depended on church membership. Their children, however, baptized as "halfway" members, could not receive the Lord's Supper or participate in church elections.

Such events reflected that spiritual vitality was waning in New England, and the number of members in full communion with the church declined. To many it seemed that the judgment of God was being poured out on a sinful people. Preachers responded by publishing jeremiads (named after the Old Testament prophet), calling New England back to its holy "errand in the wilderness." Even poets added their voices to the lamentation. In an epic poem written in 1662 titled *God's Controversy with New England,* Michael Wigglesworth (1631–1705) has God wondering about his now profligate people:

> What should I do with such a stiff-neckt race?
> How shall I ease me of such Foes as they?
> What shall befall despizers of my Grace?
> I'll surely beare their candlestick away!
> And Lamps put out Their glorious noon-day light.
> I'll quickly turn into a dark Egyptian night.[1]

The vision of the founding fathers was fading. The efforts of Boston's great Puritan preacher Cotton Mather (1663–1728), who combined piety and intellect in summoning the Bay Colony back to its spiritual heritage, had little effect. He authored the most important work of historiography in the New England colonies, the *Magnolia Christi Americana* (1702), and recounted the wonderful works of God in the New World across the sea, but the challenges he laid down had little effect in bringing the people to repentance. Most people turned their attention to commerce and worldly gain, and New England became less a religious refuge and more a land of economic opportunity.

1. *Proceedings of the Massachusetts Historical Society* 12 (1873): 83–93.

Cotton Mather (1663–1728). Courtesy
of the Billy Graham Museum, Wheaton,
Illinois.

Although it had largely lost its defining authority by 1720, the Puritan tradition persisted in such distinctively American qualities as respect for lawful
government, the value of useful work, civic participation and responsibility,
concern for education, and the sense that the nation under divine guidance
had a special mission in the world. It also provided the religious background
for many of the moral and social reform movements that emanated from
New England in the nineteenth century.

4

Rekindling the Spiritual Vision

In the eighteenth century, America was drawing immigrants from all over western Europe, while at the same time the religious ardor that had marked its early years was cooling. As the prospects for economic advantage expanded, Puritans became Yankees and Anglicans evolved into country gentlemen. Still, the Jeremiahs persisted in preaching, and their lamentations gained intensity. In the second quarter of the eighteenth century, their proclamations finally bore fruit in a new wave of religious devotion called the Great Awakening.

The Great Awakening in America was one of many awakenings occurring in the Protestant world during the eighteenth century. England, Scotland, Wales, and Germany all experienced scattered revivals of religious life. Most noteworthy were the evangelical revival within the Anglican Church and the more Arminian-oriented Wesleyan movement. Churches from many denominations were affected by this resurgence of religious ardor.

Besides the waning of spiritual interest in favor of material gain, other conditions contributed to making America ripe for revival. Conflicts with the French and the Indians created unrest among the settlers. British interference in colonial affairs exacerbated fears about the future and made politics a central topic of conversation as well as a divisive influence. These disturbing conditions occupied public attention at the expense of moral and religious affairs. Winds of the rationalistic European Enlightenment also crossed the Atlantic, penetrating the minds of church leaders and contributing to a decline in spiritual zeal.

Awakening in the Middle Colonies

The initial signs of awakening in America occurred among the Dutch Reformed and the Presbyterians of New Jersey. The first movement toward spiritual revitalization took place in Raritan, New Jersey, under the fervent preaching of Theodore Frelinghuysen (1691–1748), a Dutch Reformed minister who had been inspired by Continental Pietism before assuming a pastorate in New Jersey in 1720. Emphasizing personal conversion, holiness of life, and high standards for partaking of the Lord's Supper, Frelinghuysen directly influenced William Tennent and his sons, who led a renewal among New Jersey Presbyterians. These events marked the beginning of the Great Awakening.

Presbyterianism, with its emphasis on a church governed by elders (presbyters) elected by the people of a congregation or a group of congregations, prevailed in the Netherlands, parts of Germany, Switzerland, France, and Scotland. Immigrants from these countries settled in the American colonies. The main strength of American Presbyterianism, however, derived from the migrations of Scots from Northern Ireland in the eighteenth century. In an effort to displace the Roman Catholic population of Northern Ireland, James I confiscated their property and turned it over to Scots, who were resettled there. But trouble plagued the new arrivals. Leases were rearranged to their disadvantage, government restrictions on wool production choked the economy, and the Anglican-controlled Irish Parliament passed legislation in 1704 that denied Presbyterians the right to hold public office. These grievances convinced many to go to the New World.

Scotch-Irish immigration grew rapidly after 1710. A large number arrived in New England in 1718, and by mid-century, one-fourth of all Pennsylvanians were Scotch-Irish. The first Scots presbytery in America was organized in 1706 in Philadelphia under the leadership of Francis Makemie (1658–1708), an itinerant preacher. In 1716, a synod was formed containing three presbyteries, Philadelphia, New Castle, and Long Island.

Two problems confronted the young church: No ministerial training was available in America outside New England, and the procedures for examining immigrant ministers were inadequate. The latter was resolved by the Adopting Act of 1729, which required all ministers to assent to the Westminster Confession. Then new difficulties arose as a result of a group led by William Tennent Sr. (1673–1746), a Scottish minister educated at Edinburgh University, and his sons, Gilbert, John, and William Jr. They settled in New Jersey and fostered an experiential form of evangelical Calvinism, teaching that a definite experience of regeneration was the indispensable mark of a Christian. Many Presbyterian clergy disapproved of the Tennents' emotional style of preaching, but the revival party was aided by the establishment of a seminary at Neshaminy, near Philadelphia, in 1727. The "Log College," as its enemies called it, produced nearly a score of pietistic revivalist ministers for the Presbyterian churches.

In 1739, the youthful and zealous English preacher George Whitefield (1714–70) made a mission tour of the middle colonies and by so doing linked the English and the colonial awakenings. Whitefield's many preaching tours to America and his extensive ministries across the widely scattered territories made him one of the most widely known figures in the colonies.

George Whitefield (1714–70). Courtesy of the Billy Graham Museum, Wheaton, Illinois.

The impact of Whitefield's emotionally poignant, graphic, and plainspoken preaching style on future American revival rhetoric was substantial. Whereas traditional sermons, even conversion-oriented ones, tended to be carefully drawn theological and exegetical treatises, Whitefield's powerful oratory probed the feelings and emotions of ordinary listeners. Both in church buildings and at huge outdoor gatherings, he proclaimed religion as a matter of the heart. At times acting out biblical narratives and on other occasions shedding tears, he portrayed the hope of heaven and the terror of damnation with equal importunity. In the middle colonies, his preaching invigorated the revivalists and resulted in a large increase in their numbers. The anti-revival faction was unhappy with this development, and a split among Presbyterians occurred between the "Old Side" and the "New Side" in 1741. The revivalist New Sides sought to strengthen their cause by founding the College of New Jersey (later Princeton) in 1746. After some initial setbacks (five presidents died within twenty years, including Jonathan Edwards), the new institution emerged as the educational mainstay of the entire region.

The Great Awakening in New England

The same forces that sparked revival in the middle colonies were at work in New England. The northern phase was initiated by the preaching of Congregational pastor Jonathan Edwards (1703–58) at Northampton, Massachusetts, in 1734.

Jonathan Edwards (1703–58). Joseph Badger, *Reverend Jonathan Edwards*. Courtesy of the Yale University Art Gallery. Bequest of Eugene Phelps Edwards.

Edwards was the son and grandson of Congregational ministers, a man of extraordinary intellectual gifts and intense religious piety—that rare combination of scholar and saint. Educated at Yale, he began his career as the assistant pastor to his grandfather, Solomon Stoddard, at Northampton in 1727. Two years later, when Stoddard died, Edwards assumed full pastoral duties. It is difficult to imagine how Edwards's meticulously logical sermons, read by a man of such slight frame, could rouse a congregation to anything beyond complacent assent. But the message itself and the sincerity with which it was delivered pierced his listeners' hearts. A sense of anxiety and fear of God's wrath gripped Northampton during 1734. Within six months, three hundred people were converted and received into the church. The revival spread through the Connecticut Valley and to Long Island, where it was taken up by other preachers.

In 1740, Whitefield came to Northampton, and his preaching led to two years of continuous revival. Whitefield, along with Gilbert Tennent, Eleazer Wheelock, and Joseph Bellamy, toured the region as itinerant "New Light" evangelists, preaching to thousands. By 1742, twenty-five to fifty thousand people had been added to the New England churches, nearly a quarter of the total population of the area.

Edwards was more than the leader of a revival; he was also a theologian and a philosopher, perhaps the greatest mind of the colonial era. Amid his duties as father, husband, and pastor, he managed to write a number of significant books: *A Faithful Narrative of the Surprising Work of God in the Conversion of Many Hundred Souls in Northampton* (1737), *The Distinguishing Marks of a Work of the Spirit of God* (1741), *Freedom of the Will* (1754), *The Nature of True Virtue* (1755), and *The Great Christian Doctrine of Original Sin Defended* (1758). The first, *A Faithful Narrative*, had a profound effect on both John Wesley and Whitefield. Most of Edwards's theological labor defended traditional Calvinistic orthodoxy against the seemingly relentless inroads of Arminianism. In other words, he endeavored to reconcile the revival with Calvinism. Although he supported a declining cause, his work was a seminal influence on the whole course of American theological development, as indicated by the fact that his writings are still in print and widely read and appreciated.

Revival in the South

In the first half of the eighteenth century, the Baptists were a relatively weak and scattered denomination, especially in the South. The picture changed, however, with the coming of the Great Awakening, which had largely run its course in the middle colonies and New England by the end of the 1740s. Influenced by the revival in New England was a group known as the Separate Baptists. Led by Shubal Stearns, originally a New Light Congregationalist, they arrived in North Carolina in 1755 and settled in the Sandy Creek section of Guilford County. From the mother congregation at Sandy Creek sprang a number of Baptist churches.

The Baptists had much success on the frontier because they went to the people and spoke their language. The more traditional denominations, which insisted on an educated clergy and dignified worship, could scarcely impress the tough and barely literate frontier residents. Baptist preachers, on the other hand, immediately established rapport with the rural folk, coming as they did from similar social backgrounds. Although criticized as overly emotional and anti-intellectual, they eventually founded schools and accorded the life of the mind a more valued place in their congregational life. At the same time, the Baptists, with their views of the strict separation of church and state and their disregard for colonial laws requiring a licensed clergy, conflicted with the existing denominations. Not only local governments but also angry mobs harassed the Baptists, often resorting to brutality. Persecution, however, actually stimulated Baptist growth, and by 1776 the denomination claimed ten thousand adherents.

Methodism took its name from the disciplined and methodical Christian life that Anglicans John (1703–91) and Charles (1707–88) Wesley modeled for their followers. The Wesleys' teachings were a combination of Anglicanism, Puritanism, and German Pietism. They believed that salvation was not merely a gift received through the power of the Holy Spirit at conversion but the Christian life itself, a present reality reflected through the expression of perfect love and pure motives. Once converted, a person was to be vividly conscious of the Spirit's work, which expressed itself in joy, enthusiasm, and devotion. Evidence of conversion included the act of renouncing the usual pleasures of society, such as card playing, dancing, gambling, and theater going. These proscriptions would profoundly influence evangelical Protestant conceptions of morality in both England and America.

Although John Wesley had briefly served as an Anglican missionary to Georgia between 1736 and 1738, Methodism as such was brought to America in the 1760s by lay preachers. Thus, the Methodist expansion occurred after the Great Awakening had subsided. The rapid dissemination of the Methodist faith in the colonies was the result of the itinerant ministry of its preachers. With nothing but a horse and a Bible, the circuit riders roamed throughout Maryland, Virginia, and North Carolina, preaching to any who would hear. In 1770, there were Methodist societies in these three colonies as well as in New York, Delaware, and Pennsylvania.

By the outbreak of the Revolution in 1775, the Methodist revival in the South had made significant inroads. At this time, the membership of colonial Methodism totaled 6,968; of these only 764 lived north of the Mason-Dixon line. John Wesley sent some of his ablest associates to America, the most important being Francis Asbury (1745–1816), who became the guiding genius of the denomination. Because Methodism was officially linked to the Anglican Church, however, during the Revolution (which John Wesley opposed), Methodists were seen as Tories and loyalists, especially in the North. Not until Methodists formed an independent denomination did their numbers begin to increase significantly throughout America.

The Impact of the Awakening

Some historians question whether the term *Great Awakening* accurately describes the religious dynamics of the era and instead emphasize the variety of religious and folk practices of the colonials. Nevertheless, the religious developments of the period provided Americans with their first truly national experience. Nothing in their previous history had united all Americans. Travel was difficult, intercolonial communications were undeveloped, and most people kept to themselves within their ethnic communities. Nourished by itinerant revivalists, however, the Great Awakening cut across regional, ethnic, and religious boundaries. This national movement helped prepare Americans for the Revolution that would follow, for religious cooperation opened the way for political and military cooperation. On the community level, the Awakening challenged traditional religious authorities and unleashed an individualistic, democratic impulse. It also figured prominently in the upsurge of humanitarian expression. In every section of the colonies was evidence of a deeper concern for and a wider commitment to ameliorating human suffering. Schools and orphanages were founded, missions to the Indians were revitalized, and objections to slavery were raised for the first time.

In New England, where missionary work had been dormant since King Phillip's War, a new effort to reach Native Americans surfaced. Through the labor of Edwards, John Sergeant (1710–49), and especially the Brainerd brothers, David (1718–47) and John (1720–81), Indian missions were established in western Massachusetts, New York, Pennsylvania, Delaware, and New Jersey. The Congregational missionary Eleazer Wheelock (1711–99) secured a charter for a school for Indians in New Hampshire that eventually became Dartmouth College. In the middle and southern colonies, the Presbyterians, Anglicans, and Moravians engaged in ministry to the Indians. Out of the Moravian labors came numerous Christian Indian settlements, ranging from southern New England to the Ohio country in the west. Their most noteworthy worker was David Zeisberger (1721–1808). The peaceful Moravians adapted to Native American ways, communicated Christianity with cultural insight, and did not tie belief in Christ to acceptance of a European lifestyle. Unfortunately, the westward movement of whites engulfed the peaceful Christian communities, resulting in strife and massacres, the worst being the tragic destruction of the Gnadenhütten village in Ohio in 1782. Zeisberger eventually led a remnant of Christian Indians to safety in Ontario.

Between 1714 and 1760, the number of black slaves in America jumped from 58,850 to 310,000, largely because the supply of white indentured servants diminished to almost nothing. Even though slavery was not extensive in the North because of its limited economic usefulness, many New England merchants sought wealth in the slave trade. Because several British courts had ruled that baptized slaves must be freed, many American slave owners approached the question of evangelizing blacks with great reticence. Even though colonial legislatures affirmed that baptism did not confer the right to freedom, little evangelism occurred among slaves prior to the Great Awakening. The Anglican Church, through its Society for the Propagation of the Gospel in Foreign Parts, was the first to devote attention to the blacks. However, few Anglicans residing in the colonies took up the task; it was the missionaries, catechists, and schoolmasters sent from England who felt called to reach the blacks.

During the Great Awakening, various itinerant preachers, including George Whitefield, who owned a slave, sought to bring the gospel to blacks. Particularly noteworthy was Samuel Davies (1723–61), a Presbyterian from Virginia who wrote hymns for African-Americans and encouraged their presence in white church services. Revivalistic Christianity, with its emphasis on divine grace, heavenly hope, and spiritual experience, resonated with many slaves, who began to establish fellowships of their own, despite obstacles and prejudice. In the early 1770s, the first black church was founded by the African-American pastor David George (1742–1810) in South Carolina.

The initial public opposition to the slave trade originated among the Society of Friends (Quakers) and the Mennonites of Germantown, Pennsylvania. The chief spokespersons against slavery were the Quaker mystic and humanitarian John Woolman (1720–72) and Anthony Benezet (1713–84), a Huguenot Quaker. As a result of their influence, the Philadelphia Yearly Meeting of Friends in 1758 condemned slavery and by 1775 denied fellowship to any Quaker who refused to emancipate his slaves. Both men published significant books condemning slavery, and Benezet influenced John Wesley, who adopted an antislavery position. Although Jonathan Edwards and George Whitefield had no objection to slavery, some in the next generation of theologians, such as Samuel Hopkins (1721–1803) and Ezra Stiles (1727–95), both ministers in Rhode Island, opposed the institution as contrary to Christian ideals. The clash between the Christian faith and slavery occurred repeatedly during the next century, achieving its climax in the Civil War.

Apart from the rapid increase in new congregations, the major institutional impact of the Great Awakening was the creation of colleges to train the swelling numbers of ministerial candidates. The Presbyterians were especially active, establishing the aforementioned College of New Jersey in 1746 and Hampden-Sydney College in Virginia in 1775. The Baptists founded Rhode Island College (later Brown University) in 1764. In 1766, the revivalists among the Dutch Reformed obtained a charter for Queens College (now Rutgers University) in New Jersey. Dartmouth College, sponsored by pro-revival Congregationalists, was chartered in New Hampshire in 1770.

The Awakening also contributed to the divisive character of American denominationalism. Not everyone went along with the new religious tide, especially its excesses. In addition to the Presbyterian split into Old and New Sides, schism occurred in New England Congregationalism. The Old Light group, led by Charles Chauncy (1705–87), pastor of the First Church of Boston, opposed itinerant revival preachers and the antinomian doctrines they allegedly preached. The New Lights, headed by Edwards, favored revival, lay exhorters, and a looser church structure. The Baptists also divided into Regular and Separate factions. The former were Calvinistic anti-revivalists, while the latter were pro-revival and more flexible in their evangelistic methods. An Arminian group, the Free Will Baptists, and the sabbatarian Seventh-Day Baptists also emerged during this period.

The Awakening created a distinctly revivalist tradition. Its evangelistic thrust emphasized sin, salvation, and a clear-cut conversion experience. In congregational life, less emphasis was placed on ecclesiastical authority, complex theological creeds, and the sacramental elements of worship. This phenomenon surfaced and subsided frequently throughout the history of American Protestantism and was a major factor in what came to be known as the evangelical tradition.

5

The Church in the Midst of Revolution

The European Enlightenment, which emphasized that reason would lead people to knowledge, help them understand nature, and aid in reforming society, penetrated the American colonies early in the eighteenth century. Although traces of Enlightenment thought appeared earlier, most historians date its beginning to the publication of Isaac Newton's *Principia Mathematica* (1687) and John Locke's *Essay Concerning Human Understanding* (1690). In the next years, English and Continental thinkers made a self-conscious effort to cast off the constraints of traditional religion. By the 1750s, these optimistic concepts gained an American foothold, resulting in a "third way" in American theology, one situated between trinitarian orthodoxy and rationalistic naturalism.

The Enlightenment and Changing Patterns in Theology

Enlightenment ideas appeared in the writings of American clergymen, including those who participated in the Great Awakening. Jonathan Edwards, for example, carefully read Locke while at Yale and appropriated much of his theory of knowledge in his own philosophical writings. Edwards also declared enthusiasm for the works of the "incomparable Mr. Newton." He, however, remained a champion of scriptural authority against the more secular implications of Enlightenment thought, which emphasized mind over heart, reason over revelation, and ethics over personal salvation.

Later exponents of Edwards's theology adjusted it even further to accommodate Enlightenment insights. Joseph Bellamy (1719–90) and Samuel Hopkins (1721–1803), two of Edwards's students, modified the Calvinistic emphasis on the inherited nature of original sin and opened the way for a larger role for human volition in the experience that results from the divine act of regeneration. They thus sought to make intellectualism and revivalism acceptable to American thinkers of the day.

Meanwhile, a decidedly more liberal position developed in contrast to the theology of Edwards and his followers. Its roots were found in the teachings of the English Presbyterian John Taylor (1694–1761) and other foes of covenant theology. They rejected the doctrine of original sin altogether, maintaining that sinfulness comes by choice rather than by inheritance. These views were attractive to Boston Congregationalist ministers such as Charles Chauncy and especially Jonathan Mayhew (1720–66), who sharply criticized revivalism and rejected Calvinism. Mayhew's writings later provided religious and civil arguments for the revolt against Britain.

The most generalized religious adaptation of Enlightenment ideas was Deism. Unlike theistic religion, Deism minimized active participation by God in the everyday affairs of humankind. Deists recognized divine creation of the universe and emphasized moral law, natural religion, man's innate ethical potential, and revelation tested by reason. They revered Jesus as a moral teacher rather than a divine miracle worker and savior. These views spread to the colonies and first surfaced in the colleges.

Many Deists maintained nominal connection with a church without fully adhering to its doctrines. One example is George Washington (1732–99). Others, such as Benjamin Franklin (1706–90) and Thomas Jefferson (1743–1826), displayed friendliness toward organized religion without becoming church members. None, however, affirmed what today would be considered biblical orthodoxy. An anti-supernaturalism marked their views, and Jefferson went so far as to prepare his own version of the Gospels shorn of all references to miracles or theological statements.

The early Deists envisioned an ideal society ruled by reason, ennobled by benevolence, and blessed by freedom. The Deist mood that characterized many of the Revolution's leaders was moderate and ethical, shaped by Protestant Christianity. This contrasted sharply to Voltaire in France, who strongly condemned the church. Without directly attacking the churches, American Deism advanced the cause of human autonomy by downplaying God's present activity and authority in the world.

These philosophical and theological ideas soon evolved into a new American denomination: Unitarianism. Denying both the Trinity and the full deity of Christ, Unitarians preached the unity of the Godhead and tailored their liturgy accordingly. They also sought to demonstrate that a genuine religious and moral community could exist without doctrinal conformity. Ironically, the first Anglican (Episcopal) congregation in Boston (King's Chapel) became in 1785 the first American church to openly declare itself Unitarian. Not accountable to any ecclesiastical structure, many Congregational churches in eastern Massachusetts soon followed suit. By the early nineteenth century, Harvard College emerged as the bastion of American Unitarian thought. A separate denomination was finally established in 1825, the American Unitarian Association.

The Churches in the Revolution

While the Unitarians and the Deists were revolutionizing theology, social and political upheaval was also brewing. From 1760 to 1775, relations between the American colonies and England steadily deteriorated. British efforts to tighten control over their empire and to make the colonies responsible for funding their own governments and defense led to such unpopular economic measures as the Sugar Act (1764), the Stamp Act (1765), and a variety of navigation laws limiting free trade. These aggravated the colonists, who had to this point enjoyed a high degree of autonomy. Sentiment favoring resistance grew, while British efforts to enforce the new policies only increased tensions. Also contributing to American hostility was the Anglican demand for an American bishop. John Adams stated that this agitation contributed "as much as any other cause, to arouse the attention not only for the inquiring mind but of the common people and urge them to close thinking on the constitutional authority of parliament over the colonies."[1] On April 19, 1775, at Lexington Green and Concord Bridge, the War for Independence broke out.

What role did the churches play in this violent revolution? Both English and American Protestants had long engaged in political theorizing. Although sensitive to Paul's admonition that Christians should be subject to the existing powers, they were not inclined to accept what they regarded as oppression if a plausible religious reason could be found for resisting. Colonists of British origin easily recalled the Puritan Revolution of the 1640s and the Glorious Revolution of 1688–89, both popular movements that challenged the power of the British crown. Such precedents encouraged people to consider revolt. By combining ideas from both natural law and the Calvinistic concept of government as a compact under God between the ruler and the ruled, the colonists formulated a doctrine of active resistance.

---

1. Charles Francis Adams, ed., *The Works of John Adams,* vol. 10 (Boston: Little, Brown, 1856), 185.

But not all Christians were of the same mind about rebellion. Some, especially the Quakers and the Mennonites, were unable to justify armed revolt on any grounds. Others felt that a certain measure of reform was necessary but wished to see it accomplished through redress of grievances rather than through a resort to arms. Still others, clergy included, who had been on the sidelines in the political debates, wholeheartedly endorsed war when it began.

The Established Churches

No religious body surpassed the New England Congregationalists in contributing to the revolutionary cause, and the clergy were the primary catalysts. Besides acting as recruiters, most New England clergy supported the war with their pens and meager salaries. For generations, ministers had educated their parishes in the principles of civil government on election days, special days for "fasting and humiliation," and thanksgiving days. Jonathan Mayhew of Boston, for example, warned his people against the insidious growth of tyranny: "Civil tyranny is usually small in its beginning till at length, like a mighty torrent, or the raging waves of the sea, it bears down all before it, and deluges whole countries and empires."[2] At each point of crisis in the decade from 1765 to 1775, the New England pulpiteers dwelt on the rights of the provincial populace. Enriching their vocabularies with biblical terminology and examples, the clergy made the preservation of colonial rights and the necessity for resistance holy causes. Earnest laymen such as Samuel Adams (1722–1803) furthered the ideals of the revolutionary cause through their eloquent writings and oratory.

The Anglican Church, although it produced some of the Revolution's most ardent proponents, was, of all the denominational groups, the most loyal to Britain. Nevertheless, most of its laity supported the rebellion, even though the clergy had pledged their support to the crown and were largely loyalist. In fact, it was so dangerous for some ministers to proclaim loyalist convictions from the pulpit that Jonathan Boucher of Virginia deemed it necessary to preach with loaded pistols lying on a cushion. In the northern colonies, especially Connecticut and New York, the Anglican clergy were even more inclined toward loyalty than those farther south. Many were forced to flee or risk being tried for high treason by the new patriot governments. Thus, it was through laymen such as Washington, James Madison, Patrick Henry, John Marshall, and Alexander Hamilton that Anglicanism made its deepest and most lasting contribution to the American patriotic cause.

2. Jonathan Mayhew, *A Discourse Concerning Unlimited Submission and Non-Resistance to the Higher Powers* (Boston: D. Fowle, 1750), vi.

The Voluntary Bodies

The role of the nonestablished churches during the Revolution is complex. Each had its own unique history, and none was entirely loyalist in its attitudes and actions.

Presbyterians, mostly of Scotch-Irish derivation, still burned with resentment toward England for the wrongs that had precipitated their migration. Most, therefore, welcomed the chance to unite behind the revolutionary

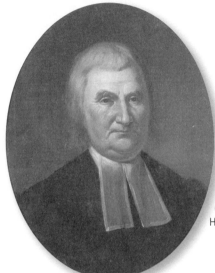

John Witherspoon (1723–94).
Courtesy of Independence National
Historical Park.

banner. Outstanding among Presbyterian patriots was John Witherspoon (1723–94), who had come to America in 1768 to assume the presidency of the College of New Jersey (later Princeton). As one of five delegates representing New Jersey in the Continental Congress, Witherspoon was the only clergyman to sign the Declaration of Independence.

The Baptist churches, steeped in a long tradition of a compact theory of government and of strong advocates of religious liberty, wholeheartedly supported the patriot cause. Their solidarity against British intrusions won them the favor of their former ecclesiastical oppressors in New England and Virginia and gained for them the legitimacy they had been seeking for over a century.

The Methodists, however, were not as united. John Wesley himself remained loyal to King George III and advised his American ministers to stay neutral. Doing so resulted in local pressures that forced nearly all of them, except Francis Asbury, to return to England by 1778. Colonial Methodists were severely harassed for their supposed Toryism. Some were jailed, others beaten, and many more fined. Such episodes underlined the reality that Christians who believe the same creed and the same Bible often hold different conclusions concerning the political expression of their faith. Despite persecution, Methodist numbers increased during the revolutionary period, tripling by 1780 to thirteen thousand.

Henry (1711–87) and Peter (1746–1807) Muhlenberg. Courtesy of the Concordia Historical Institute.

Like the Baptists, the Dutch Reformed were intensely patriotic, but because their churches were located mainly in the Hudson Valley, lower New York, and New Jersey, places where the British were most active, they became prime targets for violence. Churches were scattered, ministers imprisoned, and property destroyed. Laypeople gathered where they could and sustained their church life in small groups, setting aside certain days for fasting, prayer, and thanksgiving.

The Lutherans and the German Reformed were largely of patriot sentiment with only a small loyalist minority. By all standards, the Muhlenberg family was the most influential among Lutherans during this period. Henry (1711–87), the father, exercised an informal governorship over all the churches from New York to Georgia. Although he himself claimed neutrality, his sons were ardent patriots. One of the colorful incidents of the period was the action of Peter Muhlenberg (1746–1807), a pastor in Woodstock, Virginia. In a farewell sermon to his congregation, after describing the colonial situation, he announced, "In the language of Holy Writ, there is a time for all things. There is a time to preach and a time to fight; and now is the time to fight." Then he stripped off his gown, stood before his parishioners in a colonel's uniform, and went off to war.[3]

Colonial Roman Catholics generally affirmed the patriot cause and in fact organized several regiments throughout the colonies. Catholic signers of the Declaration of Independence and the Constitution included Thomas Fitzsimmons, Daniel Carroll, and Charles Carroll. Although Catholics were relatively few, they emerged from the Revolution in a favorable light and thereby advanced their cause to secure religious freedom and acceptance. The three thousand Jews, largely residing in New York and Rhode Island and the largest European non-Christian religious group in the colonies, wholeheartedly supported the Revolution with both funds and military enlistments.

Church groups such as the Quakers who sought to honor Jesus' words about "turning the other cheek" were unable to offer any direct military aid, but they did provide humanitarian assistance. Many "conscientious objectors," especially among the Quakers, were persecuted for their convictions. In Pennsylvania, some pacifists who tried to stay neutral received harsh treatment, including confiscation of their farms. The Moravians also suffered, although many rendered indirect service to the cause of independence. It is through their missions that Moravian fortitude is best remembered. Moravian Native American leaders persuaded their tribes to be sowers of peace and to resist taking sides. This, of course, was misinterpreted by both the British and the Americans, who were already biased against the Indians. Moravian Native American believers were treated with cruelty and in several instances were butchered in cold blood by American militiamen. Such acts undermined the credibility of missions to the Indians for years to come.

For African-Americans the Revolution provided mixed experiences as well as profound disappointment. Ironically, American patriots, while rebelling against British "tyranny," did not include blacks in the human rights proclaimed in the Declaration of Independence, though blacks fought in the war. In framing their constitutions, however, the states from Pennsylvania and New Jersey northward abolished slavery.

In spite of intense prejudice, African-Americans founded independent churches, the first being the Silver Bluff congregation gathered by former slave David George in South Carolina. Because the British army promised emancipation in areas it controlled during the war, George retreated with the British into Nova Scotia and eventually led a party of blacks from there to the new Sierra Leone settlement in West Africa. With his wife, Hannah, Andrew

3. David F. Wells et al., eds., *Christianity in America: A Handbook* (Grand Rapids: Eerdmans, 1983), 143.

Bryan (1737–1811) founded the First African Baptist Church in Savannah, a fellowship that spun off numerous other congregations and experienced severe harassment, including the imprisonment of several members by local governmental authorities. At the same time, in the midst of a revolution for liberty fought with religious fervor, many African-Americans found in Christianity a message of forbearance and hope, even though they were suffering extreme deprivation.

The revolutionary experience had a profound effect on how American Christians came to view their newly independent country. Some believers worked for the Revolution with measured restraint. They claimed that their highest loyalty belonged to a God who stands above all and judges all earthly societies, each of which reflects the frailties of humankind. Other revolutionaries, however, sanctified the American effort with biblical imagery and ascribed to the struggle with England a sacredness and a purity of purpose borrowed from Christianity. Some historians have seen in this tendency to glorify the new state the beginning of American civil religion.

Religion and Politics in the Framing of the Republic

To legitimize the social structures and endow their actions with divine sanction, the early Americans constructed a national framework with materials drawn from both the Christian religion and the English political heritage. Although a separation between church and state was written into the federal Constitution, Christianity played a crucial role in supplying values, vocabulary, and symbols to undergird the national purpose.

This wedding of religion to politics had deep roots. The Puritans drew heavily on biblical imagery to make sense of their lives and circumstances; through repeated practice this custom was dyed deeply into the American fabric. It recurred with renewed force during the Great Awakening. In fact, in his *Thoughts on the Revival of Religion in New England,* Edwards related that he was seeing the coming of the millennium on American soil.

A distinctive feature of this tradition was the idea that America was singled out from among the nations for a special mission and destiny, a phenomenon that historians have labeled "American Exceptionalism." Throughout most of the colonial period, England too was included in this sense of divine purpose, but after the Revolution, Americans began to view themselves exclusively as God's "New Israel." Laymen Jefferson, Franklin, and John Adams were as vigorous as any clergyman in affirming that the United States had come into being as a grand design of providence for the illumination of the ignorant and the emancipation of enslaved mankind everywhere. These sentiments were preserved for posterity in the contemporary mottoes *E pluribus unum—Annuit coeptis* and *MDCCLXXVI—Novus ordo seclorum* ("Out of many, one—He [God] has smiled upon our undertakings" and "1776—a new order for the ages"). Reflecting the spirit of the eighteenth century, the new age did not include Native Americans, blacks, or women in its agenda, at least not yet.

When the conflict ended in America's favor, many regarded the outcome as a sign of "chosenness" or God's special affection for his people in the New World. In 1783, Ezra Stiles, president of Yale, observed how "the wonder-working providence of God" had been displayed in the events of the war and looked ahead to the coming freedom, prosperity, and splendor of the United States. Thus, the perspective of American Christians shifted from that of a chosen *people* challenged to carry out a special task to that of a chosen *nation* as the recipient of divine favor. In the words of H. Richard Niebuhr, "The Kingdom of God in America [became] the American Kingdom of God,"[4] with the emphasis on American.

The tension inherent in this mixing of religion and nationalism had implications for the society that claimed such high ideals and a special providential mission.

4. H. Richard Niebuhr, *The Kingdom of God in America* (Chicago: Willett, Clark, 1937), 9.

PART 3

THE NATIONALIZATION AND EXPANSION OF THE CHURCHES (1784–1860)

6

New Churches for a New Society

U ncertainty, experimentation, and adjustment marked every aspect of the new republic as Americans faced the responsibilities of independence with few precedents to follow. Both the churches and the nation had to establish their own bounds within the realm of freedom. Most significantly, out of the revolutionary struggle came a profound departure from the previous millennium of European church history. No longer would an officially established church leading a religiously uniform society be the accepted social order. A truly revolutionary idea, liberty of personal choice, was now the organizing principle in American Christianity. The churches were called upon to make this dramatic adjustment in a nation that was rapidly redefining itself according to new concepts that arose from the revolutionary experience. Committed to republican political ideals, decentralized government, democratic participatory politics, and free-market economics, the emerging social and cultural order inevitably influenced the churches and was in turn influenced by the Christianity the people expressed.

Grappling with the New Religious Freedoms

Since the seventeenth century, the desire for religious freedom had been growing. As shown in chapter 2, toleration of minority religious opinions and freedom of worship were still extremely radical ideas, and in Europe only the Dutch actually allowed such liberty. A person such as Roger Williams, who called for religious freedom and made it a distinctive feature of his colony of Rhode Island, was an isolated exception. But the emergence of the English Baptists in the early seventeenth century and the sectarianism prevalent in the English civil war had been heralds of change. After the restoration of the monarchy in 1660, many English leaders realized that continuing political health was possible only if the destructive energies of religious conflict were checked through a more moderate attitude toward Protestant dissenters. Thus, the Toleration Act of 1689 granted Nonconformists substantial liberty to worship as they saw fit.

The religious minorities, for whom freedom was a basic element of their convictions, had a leavening influence both in Europe and in America, which became a haven for radical groups such as the Baptists, Quakers, and Mennonites. Where the minorities flourished, diversity of theological opinion increased. Moreover, the Great Awakening tempered the strict Calvinism of the early colonial fathers and encouraged a more experience-oriented Christian life. The secularizing force of rationalism further undermined religious uniformity. In fact, Deism and Unitarianism, which rejected miracles and other traditional dogmas, substituted a vague lowest-common-denominator religion for traditional Christianity.

These influences led to the enshrinement of religious freedom in the federal Constitution. Article 6 states that "no religious test shall ever be required as a qualification to any office or public trust under the United States." This was a response to the English Test Act of 1673, which restricted public offices to those who took communion according to the Anglican rite and thus belonged to the established church. The First Amendment specifies that "Congress shall make no law respecting an establishment of religion, or prohibiting the free exercise thereof."

The Constitution clearly prohibited the American government from sponsoring any one religious body; however, it did not exclude religious values from politics or forbid the national government from encouraging religious ideals in general. The complex American relationship between religion and politics can be clarified by comparing it with other judicial definitions of separation, such as that of France. A 1905 law there mandated a complete separation of church and state; that is, the regime could not engage in any religious activity and could not provide any support whatsoever. The difference between these two approaches is a product of the countries' histories: the rationalist and anticlerical tradition of French revolutionary republicanism and the origins of American democracy, which were not antireligious in character.

The new religious freedom shaped the future course of the churches. The Constitution assured the rightful participation of a minority sect in the democratic process, thereby giving all religious bodies equal protection under the law. Further, the provisions extended theoretically to non-Christians and even to the nonreligious. It followed that churches were to be wholly voluntary institutions, dependent exclusively on their ability to reach and persuade free people to join and support them. The state took on the role of a benevolent but impartial guardian of order among independent churches and their denominational competitors.

Religious liberty and pluralism had long-range consequences for the American churches. Former religious monopolies (establishments) could no longer take for granted the allegiance of their client populations. Participation was voluntary. As a result, the religious tradition, which previously could be authoritatively imposed from above, now had to be marketed. It had to be "sold" to a clientele that was no longer constrained to "buy," resulting in a competitive situation in which religious institutions were market oriented and the services offered by churches were consumer conscious. These dynamics meshed well with the developing managerial and market environment of the new economic and social order. In practical terms, for American churches, this meant an emphasis on results, bureaucratic structures, a susceptibility to trends, and the desire for a more entrepreneurial rather than pastoral style of leadership.

Most Americans welcomed the new religious pluralism, but at the state conventions for ratifying the Constitution, some resisted the elimination of religious tests. In Massachusetts, critics complained that non-Protestants and pagans would connive their way into office. Especially feared was Roman Catholic "Popery." The protest revealed the tension that permeated American society. Resentment mounted as other religious faiths found a place in America and the dominance of the "Protestant establishment" gradually eroded. Freedom increased opportunity, and over time nonwhite and non-Protestant Americans gradually gained access to areas of influence from which they had formerly been barred.

The removal of official support for the churches forced a rediscovery of personal responsibility and financial commitment. People now made up their own minds about Christianity, without the government dictating their ecclesiastical choice. Although many still attended church out of habit or for the sake of respectability, actual membership as well as active participation in congregational life fell off significantly. This waning of spiritual life was already well underway during the Revolution, and when it continued following the war, some clergymen began calling for another awakening.

Church Disestablishment at the State Level

The ending of establishment at the state level took place as well. In a broad sense, disestablishment may be viewed as an acceleration of the general democratization process in American culture. Voluntarism in religion was essential to the process. Nevertheless, in one way or another, a few states clung to their traditional religious establishments.

In Anglican Virginia, where more than half the population was non-Anglican, protest against the official church had been seething for half a century. Of all the dissenting groups, Baptists and Presbyterians were the most determined to bring about Anglican disestablishment. Political leaders such as James Madison and George Mason were equally insistent about this. Decisive in this process was Thomas Jefferson's Bill for Establishing Religious Freedom, first presented in 1779 and adopted seven years later. Jefferson regarded it as one of the most significant achievements of his life. Aiding its passage was Madison's celebrated *Memorial and Remonstrance,* which argued against a tax to support teachers of religion. While this was a landmark document in the history of religious liberty, it took another fifty years and numerous other legislative measures to bring about a functional separation of church and state in Virginia.

Other states also moved to terminate formal connections with Anglicanism. Maryland's Declaration of Rights of 1776 guaranteed full religious freedom to all Christians, but that state did not grant full political rights to Jews until 1826. The Halifax Congress in North Carolina (1776) adopted a constitution prohibiting the establishment of a particular church in the state. It did, however, restrict the holding of public office to persons who affirmed "the truth of the Protestant religion." South Carolina in 1790 affirmed that it recognized no establishment of any kind. Georgia abolished the Anglican relationship in its first constitution of 1777. In New York, the only state north of the Mason-Dixon line where Anglicanism prevailed, the tenuous bond between church and state was dissolved in 1777.

The situation in New England was quite different. Because the Congregational establishment overwhelmingly lined up on the patriot side, the severance of ties with England had little bearing on the church-state situation. Despite pressures for disestablishment, Congregationalism prevailed the longest in Massachusetts. The state's first constitution (1779) asserted the government's right to make provision "for the institution of the public worship of God, and for the support and maintenance of public Protestant teachers of piety, religion and morality." Dissenters, however, were given the privilege of directing their religious tax to their own denominations. The Congregationalists continued to exert official influence, and it was only after years of heated debate that the state finally approved a bill in 1833 that ended the oldest religious establishment in New England.

Connecticut kept its old royal charter and refused to draft a new state constitution for more than forty years after independence. As protests mounted, Baptists and Methodists, joined by Unitarians, Universalists, Quakers, and Episcopalians, worked with the Jeffersonian Democratic Republicans to oppose the conservative Federalists and by this means exerted a more liberalizing influence in the state government. As a result, in 1818, a constitutional convention at Hartford drew up a document stipulating that "no preference shall be given by law to any Christian sect or mode of worship." The previous year New Hampshire had adopted a similar policy.

Denominational Readjustments

The end of government sponsorship forced the churches to reevaluate their resources and goals. Yet disestablishment was only one element of the changing religious climate. Theological liberalism also flourished, especially along the northeastern seaboard. Because the European Enlightenment reached America relatively late, its full impact was softened by the pressing political concerns of the times. Enlightenment ideas nevertheless attracted some of the best minds in the youthful nation, and they even permeated popular thinking as well. Books such as Ethan Allen's *Reason the Only Oracle of Man* (1784) and Thomas Paine's *Age of Reason* (1794) were widely read by laypersons as well as clerics.

With some exceptions in rural areas, attendance at worship dwindled, and most congregations added a mere four or five new members a year. In 1798, the Presbyterian General Assembly noted with alarm "a general dereliction of religious principles and practice among our fellow citizens . . . and an abounding infidelity, which in many instances tends to atheism itself."[1] Conditions were even more depressing on the frontier. Cut off from the more stabilizing social life of the East and concerned chiefly with eking out a bare material existence, the pioneers found little time for things of the spirit or the life of the mind.

All religious bodies had to reassess their relationships to this new social situation. The Anglican Church Americanized itself, appointed local bishops, and renamed itself the Protestant Episcopal Church in 1783. Connecticut loyalist Samuel Seabury and others were consecrated as bishops in Scotland (because the mainline Church of England was reluctant to do so), thus preserving the Anglican principle of apostolic succession. Methodism, still considered a religious society within the Anglican Church, had begun forming independent congregations during the Revolution. In 1784, Francis Asbury, who had originally gone to America at Wesley's behest in 1771 to aid the fledgling Methodist work, was the acknowledged leader of the group in the new republic. He refused to accept an appointment by Wesley as general superintendent of the American church and called a conference of preachers in Baltimore in 1784 to carry out the task, an action that demonstrated the

---

1. E. H. Gillette, *History of the Presbyterian Church in the United States of America,* vol. 1 (Philadelphia: Presbyterian Publication Committee, 1864), 297.

autonomy of American Methodism. They named themselves the Methodist Episcopal Church, making Wesley's authority purely nominal. Methodism continued to gain new adherents and experienced great growth during the Second Awakening a few years later.

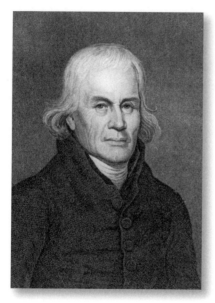

Francis Asbury (1745–1816).
Courtesy of the Billy Graham Center Museum, Wheaton, Illinois.

Unlike expansionistic Methodism, New England Congregationalism, secure in its regional heritage, assumed a more restrained attitude toward the rest of the nation. Doctrinal disputes resulted in numerous factions, and Jonathan Edwards Jr. (1745–1801) and Timothy Dwight (1752–1817) championed trinitarian orthodoxy against the inroads of Unitarian thought. A lack of unity made it impossible for Congregationalists to forge any kind of major undertaking on the national level.

The unprecedented growth of Presbyterianism in the postwar years demanded a more efficient organization. Under the able leadership of John Witherspoon and others, a General Assembly was called in 1789 and rules for discipline and doctrine were adopted. Although marked by vigorous theological conservatism, Presbyterianism reflected a highly rationalistic style of theology, a trend seen, for example, in the substitution of Scottish Common Sense Realism for the traditional Edwardsean theology at Princeton. The Common Sense philosophers assumed that one could assuredly and intuitively know the first principles of morality and reality and that there was no discontinuity between inner thought and outer reality.

The Baptists, with the battles over religious freedom behind them, made rapid gains throughout the new nation. The divisions between the Separate and Regular Baptists had largely healed, and although their church polity was thoroughly voluntaristic, they saw value in cooperation. By 1800, roughly fifty Baptist associations existed, but no national or interregional structure existed to bind these local bodies together. The first wider link was the foreign missionary society formed in 1814 commonly known by its short title, the Triennial Convention.

Other American churches adjusted to the new national environment. Lutherans created regional synods to recruit, train, and ordain ministers, and the General Synod, formed in 1820, brought together the heterogeneous elements of American Lutheranism. The Dutch Reformed Church severed its formal organizational tie with Holland in 1792, organized as an independent American body, and renamed itself the Reformed Church in America in 1867.

Although Roman Catholicism was in a stronger position after the war, it too had its problems, particularly a low ratio of priests to communicants (thirty to twenty-four thousand). It gained a firmer footing in the country after the consecration of John Carroll (1735–1815), from the distinguished Maryland family, as bishop of Baltimore. He was the first American bishop, and his many achievements included the founding of Georgetown College in 1789 (now Georgetown University) for the training of priests. By 1808, there were suffragan sees in Boston, New York, Philadelphia, and Bardstown (now Louisville), Kentucky, along with a metropolitan see in Baltimore. Carroll worked assiduously to interpret America for the Vatican and the Vatican for America. He championed the concept of religious toleration and demonstrated that the founding of the new nation was not exclusively a Protestant venture.

America's new democracy not only permitted the continuance of the old divisions of the Christian church but also encouraged the growth of new groups. As previously noted, the Great Awakening (a leveling and therefore democratic movement) had the effect of splintering many of the established churches. Most of its proponents preached in English to English-speaking audiences. A large German-speaking population stood apart because of the language barrier, but by the late eighteenth century, they too were receiving the biblical message in their own tongue. Philip Otterbein (1726–1813), a minister of the German Reformed Church, arrived in America in 1752 and adopted the techniques of Francis Asbury in organizing class meetings and lay leadership among his German-speaking converts. He joined forces with Martin Boehm (1725–1812), a Mennonite, and together they founded the United Brethren in Christ in 1800, which was distinguished by Methodist polity and doctrine. Likewise, Jacob Albright (1759–1808) of Pennsylvania, originally a lay Methodist preacher, founded a German-speaking denomination known as the Evangelical Church. These two groups of German origin combined in the twentieth century to become the Evangelical United Brethren Church.

Free blacks in northern cities formed independent congregations in the new republic, demonstrating that African-Americans were determined to create and sustain their own institutions. For the next 150 years, these churches were the most durable self-directed social structures in the black communities. Especially significant was the work of Richard Allen (1760–1830), a former slave, who organized the African Methodist Episcopal Church in 1814 in Philadelphia. He also cofounded the Free African Society, the first benevolent organization in America run by blacks for blacks.

Richard Allen (1760–1830).
Courtesy of the Billy Graham
Center Museum, Wheaton, Illinois.

Some slaves, always under close supervision by their masters, attended church services but were normally seated in separate galleries. At the same time, an "invisible institution" was arising among the slaves, a genuine folk religion composed of Christian elements adapted in texture and tone to the new practitioners. This was the slaves' counter church, and its theology was expressed through spirituals, songs of longing and hope for both heaven and present liberation. Preaching was more exhortation than discourse, and the call-response pattern characteristic of traditional African ceremonies found expression in the active participation of congregational members. The emotional and demonstrative character of Baptist and Methodist worship was attractive to African-Americans, but conformity to the racial customs of the day prevented them from being assimilated into these parent churches. White parishioners simply chose to separate or even exclude black worshipers and then justified their actions with such spurious theological arguments as the "curse of Ham."

By 1850, a United States citizen could reside in any of thirty-one states, even as far west as California. However, the same person could join a church in three times that many religious denominations. Such a phenomenon raised the question as to why there was such an array of American denominations, all calling themselves Christian and all professing adherence to the same Bible. Why had these denominations emerged, and what was their significance for Christianity in America?

In *The Social Sources of Denominationalism,* H. Richard Niebuhr tackled this difficult question. While conceding that theological, ethnic, and nationality factors were involved in the growth of denominations, he suggested that they were as much the products of social and economic factors as religious factors. Niebuhr interpreted American denominationalism as "the accommodation of Christianity to the caste-system of human society."[2] This was in contrast to Jesus, who revolted against the class distinctions of his day. Thus, Niebuhr saw the European magisterial Reformation as reform mainly for the middle and upper classes. It was only a matter of time before its inherent inequalities were challenged by the less powerful groups of the Radical Reformation. In a relatively short time, Europe and later America were dotted not only with Episcopalian, Lutheran, Dutch Reformed, and Presbyterian churches but also with Anabaptist and Quaker groups. The first cluster represented the more secure and leadership classes and the second the common people.

The same could be said of the Methodist and Baptist movements, which appealed largely to those groups that felt alienated from the more privileged communions. Later, the political and social upheaval that resulted finally in the Civil War further divided churches and created additional American denominations. Niebuhr did not seek to reduce all ecclesiastical distinctions to social causes, but his study illuminated the way human concerns and cultural bearings conditioned people's preferences for church life and, in particular, how denominationalism came to flourish on American soil, where individual freedom of choice was maximized.

A similar observation is offered by Mark Noll in *America's God from Jonathan Edwards to Abraham Lincoln* (2002). He calls the Episcopalian, Lutheran, Dutch Reformed, Congregationalist, and Presbyterian denominations "formalist." They maintained their identity through their European Reformation origins and worship styles, an educated clergy whose writings were widely published, and a proprietary attitude toward the social order. They were more heavily located in northern regions and included agriculturalists, businessmen, and commercial figures. Politically they tended to support Federalist, Whig, and later Republican Party priorities. Some supported the antislavery movement. In contrast were the "anti-formalists," best represented by the Methodists and the Baptists along with new denominations emerging out of the Second

2. H. Richard Niebuhr, *The Social Sources of Denominationalism* (New York: Henry Holt, 1929), 6.

Awakening. They tended to be more sectarian, informal, emotional in their worship style, and conversionist oriented. They were led by a more itinerant and less educated clergy, drew from lower-middle and rural classes, and were numerically strongest in the South and the West. They opposed any sort of religious establishment, championed spiritual liberty, and advocated localness in politics and economics, which drew them toward the Democratic Party.

It would be far too simplistic to link denominational loyalty with political party allegiance in antebellum America, but regional, ethnic, and class sympathies could be discerned that would influence the eventual responses of the churches to the slavery issue and the Civil War.

7

The Second Awakening

It was a wintry season for the churches of the postrevolutionary period. A historian of the Episcopal Church characterized the era as one of suspended animation and as "the lowest ebb-tide of vitality in the history of American Christianity."[1] Lyman Beecher (1775–1863), who was a student at Yale in 1795, described the religious conditions there in his autobiography: The college "was in a most ungodly state. The college church was almost extinct. Most of the students were skeptical, and rowdies were plenty. Intemperance, profanity, gambling, and licentiousness were common."[2] A Presbyterian writer decried "the profligacy and corruption of the public morals,"[3] and in Baptist circles there was a sense of waning spiritual vitality. The western frontier was populated by "experimenters," individuals who had escaped the restraints of society and had migrated in search of new opportunities. Life there relied more on primitive instincts than on religious piety. Ministers were few and churches even fewer. Frontier evangelists such as Presbyterian David Rice acknowledged that there was little creditable profession of religious faith. The times were clearly ripe for a renewal of vital religion.

Many historians have suggested that the revivalist preachers of the nineteenth century were the natural successors of the patriotic orators of the

1. James T. Addison, *The Episcopal Church in the United States, 1789–1931* (New York: Scribners, 1951), 76.

2. Lyman Beecher, *The Autobiography of Lyman Beecher,* vol. 1, ed. Barbara M. Cross (Cambridge: Harvard University Press, 1961), 27.

3. L. W. Bacon, *A History of American Christianity* (New York: Christian Literature Co., 1897), 231.

Revolution and the religious exhorters of the Great Awakening before them. The Revolution had been preached with religious zeal and had, of course, succeeded. Now new spokesmen picked up at the close of the 1790s where the patriotic orators had left off. They were sustained by a strong sense of continuity with their religious and political predecessors.

The new generation of clergy could not speak for the collective conscience of American Christians. The America of 1800 was too large, sprawling, and diverse to support any utopian ideas of national religious uniformity. Church leaders felt that the centrifugal forces of an expanding society had to be balanced by the centripetal power of a widespread faith commitment, and they refashioned the technique of revivalism to serve this function. Calling Americans again to repentance, preachers sought to bring souls to God and assert the unity of a culture threatened by fragmentation. In the new nation, redeemed individuals would transform society.

The Eastern Phase of the Awakening

Signs of revival appeared first in the East. Almost imperceptibly, people began taking new interest in religion; fresh converts strengthened churches, and new congregations, especially in New York, Long Island, and New Jersey, were established. The revival fires kindled first among college students. As early as 1787, the students of Hampden-Sydney College and Washington College, Presbyterian institutions in Virginia, experienced awakening; a number even decided to enter the ministry. The thirty or forty men who sought ordination eventually served Presbyterian churches on the frontier.

The expansion of New England Methodism, with its strong evangelistic emphasis, contributed to the spiritual advance in that region. By 1796, a New England Methodist Conference with three thousand members existed, and a network of circuits soon covered the entire region. Before long, in central and western New York, the revivals were of such a scope that local analysts began referring to the region as the "burned-over district" (burned by the flame of the Holy Spirit).

Events at Yale College illustrate the changing religious context. Timothy Dwight (1752–1817), grandson of Jonathan Edwards, was elected president in 1795 and immediately set about upgrading the educational and religious climate of the institution. He met the students on their own ground and held a series of frank discussions on timely issues. His chief concern was infidelity, and he launched a four-year cycle of discourses on the Christian religion in which he expounded the main doctrines and pointed out their moral implications. More than one-third of the student body professed faith in Christ. Similar awakenings followed at Dartmouth, Williams, and Amherst Colleges.

Dwight's role in the Yale revival helped heal the breach with the old, anti-revivalist Calvinists. The revival also produced such evangelical leaders as Lyman Beecher, who became the organizer and promoter of the Second Awakening in New England, and Nathaniel Taylor (1786–1858), its theologian. Events at Yale were the catalysts for the involvement of other eastern colleges. Graduates of these schools then went forth to found new colleges and churches in the West.

The Western Phase of the Awakening

The frontier phase of the Second Awakening differed greatly from that of the East. The seaboard revivals were quiet, orderly, and restrained; those in the West exploded with religious excitement and emotional outbursts. Revivalist preachers on the frontier were dealing with people on the move. Conditions did not allow for the long-term Christian training practiced in the East. There was a greater urgency in proclaiming the gospel message.

Those who sparked the frontier revival were mostly Presbyterians in the Appalachians. James McGready, Barton W. Stone (1772–1844), and William McGee worked with their Baptist and Methodist colleagues in a cooperative effort to reach the unchurched. They were intensely concerned with salvation and proclaimed the message to all who would listen. They attracted more people than the small churches could hold, necessitating outdoor meetings.

Barton W. Stone (1772–1844). Courtesy of Disciples of Christ Historical Society, Nashville, Tennessee.

Participants brought their provisions with them and came prepared to spend several days on the site. Thus was born the frontier camp meeting.

The revival flames spread rapidly through Kentucky and Tennessee into North and South Carolina, western Virginia and Pennsylvania, and thinly settled regions north of the Ohio River. The Cane Ridge Camp meeting of August 1801 was the most spectacular of the Kentucky meetings. Nearly twenty thousand people were present, some from as far away as Ohio. Evangelists mounted their stands among dusty travelers in crude makeshift tents and pleaded with them to be converted. The loneliness of the farmer's life contrasted sharply with the exhilaration of fellowship he felt with thousands like himself.

The meeting was marked by extraordinary outbursts of feeling. One Methodist preacher reported that as he preached, hundreds fell prostrate, writhing in spiritual agony before him. Some jerked their heads, while others uncontrollably leaped as they experienced the smiting power of the Holy Spirit. These accounts were probably exaggerated by both friendly and hostile witnesses, but they were sufficiently numerous to arouse misgivings in the minds of many. The Presbyterian General Assembly of 1805, while recognizing the power of the spiritual revival, also cautioned against disorder and irreverence. The assembly was also alarmed by the tendency of Presbyterian revivalists to accept a Methodist doctrine of grace and their laxity regarding ordination requirements.

These issues led to divisions among the Presbyterians between 1803 and 1805. Most notable were the departure of the pro-revivalist Cumberland Presbyterians from the Kentucky Synod, and the Christian Church or New Light schism led by Cane Ridge minister Stone. The Baptists and the Methodists, whose theologies fit much better with revivalism than did the Presbyterians' Calvinism, did not experience such splits. For them the camp meetings were harvest times.

Sporadic revivals continued throughout the 1820s and 1830s. As the camp meetings became more routine, much of the early excitement disappeared. By 1840, the frontier camp meetings had evolved into summer Bible conferences where the faithful could gather to hear inspirational addresses. The final thrust of the Second Awakening, however, was yet to occur in the North.

Charles Finney and the "New Measures"

As Mark Noll points out, with the adoption of more aggressive evangelistic strategies during the Second Awakening, an important shift took place in the nature of American revivalism.[4] This was highlighted above

---

4. Mark A. Noll, *The Old Religion in a New World: The History of North American Christianity* (Grand Rapids: Eerdmans, 2002), 96.

all by the career of Charles Grandison Finney (1792–1875). Born in Connecticut and reared in western New York, he was trained as a lawyer. In 1821, he had a dramatic conversion experience and immediately redirected his energies toward preaching the gospel of "free and full salvation." In the fashion of legal training of the day, he "read theology" with a Presbyterian minister but never attended a theological school. Only reluctantly did the St. Lawrence Presbytery agree in 1824 to ordain him as a "home missionary," for it had reservations about his belief that the atonement was for all rather than an elect few and about his apparent leanings toward Christian perfectionism.

Mr. and Mrs. Charles Grandison Finney (1792–1875). Courtesy of the Billy Graham Center Museum, Wheaton, Illinois. Used by permission of Oberlin College.

Finney began preaching under the auspices of the Female Missionary Society, first in small towns and then larger ones in upstate New York, and had astonishing success. He aroused antagonism from local pastors for criticizing the "settled ministry" as being too restrictive in character. In 1830–31, he was catapulted into the national spotlight through his remarkable revival in the major city of Rochester, New York. He then began holding meetings in the eastern cities of Boston, Philadelphia, and New York.

After a brief stint as a pastor in New York City, Finney relocated in 1835 to Oberlin College in Ohio, a college that had just been founded by Congregationalist evangelicals and immediately proved to be on the cutting edge of revivalism and social reform. The college admitted women and blacks and stood in the forefront of the fight to abolish slavery. The Old School Presbyterians at Princeton, who had strong misgivings about Finney's evolving Arminianism, were more than delighted when he transferred his membership to the Congregational Church in 1836. Oberlin would be his home base for the remainder of his life.

The most controversial aspect of Finney's ministry was his so-called new measures, many of which he had appropriated from the Methodists. They were spelled out in addresses given to his New York Presbyterian congregation in December 1834 and published as *Lectures on Revival* in 1835. As William McLoughlin pointed out, they defined the philosophic or scientific principles on which all modern revival techniques since his time have rested and thereby made the principles of conversion and revivalism systematic and pragmatic. These principles transferred the revival from the realm of the miraculous to that of practical action. In fact, Finney declared bluntly that a revival is "not a miracle, or dependent on a miracle in any sense. It is a purely philosophical result of the right use of the constituted means." The new measures were enjoined by God "for the production of a revival" and "have a natural tendency to produce a revival."[5]

In more specific terms, the measures Finney utilized in his meetings included singling out sinners by name while preaching, using "you" instead of "they" when speaking of the wicked, encouraging those who were under conviction and sorry for their sins to come forward to the "anxious bench" where attention could be centered on them and they could pray for the divine grace that would bring about conversion, holding prayer meetings at "unseasonable hours," and allowing women to testify and pray at the public meetings. He also popularized "protracted meetings" that could last for weeks or even months. He insisted that the Calvinist idea of the sovereignty of God that caused one just to wait for a revival to happen was wrongheaded. The sovereign God has provided his people with the means to carry out his work. Revivalism should not lead to ascetic withdrawal or spiritual contemplation but to religious activism and the achievement of measurable results. The reputation of a revivalist depended on the number of converts that resulted from his ministry.

Finney brought the camp-meeting revival to the city. Wherever he traveled, congregations were held spellbound by his piercing eyes and stentorian voice, which he used with theatrical effect. His activity in urban centers caused

---

5. William G. McLoughlin, *The American Evangelicals, 1800–1900* (New York: Harper & Row, 1968), 86–87.

conflict with the more restrained evangelical ministers, especially Lyman Beecher, who attacked his blunt methods, unconventional procedures, and perfectionist theology. Finney and the founders of Oberlin had hoped to bring about a great national transformation, after which the revived and converted Christians would move on to change society. This desire lay behind the enormous impetus for social reform, but the evangelical movement soon began to fragment, and the emphasis on reform increasingly took precedence over the call to conversion. At the same time, Finney's preaching more and more emphasized Christian perfection, the transformation of the inner life. Thus, his actions fed into the Holiness movement, which emerged in the 1840s.

The last phase of the revival in the North coincided with the financial crash of 1857, which triggered a severe depression and hardship among businessmen and factory workers alike. The distinctive feature of the revival during 1857 and 1858 was its absence of evangelists. Instead of preachers imploring the hearers to repent, thousands of clerks and businessmen began coming together spontaneously for midday prayer and Bible study. The first such gathering occurred at the Old Dutch North Church on Fulton Street in New York City on September 23, 1857. Newspapers devoted large sections to accounts of the revival, and soon the businessmen's prayer meeting was a regular activity in small towns and large cities from Indiana to Quebec. As one enthusiast put it, God drove out mammon that he himself might reign. "He made poor the merchant princes that they might be rich in heavenly gain." When the wheels of industry ground to a halt and the countinghouses in the city were deserted, the voice of God called the faithful to rest, pray, and find health.[6]

The Consequences of the Second Awakening

The Second Awakening had numerous consequences for American religion. First, it resulted in a swelling of church membership, especially in the South, where evangelical Protestantism became the dominant religious ethos. In Kentucky alone, between 1800 and 1803, the Baptists gained more than ten thousand new members and the Methodists an equal number. It also represented a shift from strict Calvinism as the primary theological mode in American religious life.

Moderate critics often accused the revivalists of allowing emotion the upper hand over reason and logic, something that Finney, who with his legal mind strongly believed in the power of prayer and the work of the Holy Spirit in bringing about revival, certainly did not want. Actually, the new emphasis

6. W. F. P. Noble, *1776–1876: A Century of Gospel-Work* (Philadelphia: H. C. Watts, 1876), 418.

was on divinely directed, disciplined human effort to achieve revival, not on passively waiting for the providential outpouring of the Spirit, whenever in God's due time that might take place. The new measures in the promotion of revival involved intense prayer, the use of proper techniques, and the expectation of measurable results. From this time on, revivalism would be an ongoing feature of American Christianity.

The Second Awakening also had the unintended effect of splintering churches, much as had happened in the wake of the Great Awakening a century earlier. Revivalism resulted in controversy and even schism in the Lutheran, Congregational, Reformed, and Presbyterian churches. Directly or indirectly, the revivals were instrumental in the emergence of more than a dozen new denominations.

The most outstanding consequence of the Second Awakening was the enormous increase in humanitarian and reform efforts. Those touched by the revival spirit poured their lives into foreign and home missions, social and educational reforms, and the struggle against the greatest evil of the day, slavery. New social opportunities for women allowed them to participate in church life and social reform organizations.

8

Envisioning a Christian Social Order

In spite of its diverse character, the Second Awakening helped to forge a mainstream tradition for American evangelical Protestantism. Essentially orthodox in theology, experiential in faith, and Puritan in outlook, this tradition dominated the social and religious life of nineteenth-century America. The effects of religious fragmentation were offset by a conscious blurring of doctrinal distinctions among the competing denominations. Confidently evangelical, they proclaimed a life-transforming faith based on an authoritative Bible, a personal Savior, and a moral universe having its origin in the Triune God. The various religious groups also espoused a common identity with the nation, and they worked to unify the culture more than any legal establishment of religion ever could have.

Throughout the first half of the nineteenth century, most churches resisted the secularizing impulses of the age and enabled the republic to maintain its basically Christian identity. Political and religious leaders alike maintained that the success of the American experiment depended on the moral and intellectual character of its people. To this end, educators, revivalists, popular orators, and essayists combined their talents to shape and direct the developing American character and overall cultural ethos.

One result of their labors was the sprawling array of "interlocking directorates" and reform societies that some historians call the Benevolent Empire. At a ministers' meeting in Boston in 1812, Lyman Beecher labeled these groups "a disciplined moral militia,"[1] and terms such as *battle, campaign,* and *crusade* were enlisted into the rhetoric of reform.

---

1. Vincent Harding, *A Certain Magnificence: Lyman Beecher and the Transformation of American Protestantism, 1775–1863* (Brooklyn, N.Y.: Carlson, 1991), 79.

The voluntary societies that carried out these reform efforts were interdenominational in character and national in scope, thereby allowing churches to pool their efforts to meet particular needs. Also, by concentrating on a single objective, these societies enjoyed a broad level of support and avoided potentially divisive theological issues. Founded as nonprofit agencies, they harnessed lay energies, and because they did not have to wait for decisions from an official ecclesiastical body, they were ideal instruments for quick, concerted action.

Many Christians believed that God would accomplish "the glorious things foretold in the Bible." Most did not look for the immediate dawning of millennial glory, but they did believe that humanitarian efforts would ultimately bring about the kingdom of God on earth. Such a millennium could not simply be prayed for; it would be introduced, said President Eliphalet Nott of Union College, "by human exertions."[2] In giving the millennium such a temporal and material character and by identifying the kingdom of God with the prospects of the republic both at home and abroad, Protestant spokesmen contributed immensely to the American concepts of progress and national mission.

Missions

The tens of thousands who poured over the mountains into the western lands caused alarm among the eastern clergy. Who would feed and care for these wandering sheep? Denominations realized they had to develop strong missionary programs if frontier society was to be won to Christian ideals and practices. The home missionary movement was the means whereby the West, the nation, and ultimately the world could be redeemed from the effects of immorality and undisciplined greed. As Andrew Walls pointed out, the greatest mission success of the English-speaking community in the nineteenth century was the evangelization of the American frontier west of the Appalachians. The roving evangelists preached the gospel, planted and pastored churches, and brought Christian civilization to the disorder of the West.[3] The outstanding domestic effort was the American Missionary Society, formed in 1826. Its personnel were young men trained and sent forth from colleges and seminaries to spread Christian morality and institutions on the frontier. At its height in 1850, the society sponsored 1,065 missionary workers.

Diligent efforts were also launched to win Native Americans. The New York Missionary Society, formed in 1796 by Presbyterians, Dutch Reformed, and Baptists, carried the gospel to the southern tribes. In New England, a

2. This is the summary argument of his *Lectures on Temperance* (New York: Sheldon, Blakeman, 1857), 277–81.

3. Andrew Walls, "The American Dimension in the History of the Missionary Movement," in *Earthen Vessels: American Evangelical and Foreign Missions, 1880–1980,* ed. Joel A. Carpenter and Wilbert R. Shenk (Grand Rapids: Eerdmans, 1990), 1–25.

Methodist circuit rider.
Courtesy of the Billy Graham
Center Museum, Wheaton,
Illinois.

number of Congregational mission societies emerged, the earliest being the
Connecticut Missionary Society, founded in 1798. It proposed to "Christian-
ize the heathen in North America, and to support and promote Christian
knowledge in the new settlements within the United States."[4] From 1820
onward, the federal government assisted the work through annual subsidies
given to agencies engaged in tribal missions.

Missionary efforts among Native Americans had ambiguous results, as
the ironic experience of the Georgia Cherokees exemplified. Following the
1794 tribal treaty with the United States government, several denominations
sent missionaries to found Cherokee churches. Many of the tribes responded
positively, establishing congregations, developing a written language, and se-
lectively adopting American ways while taking care to avoid full assimilation.
The Cherokees even lived under a self-governing constitution and produced
their own books and newspapers.

Sadly, these achievements came to an end when whites moved to take
over reservation lands. President Andrew Jackson defied a Supreme Court

---

4. *The Constitution of the Missionary Society of Connecticut* (Hartford, 1800), cited in James R.
Rohrer, *Keepers of the Covenant: Frontier Missions and the Decline of Congregationalism, 1774–1818*
(New York: Oxford University Press, 1995), 62.

decision in favor of the Cherokees and ordered them to move west of the Mississippi River. Thus began the infamous "trail of tears" in 1838. Some missionaries assented to the removal, but the courageous Samuel Worcester and Elizur Butler were jailed for civil disobedience when they supported the Cherokees against the rapacious demands of the Georgia government. Others made the long and arduous journey with the Cherokees to the Oklahoma Territory and continued ministering to them. This event marked one of the most tragic episodes in the history of relations between Native Americans and whites.

As world trade and geographic knowledge expanded in the post-Reformation era, both major branches of Christianity developed a missionary outreach. The most extensive was the Roman Catholic work in North and South America, sub-Saharan Africa, and south and east Asia. The Protestant effort was less spectacular, with a variety of works in areas where trading companies were active, such as India and the East Indies (Indonesia), a few isolated ventures by lone-wolf types, and the much larger outreach generated by German Pietism. The latter was seen in the globally oriented Moravian missions that Count Nicholas von Zinzendorf launched in the 1730s and the work of missionaries trained at the Francke Institution in Halle who served in India and colonial North America. The most notable of these missionaries was the aforementioned Henry Muhlenberg, who arrived in Pennsylvania in 1742.

The evangelical revivals in Britain and Europe in the later eighteenth century combined with a new wave of European imperialism, which enabled the transmission of the Protestant faith to vast numbers of people around the world. European Protestants formed voluntary mission societies, beginning with the Baptist Missionary Society (1792), the London Missionary Society (1795), the Netherlands Mission Society (1797), and the Basel Mission Society (1815). The American churches soon followed their lead.

As American ships traded in far-off lands and British Christians opened new ministries abroad, Americans began to sense the need for foreign mission involvement. The dedication of a group of students at Andover Theological Seminary in 1810 activated this concern. Led by Samuel J. Mills Jr., the group, which included Adoniram Judson (1788–1850), Samuel Newell, and Samuel Nott, petitioned the Congregational General Association of Massachusetts to initiate a foreign mission and offered themselves as candidates. The association received the proposal warmly, and soon donations flowed in to the newly founded (1810) American Board of Commissioners for Foreign Missions (ABCFM). The young missionaries were ordained and sent to India in February 1812. Some of them were Williams College graduates who had pledged themselves to foreign service in 1806 during a prayer meeting in the midst of a thunderstorm.

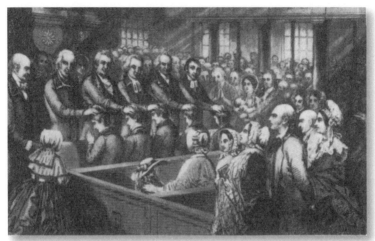

Consecration of the first American foreign missionaries. Courtesy of the Franklin Trask Library, Andover Newton Theological School.

Other foreign mission societies followed. When Judson decided from his study of Scripture that believers' baptism was the proper mode, he resigned from the Congregationalist board and sought certification as a Baptist. Accordingly, Baptists from eleven states gathered at Philadelphia in May 1814 and launched the General Missionary Convention of the Baptist Denomination of the United States of America for Foreign Missions. Popularly known

Adoniram Judson
(1788–1850)

as the Triennial Convention because it met every three years, this was the first broadly based organization of American Baptists.

The Congregationalist ABCFM dispatched nearly seven hundred missionaries in its first thirty years. Among its most notable achievements was the introduction of Christianity to the Hawaiian Islands in 1820. In 1821, the Domestic and Foreign Missionary Society of the Protestant Episcopal Church, which concentrated its efforts in the Northwest, was organized. By 1860, American missionaries were serving in many nations and on nearly every continent.

Mission agencies received vital support from the Bible and tract societies that were founded during these years, since distribution of Bibles and Christian literature went hand in hand with missionary outreach. The American Bible Society was organized in New York in 1816, and its sister organization, the American Tract Society, was begun in 1825. Agents from these two societies crisscrossed the North American continent, supplying people with religious literature. The growth of denominational publishing houses, such as the Methodist Book Concern (1789) and the American Baptist Publication Society (1840), complemented the literary work. New printing technology enabled the publication of more than 850 religious periodicals in 1840, 250 of which originated in the western states and frontier territories. These were a primary means of bringing Christian knowledge into homes and of influencing the lives of thousands. It is impossible to overestimate the importance of this cascade of religious literature for the nurturing of faith in the increasingly literate society.

Education

An important by-product of the era of benevolence was a passion for learning. Church leaders believed that without vigorous education in Christian principles America would not achieve its destiny. The West, once again, was the primary focus. Lyman Beecher, aroused by the influx of Catholic immigrants, whom he pictured as subverters of republican institutions, campaigned to educate the West: "For population will not wait, and commerce will not cast anchor, and manufacturers will not shut down the gate, and agriculture, pushed by millions of freemen on their fertile soil, will not withhold her corrupting abundance. We must educate! We must educate! Or we must perish by our own prosperity."[5]

The period from 1780 to 1860 is recognized by historians as the "denominational era in American higher education." During these eighty years, the number of colleges in the United States increased from 9 to 173. Congre-

_____
5. He made this statement in his 1834 tract, *A Plea for the West.*

gationalists, Presbyterians, and Episcopals led the way in starting colleges, followed by Methodists, Baptists, and other denominations. Staffed primarily by ministers and with clergy as presidents, these denominational colleges were the backbone of American higher education prior to the Civil War.

The founding of theological seminaries was another innovation of antebellum Protestant education. Traditionally, those aspiring to the ministry attended an eastern college such as Yale or Princeton and then joined themselves to clergymen with whom they lived and worked, gaining practical experience. By 1800, however, with the expansion of American society and the proliferation of churches, graduate professional schools were formed to credential the needed clergy, thus ensuring a more scholarly ministerium in the older denominations.

In 1807, orthodox Congregationalists founded the first permanent theological seminary at Andover, Massachusetts, in reaction to Harvard's drift toward Unitarianism. The Presbyterians opened their first seminary at Princeton in 1812. New School Presbyterians were responsible for launching Union Theological Seminary in New York City in 1836, and the Episcopal Church founded General Theological Seminary there in 1824. Divinity schools at Harvard and Yale Universities were established in 1816 and 1822 respectively.

The early nineteenth century also witnessed the rise of public education, a major factor in the rising literacy rate. Where community-supported schools existed, a strong religious influence usually prevailed, as was the case with Congregationalism in New England. By 1825, however, the trend was clearly toward a more secular approach. The catalyst for this movement was Horace Mann (1796–1859), under whose leadership Massachusetts developed a system of secular schools run by the state. Mann desired a Protestant-tinged education but without sectarian intrusions. Some churchmen, especially Presbyterians, Lutherans, and Catholics, felt that such an education was theologically superficial and created alternative or parochial (parish-based) schools that shielded their youth from what they considered diluted values. Although the Presbyterian program soon passed away, the Catholic and Lutheran schools thrived.

These years also saw the flowering of the Sunday school. From its inception in 1769 in England by Methodist Hannah Ball to its popularization by Robert Raikes, the goal was to provide religious and literacy instruction to the many children who lacked access to formal schooling. The early American Sunday schools were organized and operated mainly by societies formed for that purpose. In 1804, the Union Society began to provide education for the poor female children of Philadelphia. Other large cities such as Pittsburgh, Boston, New York, Albany, Baltimore, and Charleston followed suit, and in 1824, the American Sunday School Union was founded to provide lesson materials for the classes.

The Sunday schools afforded an opportunity for women to serve churches by teaching the young, which encouraged the women's movement in its formative period. In fact, churches were the real seedbed for women's consciousness. Although a woman was viewed by the law as a nonentity and in the professions as an intruder, in church she was the same as a man: a sinner saved by grace. The influence of women was so great in nineteenth-century Protestant parishes that one historian has described this period as the "feminization of American religion."[6] These years witnessed earlier baptisms of children, the quiet disappearance of the doctrine of infant damnation, and a new emphasis on themes of submission, love, mercy, and meekness in both hymnody and the doctrine of Christ. Above all, church women stood in the forefront of the women's rights movement and helped organize the Seneca Falls (N.Y.) Convention on women's rights in 1848, which issued the first formal call for female voting rights.

Social Reform

The aim of the Benevolent Empire was not only to evangelize individuals and plant new churches but also to remake society. Hence, its supporters, in addition to encouraging revival, also championed moral and social reform and showed compassion to the weak and the neglected in society.

Some of the most noteworthy endeavors launched during this time involved prison reform, temperance, education, peace, and the abolition of slavery. The American Temperance Society (1826) spearheaded a sweeping drive for changes in drinking practices. Methodologies perfected in the winning of Christian converts were employed in battling "ardent spirits" and "demon rum." The drinking habits of the bulk of American Christians changed, and public opinion developed in favor of a total ban on alcoholic beverages. In 1846, Maine became the first state to legislate prohibition.

Britain had provided the model for the benevolent efforts of American Christians, but in forming peace societies, Americans took the initiative. Disillusionment over the War of 1812, continuing currents of Enlightenment optimism, and the nonviolent tradition of Quakers and Mennonites played a role in the development of several state peace societies. A national body, the American Peace Society, followed in 1828. For more than a decade, the society stimulated discussion on the evils of war and the possibility of a "Congress of Nations" to avoid it. During the Mexican War (1846–48), the Quakers sent a petition bearing one thousand signatures to the government asking that peace be established at once. However, internal tensions between extremists and

6. This is an argument of Ann Douglas in *The Feminization of American Culture* (New York: Knopf, 1977).

moderates weakened the movement, and the Civil War buried it completely. It did not resurface until the Spanish-American War of 1898.

Christian compassion also led to the organization of support bodies for young men and women. The Young Men's Christian Association (YMCA), which originated in London in 1844, opened its first American branch in Boston in 1851. Within a decade more than two hundred such organizations served young American adults, both male and female. The problem of female drunkenness and prostitution led to the establishment in 1830 of Magdalen Asylum in New York and in 1834 of the American Female Moral Reform Society.

The restoration of criminals to a responsible place in society was the aim of the Philadelphia Society for Alleviating the Miseries of Public Prisons, which was founded in 1787. After the War of 1812, renewed interest in prison reform led to the establishment of a new type of penal institution, such as that at Auburn, New York. It operated on the philosophy that communal labor could best rehabilitate inmates. Christians were often in the vanguard of these efforts.

The reform of economic structures had low priority in the social thought of evangelicals. They were confident that an individual freed from the grips of sin, liquor, and indolence would become prosperous. After the devastating effects of the panic of 1837, however, some Christian activists realized that the problem of urban poverty demanded attention. Unitarian Joseph Zuckerman (1778–1840) formed the Benevolent Fraternity of Churches in Boston to bring ministry and charitable aid to the city's poor. After absorbing the socialist sentiments of Robert Dale Owen, Orestes Brownson helped form the Workingman's Party in New York City and by 1836 was ministering in Boston through his own Society for Christian Union and Progress.

For the most part, however, a predominantly rural and individualistic Protestantism did not seriously address the emerging industrial and urban issues of the mid-nineteenth century. The thinking of reformers regarding economic questions was simplistic. Moral exhortation substituted for informed analysis of structural societal problems. Even when they spoke of the relationship between religion and worldly business, such Protestants focused on the ethical conduct of individuals rather than on such entities as government or corporations.

Abolition

Slavery was an ugly and perplexing blot on the record of a nation conceived in liberty. Although it had existed from America's earliest days, humanitarians both within and without the Christian community were increasingly critical of the institution, especially John Woolman and Anthony Benezet, previously mentioned. The attackers intensified their offensive, and soon after the Revolution, the northern states, where there was but a fraction of the number of slaves in the South, enacted antislavery legislation. By 1787, Rhode Island, Massachusetts, New York, Connecticut, Vermont, New Hampshire, New Jersey, and Pennsylvania had either abolished slavery or provided for phasing it out. The Northwest Ordinance of 1787 permanently excluded slavery from the yet unorganized territories in the West and north of the Ohio River. Although the Constitution was silent on slaveholding, a compromise necessary to secure its acceptance by the southern states, Congress legislated a halt to the slave trade in 1808.

Nevertheless, slavery was deeply entrenched in the South. Whereas industrialization was advancing rapidly in the North, the enormous expansion of cotton production in the South resulting from the invention of the cotton gin (1793), opening of new land to the west, and the growing demand of the British and American textile industry for raw materials contributed to the growth of an agrarian society heavily dependent on slave labor. By 1860, 75 percent of the slaves in the South were engaged in cotton production. Although several southern states before 1800 actually had worked to restrict the importation of new slaves, they now became much more defensive about what they labeled the "peculiar institution," especially after slave revolts in 1822 and 1831. Thus, antislavery agitation in the North appeared concurrently with an aggressive pro-slavery movement in the South. An ominous cloud was forming that threatened the future of the nation.

Jonathan Blanchard (1811–92).
Courtesy of Buswell Memorial
Library, Wheaton College,
Wheaton, Illinois.

Abolition societies, composed of both blacks and whites and humanitarians of various kinds, launched a vigorous campaign against human bondage. Organizations first appeared in Philadelphia (1775), New York (1785), Maryland (1790), Connecticut (1791), New Jersey (1792), and Delaware (1794); a fresh effort took shape in 1833 under the auspices of the American Antislavery Society. Outstanding clergymen, including Lyman Beecher, Charles Finney, Theodore Dwight Weld, and Jonathan Blanchard (1811–92), then president of Knox College and later the founder of Wheaton College; the New England Unitarians; and independents such as former slave Frederick Douglass and William Lloyd Garrison lent their influence to the crusade. Sarah and Angelina Grimke, Harriet Beecher Stowe (1811–96), and Julia Ward Howe (1819–1910) enlisted financial support and devoted themselves to the cause. Soon abolitionist chapters formed within churches, and several Baptist associations and Methodist conferences, particularly in New England, passed strong antislavery resolutions.

The southern response to the northern attacks reflected just how deeply rooted slavery was in that region. It is important to remember that most slave owners, Christian or otherwise, inherited the institution just as one inherits one's culture. By the early nineteenth century, slavery was so much a part of southern economic and social life that the idea of abolition threatened not only southern culture but also the security of the slaves themselves.

A historical profile may help to illustrate the situation. In his 1891 autobiography, *Recollections of a Long Life,* Jeremiah Jeter, a Virginia Baptist clergyman, recorded his anguish over the slavery question. He grew up determining never to own a slave. Then he married a woman who held slaves, and he thereby became an owner. During their engagement, they agreed that after they married, Jeter could dispose of the slaves in whatever way he thought proper. When the time came, however, the difficulty of doing so overwhelmed him. To free them would be a violation of the laws of the state. Even if they were freed, how could the slaves support themselves? What about those slaves who were married to slaves owned by other masters? Should he send those freed to Liberia, even though none of them wanted to go there? Jeter's dilemma dramatically underlined the tragic reality that slavery had become a systemic problem. To tamper with one part of the system inevitably produced undesirable consequences in another. The burden of an inherited past was heavy for those southerners who were troubled by the "peculiar institution."

On the other hand, many southerners claimed that slavery was good and argued that they had the best interests of the blacks in mind. The pro-slavery position, however, was actually based on paternalism and racial superiority. Yet ministers and laypersons alike defended slavery by using selected passages from both Testaments that recognized slavery as an institution in ancient society and said nothing in criticism of it. Although not a southerner, even the renowned Princeton theologian Charles Hodge did not see a direct biblical quarrel with slavery. Also, many northern churchgoers, although not supporters of slavery, considered blacks inferior. Thus, southerners regarded the abolitionists as unwelcome agitators.

The abolitionists appealed to a higher moral law and had no compunction about violating civil laws that they regarded as unjust. Hence, they aided runaway slaves and illegally circulated antislavery literature in the southern states. William Lloyd Garrison went so far as to declare the Constitution illegal because it sanctioned slavery, and thus, abolitionist activities on behalf of civil liberties were justified by a higher moral law.

By 1840, internal conflicts had shattered all hope of a united national front among Christian reformers. Divisions over slavery and the women's rights movement intensified divergent approaches to reform. Furthermore, while reformers fought to reshape the outward characteristics of American society, other forces were penetrating the ideas and values undergirding American Christianity. Evangelical revivalism had provided a vital, formative cultural force from the 1790s to the 1830s. By mid-century, however, a more varied and complex religious and social context had developed.

9

Diversity in Religious Life

American society in the nineteenth century underwent rapid change. Factories replaced small workshops. Slow-moving barges and sailing vessels yielded to steamships and railroads. The admission of new states doubled the size of the Union. Immigrants poured into the country, and new ideas transformed people's self-conception. The United States was a land in ferment, and developments in the industrial, commercial, political, and intellectual realms profoundly affected the church.

During the age of benevolence, denominations toned down their differences as they brought their influence to bear on the social order. But soon geographical expansion heightened sectional and sectarian interests, and religious differences resurfaced. Contributing to this trend was the liberalization of theology in the traditional denominations. Diverse approaches to the Christian faith now competed in a world in which the expanding physical and social space encouraged change.

Broadening Trends

Unitarianism appeared first among the New England clergy and businessmen in the Boston area in the second third of the eighteenth century. Significant for its prominence at Harvard University after 1800, Unitarianism grew in popularity following the publication of William Ellery Channing's (1780–1842) famous sermon "Unitarian Christianity," which articulated a middle way between orthodoxy and rationalistic unbelief. By 1825, the American Unitarian Association included 125 churches largely based in New England. An even more liberal movement developed within Unitarianism in the 1830s that Channing, who reflected an almost evangelical zeal for faith and morality, found too humanistic. It included such luminaries as Congregational minister Ralph Waldo Emerson (1803–82) and the more radical Theodore Parker (1810–60), who embraced many philosophic ideas emanating from Germany.

William Ellery Channing (1780–1842). Courtesy of the Unitarian-Universalist Association.

Often mediated through English or Scottish writers such as Samuel Taylor Coleridge or Thomas Carlyle, the German and Continental perceptions of religion as a matter of imagination and moral consciousness were becoming more accepted in some American intellectual circles. Thus, heavily influenced by European romanticism along with some traces of Buddhism, the Transcendentalists, as they were called, viewed each person as an incarnation of God and argued that reason and intuition were the guiding principles in experiencing the "unity" of all things. A subjective individualistic faith that rejected churchly religion, Transcendentalism never appealed to the masses, but it did impact wider American thought through the writings of Emerson, Herman Melville, Henry David Thoreau, Walt Whitman, Margaret Fuller, and other New England literary figures.

Closely associated with Unitarianism was Universalism, imported from England and whose first American congregation was organized in 1779 in Gloucester, Massachusetts. Although Universalists at first acknowledged most traditional theological doctrines, they soon abandoned these touchstones of the faith. The Winchester Platform of 1803 specifically affirmed the perfectibility of man, the ultimate (universal) salvation of all people, and the humanness of Jesus Christ. The two communions worked closely together and eventually merged into one denomination, the Unitarian-Universalist Association, in 1961. Though membership numbered only roughly .2 percent of the American population by the late twentieth century, Unitarian-Universalism, with its early adoption of a liberal theology, exercised an influence greater than its numbers might indicate in the saga of American religious history.

Although Unitarians and Universalists went their separate ways, ample theological diversity remained within the Congregationalist denomination. Horace Bushnell (1802–76), in *Christian Nurture* (1847), set forth a new theory of Christian education that viewed the child not as morally depraved and in need of conversion but as a person needing only a Christian rearing to grow in grace. Critics attacked Bushnell for discounting the special agency of the Holy Spirit in conversion, advocating a "moral influence only" view of the atonement, and reducing Christianity to a form of religious naturalism. Liberal Protestant thought in the next generation reflected Bushnell's humanized view of Christ as primarily a revealer of mercy, patience, and compassionate love, revealing Bushnell's influence on such future leaders as Henry Ward Beecher (1813–87) and Washington Gladden (1836–1918). Theologian Gary Dorrien argues "that Bushnell is the major theologian of nineteenth century American liberal Christianity and the key figure to its history as a whole."[1]

As mentioned earlier, women had more opportunities for expression in the nineteenth century. The revivalists insisted that the Holy Spirit's call, not necessarily education or ordination, qualified one to preach. Charles Finney allowed women to speak and pray in the presence of men, while the emerging Holiness movement included women in leadership roles. The African-American preacher Amanda Smith (1837–1915) was a leading figure on the evangelistic circuit in the United States and Britain. The Free Will Baptists had female preachers in the early nineteenth century, and in 1853, the Congregational Church became the first major denomination to formally ordain a woman, Antoinette Brown Blackwell (1825–1921), a student of Finney and a graduate of Oberlin College, that outstanding bastion of reform.

The increasing demand for greater freedom in theology, church polity, and social life led to denominational ruptures. Baptists quarreled over the question of free will versus predestination; the normally placid Quakers divided over

---

1. Gary Dorrien, *The Making of American Liberal Theology* (Louisville: Westminster John Knox, 2001), xvii.

whether the Bible or one's own "Inner Light" should be the final authority in religious life; and Methodists splintered over the call for greater lay participation in the General Conferences. Five ministers of the Dutch Reformed Church seceded from their communion, which they accused of looseness of doctrine and discipline, and formed the True Reformed Church in 1822, which later evolved into the Christian Reformed Church.

During the Second Awakening, the Presbyterians forced out those expressing Arminian tendencies. In Pennsylvania, Alexander Campbell (1788–1866) and his followers modified their Presbyterianism into a more Baptist form that emphasized the immersion of adult believers, which they considered more biblical. Campbell preached a simple message, transcending denominational distinctions, and ironically ended up forming his own denomination called the Disciples. In 1831, they joined with Barton W. Stone's Christian Church to become the Disciples of Christ. The quest to restore a pure New Testament faith, one shorn of all ecclesiastical structures, led to further fragmentation, and the primitivistic ideal found its most distinctive expression in

Alexander Campbell (1788–1866). Courtesy of Disciples of Christ Historical Society, Nashville, Tennessee.

the fiercely independent fellowships known as the Church of Christ. They rejected instrumental music in worship services and missionary societies as unscriptural.

The Sectarian Heyday

An American religious consensus hardly existed during this period. By 1830, the stalwart orthodoxy that had once judged deviant doctrines had eroded.

Americans found themselves free to worship how, where, and when they willed. Such freedom encouraged nonconformity and dissent. Resentment by the poor toward elite rule found expression in revolts against the authority structures of the existing denominations and the formation of independent assemblies directly controlled by the body of believers. The men and women who led such movements combined belief in the Bible with vigorous assertion of the worth of every individual, however poor in worldly goods.

The rejection of current social values was obvious in the millenarian doctrines that the end of the present world was at hand and that the millennial kingdom promised in the New Testament would be established. People were exhorted to forsake sin, be saved, and await Christ's imminent return. William Miller (1782–1849), a farmer and self-educated Baptist preacher in upstate New York, was responsible for the most significant millenarian group. After thirteen years of Bible study and numerological speculation, Miller concluded that on April 23, 1843, the second advent of Christ would occur.

Miller's message of doom circulated widely throughout the Northeast. As the appointed day approached, converts sold or gave away their property, and farmers deserted their plows and artisans their benches. When the actual day passed without incident, Miller revised his calculations and settled on October 22, 1844. Expectations again reached fever pitch, but nothing happened. As is the fate of all such movements, the "Great Disappointment" followed, and Millerism as such came to an end. Some of Miller's followers, however, found a new leader in Ellen Gould White (1827–1915) of Maine, who persuaded them that Christ's failure to appear was due to the neglect of proper Sabbath observance. In 1845, they formed the nucleus of what became the Seventh-day Adventist Church. It continued the practice of prophetic speculation, while avoiding specific date setting, and emphasized evangelical doctrine, healthy lifestyles, and firm commitment to religious liberty.

The most extreme expression of social alienation was the Church of Jesus Christ of Latter-day Saints, also known as the Mormons, founded in 1830 by Joseph Smith (1805–44). Smith had a vivid imagination and a great fascination with the occult implications of the dimensions of the Great Pyramid, the literal fulfillment of prophecies in the Books of Daniel and Revelation, and the prospect that American Indians were the ten lost tribes of Israel. In 1830, Smith published in Palmyra, New York, his translation of the Book of Mormon. He claimed that it had been given to him on golden tablets and that angelic informants had helped him to read it. He gathered a small group of followers into a community in nearby Fayette.

Local hostility to the Mormons erupted, however, and the group migrated to Kirtland, Ohio, in 1831. From there in 1838 they went to Jackson County, Missouri, and then in 1840 to Nauvoo, Illinois. In Nauvoo, the Mormons set about creating a cohesive community that they hoped would be a perfect society. They built a temple, organized a defense force, and established their own local government. Four years later a mob killed Smith. In an effort to avoid more bloodshed, his successor, Brigham Young (1801–77), led

Brigham Young at home with his children

nearly sixteen thousand Mormons westward across the prairies to found a new Zion. A dissenting remnant stayed behind to found the Reorganized Church of Jesus Christ of Latter Day Saints headquartered in Independence, Missouri; it rejected polygamy and claimed to be the legitimate successor to Joseph Smith.

In July 1847, Young's intrepid band reached the fertile Great Salt Lake Valley in Utah. It was removed from the "gentiles" and at the time still a part of Mexico. Here the Mormons created their own state of Deseret, a society in which self-interest was subordinated to the needs of the community. Mormons found individual expression and fulfillment in contributing to the well-being of the whole, and their society had neither unemployment nor poverty. In 1850, Deseret was incorporated into the American political system as the Utah Territory. The Mormons were gradually integrated into society, but they maintained their distinctive faith and moral values. The one major concession they had to make was the formal renunciation of polygamy. One of the most successful new religious movements in America, Mormonism, within 150 years, had over ten million adherents worldwide.

The Utopian Vision

The various utopian colonies, which attracted thousands of seekers, outrightly rejected the American social and economic order. These groups endeavored to restore a sense of community by means of shared labor and wealth. Several accepted a new role for women by proclaiming sexual equality. Some were inspired by religious ideals; others were purely secular. The depression of 1837 stimulated interest in such experiments, but even in times of prosperity some Americans questioned the morality of individualistic capitalism. The most noteworthy of the religious utopian colonies were the Shakers and the Oneida Community.

The Millennial Church, called the Shakers because of adherents' bodily shaking and ritual dancing to "shake out" sin, was one of the most radical yet successful of the utopian communities. The founder, "Mother" Ann Lee (c. 1736–84), had turned to a radical Quaker group because of an unhappy marriage and the loss in infancy of her children. She claimed to have visions and spoke in tongues; she also repudiated sexuality, considering it the source of all sin. This teaching eventually gained institutional embodiment in the Shaker practice of celibacy and segregation of the sexes.

Because of persecution in her native England, Lee and a handful of followers migrated to New York State in 1774 and established a community. During the next year, several other colonies were founded in western New England and the backcountry of Ohio and Kentucky. After Lee's death, Joseph Meacham assumed leadership, drafted a constitution for the society, and systematized Shaker doctrine. The Shakers were in a sense a Protestant expression of the institutionalized communities that monasticism represented in Roman Catholicism. The Shakers' celibacy, communal ownership of goods, simplicity

Shaker worship service. Courtesy of the Billy Graham Center Museum, Wheaton, Illinois.

in lifestyle, subordination to the authority of ruling elders, and segregation by sexes paralleled the historic monastic practices of cultivating godliness and withdrawal from the world. Since the community could not reproduce itself and depended on new people joining, the Shakers eventually died out by the beginning of the twenty-first century.

A novel attempt to adjust sexuality to perfectionistic ideals was that of John Humphrey Noyes (1811–86), a Vermont communitarian who in 1848 founded the Oneida Community in New York. Noyes advocated "complex marriage," a plan whereby every woman in the community was the wife of every man and vice versa. All sex relations, however, were regulated, and quotas were set for the number of offspring to be produced.

Noyes himself was a product of the Finney revivals and ardently embraced regeneration, perfection, and millennialism. But he went beyond the individualist conversionism of most revivalists to promote religion as communal social living. His theology was a potpourri of ideas that included the possibility of human sinlessness, the superiority of "Spirit-filled love" over static moral law, and the progressive realization of God's goodness. Coupled with his religious zeal was a Yankee shrewdness in mundane affairs, which was reflected in the economic productivity of the Oneida Community, particularly its silverware industry. Yet the community's neighbors did not react kindly to its unusual views of marriage, and in the face of bitter hostility, the Oneida Community abandoned the system of complex marriage in 1879. A year later it discontinued economic communism and converted the colony into a joint-stock company. Its fate was part of the general decline of revivalist and millennial enthusiasm in post–Civil War America, a development discussed in a later chapter.

The communitarians sought to attain the realization of the church as fellowship or *koinōnia*. They tried to perpetuate this sense of love and sanctification by expanding their church life into the world and restricting their world to the church. The very fact that the utopian experiments were tolerated at all indicates the openness of American society in the nineteenth century and a willingness to engage in social experimentation. But the tolerance was selective rather than general. Nineteenth-century America also witnessed the growth of the Roman Catholic Church as an alternative religious movement, and with its rise came intense outbreaks of nativistic, anti-Catholic hostility.

The Progress of Roman Catholicism

Several currents shaped American Catholicism in the nineteenth century. First, almost two million Irish immigrants came to the United States in the aftermath of the potato famine (1845–1848) and other economic stresses in Ireland. As a result, they greatly outnumbered French and English Catholics and replaced them in leadership positions. At the same time, much of the Irish-American hierarchy that emerged remained faithful to the earlier tradition of Americanization of the church. Catholics participated in political life, supported numerous Protestant reform movements, and even considered the possibility of educating their children in public schools with released-time provisions for religious education.

Another factor in Catholic growth was the influx of a large number of Germans, some because of the unsuccessful revolution of 1848 but far more because of economic opportunity. They settled mainly in areas north of the Ohio River. One-third of the German immigrants were Roman Catholics. Adding to Catholic numbers were tens of thousands of Hispanics who came under United States sovereignty in 1848 as a result of the Mexican War.

Of considerable importance to American Catholicism were religious orders. The pope, in 1814, allowed the Jesuits, who had been suppressed in 1773, to resume their work. Several women's orders were also active in America—older ones such as the Ursulines and Carmelites and new ones such as the Sisters of Charity, Ladies of the Sacred Heart of Jesus, and Sisters of Providence, which had numerous urban schools and convents. By 1835, every large city in the United States contained houses of the women's orders. Meanwhile, new dioceses were established in Charleston (1820), Richmond (1821), Cincinnati (1823), Mobile (1824), St. Louis (1826), and Detroit (1832). Between 1834 and 1847, Dubuque, Little Rock, Nashville, Pittsburgh, Milwaukee, Chicago, Hartford, Oregon City, Albany, Buffalo, and Cleveland established dioceses. The Roman Catholic Church numbered only 35,000 in 1789 but claimed 3.1 million adherents in 1860. It had become the largest church in the United States.

Some Catholic beliefs and customs aroused fears among native (American-born) Protestants. Anti-Catholicism in America was never purely religious, for social and economic factors aggravated suspicion. To staid Americans, the recent arrivals seemed disorderly, and they also competed for jobs. Yet this hardly justified the extreme nativist reaction. Stories of sexual excesses by clergy, which followed a formula that has never completely died in Protestant American folklore, led to the burning of the Charlestown, Massachusetts, convent in 1836. The founding of St. Louis University by the Jesuits aroused fears of Roman expansion in the West. Catholic churches were burned in Philadelphia in 1844, while a show of armed defense by Catholic congregations frightened off would-be torchers in New York. Opposition to Roman Catholicism gave rise to the Native American Party in 1837 (also called the Know-Nothings), a political organization that sought to curtail immigration and to require aliens to live in the country twenty-one years before becoming eligible for citizenship.

Despite efforts to thwart Roman Catholic gains, the church flourished. Indicative of its remarkable advance was the Plenary Council of the hierarchy held in Baltimore in May 1852. Of the thirty-two bishops present, only nine were native born. The council issued twenty-five decrees that dealt with such themes as parochial schools, administration of church property, and the standardization of discipline, but it ignored divisive issues such as slavery. The council also recognized that Catholic problems were no longer purely provincial but national in scope and that the ownership of local parishes as well as appointment of priests resided with the bishops, a policy some laity unsuccessfully challenged as un-American.

PART 4

DISRUPTION, DEVOTION, AND DEBATE (1861–1916)

10

Following the Faith in a Divided Nation

Two publications that appeared in 1851 highlighted the cleft in American Christianity caused by the slavery debate. In that year, Harriet Beecher Stowe, daughter of Lyman Beecher and wife of theologian Calvin E. Stowe, added to the popular revulsion over slavery with her best-selling *Uncle Tom's*

Harriet Beecher Stowe (1811–96)

Cabin, a thoroughgoing indictment of the nation for harboring such an evil. Her character, Uncle Tom, served as a thinly disguised Christ figure, whose greatest triumph came through his unmerited suffering and death. Southerners resented their characterization as crucifiers.

In contrast, James Henley Thornwell (1812–62), professor of theology at Columbia Theological Seminary and a prominent Presbyterian theologian, penned a biblical defense of slavery for the Presbyterian Synod of South Carolina, which it unanimously adopted. Appealing to Holy Writ, he declared:

> The Scriptures not only fail to condemn slavery, they as distinctly sanction it as any other condition of man. The Church was formally organized in the family of a slaveholder [Abraham]; the relation was divinely regulated among the chosen people of God [Israel]; and the peculiar duties of the parties are inculcated under the Christian economy [Philemon].

Consequently, to call slavery sinful was in effect to reject the Bible in favor of a rationalistic mode of thought. "Opposition to slavery," concluded Thornwell, "has never been the offspring of the Bible."[1]

Slavery and the Conflicts of Faith

In retrospect, it is evident that much of the antagonism between North and South stemmed from differing definitions of slavery. Northerners held to an abstract understanding based on a moral philosophy that viewed slavery as ownership of one man by another and, consequently, the absorption of the humanity of one individual into the will and power of another. The southern perspective, based on the thought of the Scottish philosopher William Paley, saw slavery as the obligation to labor for another man independently of the provisions of a contract. The master had a right not to the man personally but to his labor. Moreover, the master's right to the slave's labor did not deny the slave the possibility of moral, intellectual, and religious development and therefore did not deprive him of his humanity. Defenders of the practice attempted to stop abolitionists from talking about slavery in the abstract and to focus attention on slavery as it was perceived in the South. But the critics of the slave system argued that chattel slavery as practiced in the South was not the same as slavery found in the Old Testament, with its provisions for the protection of slaves. In some southern states, it was illegal even to teach a slave to read.

Finding common agreement on the authoritative teachings of the Bible that applied to the American slave institution proved impossible. The tragedy

---

1. *The Collected Writings of James Henley Thornwell,* vol. 4 (Carlisle, Pa.: Banner of Truth Trust, 1974), 393.

was that the type of biblicism that followed a flat, literalistic approach to scriptural interpretation made it difficult for well-meaning Christians to accept a critique of slavery built on broader biblical moral arguments. Whatever the complexity of the situation, however, the failure of American Christians to resolve the problem of slavery short of bloody conflict remains the greatest irony and failure of the American church experience.

The churches faced a difficult dilemma. Honorable, ethical, God-fearing people as well as self-seeking, egotistical types were on both sides of the debate, and given feelings about the issue, by the 1840s, many denominations felt compelled to take a stand. Some church bodies, such as the Congregationalists and the Unitarians, maintained their unity because they were located largely in the North. Quakers, both North and South, opposed slavery and therefore escaped schism. Other denominations, such as the Episcopalians and the Lutherans, that were determined to remain disentangled from political matters took no stance. The Roman Catholic hierarchy was unfavorably disposed toward slavery but looked for the passage of time and due process of law to bring about its termination. Thus, these churches did not separate until the war forced them to do so. When the conflict ended, their reunion was natural and spontaneous. The Presbyterians, Methodists, and Baptists, however, became embroiled in the slavery question, which strained ecclesiastical unity. Initially, they held to the doctrine of noninterference. The compromise announced at the South Carolina Methodist Conference in 1838 was repeated in most other church synods:

> We hold that the subject of slavery in these United States is not one proper for the action of the church, but is exclusively appropriate to the civil authorities; therefore, resolved that this conference will not intermeddle with it further than to express our regret that it has ever been introduced in any form, into any one of the judicatories of the church.[2]

This uneasy position lasted for only a few anxious years. As tensions deepened, the largest Protestant denominations were torn by schism.

The Methodist Episcopal Church was the first to divide. By 1843, in the South, 1,200 Methodist clergy owned 1,500 slaves, and 25,000 church members owned 208,000 more. Although northern abolitionists had tried unsuccessfully throughout the 1830s to gain a majority in the General Conference, they succeeded only in 1844. The symbolic vote on slavery centered on Bishop James Andrew of Georgia, who had possession of slaves through inheritance and marriage. The antislavery delegates insisted that he free his slaves or resign from office; the southern delegates replied that the bishop had broken no regulation of the church. After eleven days of heated debate,

2. L. C. Matlack, *The Antislavery Struggle and Triumph in the Methodist Episcopal Church* (1881; reprint, New York: Negro Universities Press, 1969), 104.

the northern interests won the vote, and the southern delegates drafted a proposal for two General Conferences, which was approved. Although relations between the two new denominations were amicable at first, strife over the allegiance of the border states and lawsuits concerning property rights heightened the strain and assured a prolonged separation. Methodists of the North and South did not reunite until 1939. The breakaway antislavery Wesleyan Methodist Church, founded in 1843, never did return to the larger denominational fold.

Fear that radical abolitionists might gain control of the missionary societies precipitated the rift among Baptists. Despite persistent antislavery agitation of Baptist abolitionists, it was apparent at the 1844 Triennial Convention that the moderates still controlled the floor. Resolutions were passed that, in effect, left the slavery question up to the individual conscience. Nevertheless, rumors circulated that the northern delegates were planning to dissolve the organization. The crucial vote again involved an individual. Southern churchmen were incensed by the rejection of a slaveholding missionary by the board of the Home Mission Society. In response, the board stated its conviction clearly: "One thing is certain, we can never be a party to any arrangement which would imply approbation of slavery."[3]

Without further ado, in 1845, the southern state conventions and auxiliary foreign missions societies seceded from the national missionary body, creating the new Southern Baptist Convention. As a result, Baptists in the South had a more formal structure linking the churches of the region than did those in the North. After the secession, the Triennial Convention reconstituted itself as the American Baptist Missionary Union (from 1910 the American Baptist Foreign Mission Society). As time passed, Baptists in the North and the West felt the need for closer organization, and in 1907, representatives from the foreign and home missions societies and the publication society met with delegates from state and city bodies to form the Northern Baptist Convention.

The Old School and the New School Presbyterian churches, having divided in 1837 over theological issues, sought to muffle the slavery controversy to prevent further fracturing. The New School group, located mainly in the North, succeeded in doing so for a time, but it finally split in 1857 when its assembly repudiated the doctrine that slavery is "an ordinance of God" and is "Scriptural and right."[4] Through astute diplomacy, the Old School Presbyterians forestalled a break until the onset of war.

The significance of these schisms for the nation's political future should not be underestimated. One by one the institutional links between North and South were dissolving. Most historians agree that the ecclesiastical divisions

3. *Baptist Missionary Magazine* 25 (1845): 222.

4. *Minutes of the General Assembly of the Presbyterian Church in the United States of America, 1838–1858* (New York: Office of the Stated Clerk, 1894), 574.

of the 1840s and 1850s paved the way for the political impasse of southern secession; some even suggest that they were the chief cause of the final break. All attempts at political compromise proved to be inadequate. By 1860, the crisis was at hand. Even the long-established Democratic Party split, opening the way for a northern Republican to become president. As soon as the presidential election returns assured Abraham Lincoln's victory, southern legislatures summoned state conventions to declare their withdrawal from the nation. On April 12, 1861, the Civil War began with the shelling of Fort Sumter, South Carolina.

The Churches amid Civil War and Reconstruction

The long agitation over slavery had prepared churches to take definite stands when hostilities began, and no American war aroused more unanimous support from the churches. In North and South, the churches gave their full support for the waging of a conflict both sides believed to be under divine control. The North fought initially to preserve the Union and later to free the slaves; the South fought to defend local institutions against the encroachment of federal power.

On both sides, chaplains served in the field and in the hospitals. They counseled homesick and frightened soldiers, wrote to families, comforted the sick and wounded, buried the dead, and tried to bring some spiritual order to wartime chaos. Some even organized regimental churches and conducted protracted revival meetings during long periods in camp. Ministers were always welcomed into the military camps. In the South, Episcopalian Robert E. Lee and Presbyterian Thomas J. (Stonewall) Jackson believed fervently that their victories were the Lord's doing and encouraged ministers to hold prayer meetings among their troops. In the winter of 1863–64, a sweeping revival broke out among the Confederate soldiers at Orange Courthouse, Virginia. Estimates are that perhaps one to two hundred thousand military men in both armies were converted during the war, and many others were strongly affected by religion in some way.

A number of northern clergymen used their influence to solicit foreign support for the Union cause, whose position dramatically strengthened with the Emancipation Proclamation of January 1, 1863. Roman Catholic Archbishop John Hughes went to Europe at Lincoln's request to win goodwill for the Union, and Henry Ward Beecher of Plymouth Church in Brooklyn visited England to do likewise.

The northern churches also responded with charitable institutions. In 1861, the United States Sanitary Commission was formed to care for the sick and wounded, provide food for soldiers, and drive ambulance wagons. The United States Christian Commission grew out of the YMCA with the purpose of distributing both religious and secular books. Volunteer workers opened libraries and reading rooms in hospitals and army camps throughout the North. By 1864, the American Bible Society had distributed close to one million Bibles among both armies. As the war progressed and Union troops pushed farther into the South, the numbers of blacks dependent on the care and protection of northern military commanders increased. This urgent need led to the founding of freedmen's relief societies to provide food, clothing, shelter, employment possibilities, and schools for the former slaves. In 1865, Congress finally established the Freedmen's Bureau to discharge this enormous national responsibility.

All of these efforts were either spearheaded or supported by church people, both ministerial and lay. Ecclesiastical endorsement of the war was overwhelming but not entirely so. Some abolitionists accused Lincoln of acting too slowly in freeing the slaves, while pockets of dissent existed among the peace-oriented Quakers and Mennonites. When the federal government resorted to conscription in 1863, most northern Quakers declared themselves conscientious objectors, refusing to fight or pay war taxes. After considerable debate, provisions were made for them to do alternative service. The South was less understanding of objectors, probably because the need for men was more acute in the Confederacy. Nevertheless, pacifists were exempted from military service if they paid five hundred dollars or provided a substitute.

During the years of war and the reconstruction to follow, Americans reflected on the terrible events that had engulfed their nation. After the rupture, America could no longer confidently promote itself as a shining example to the nations. Evasion of responsibility for the tragedy was impossible; no other country had been involved, and the instruments of peace had been cast aside to allow the war machine to settle differences between brothers. The self-righteous prayers offered up by both sides had reduced God's purposes to the level of their own sectional interests. Some, such as Lincoln, however, were self-critical and reluctant to bring matters to this level. With prophetic insight a few weeks before his assassination, the tormented leader shared his concerns in his second inaugural address:

> Both [sides] read the same Bible, and pray to the same God; and each invokes his aid against the other. It may seem strange that any men should dare to ask a just God's assistance in wringing their bread from the sweat of other men's faces; but let us judge not, that we be not judged. The prayers of both could not be answered. That of neither has been answered fully.[5]

Theologian Horace Bushnell and church historian Philip Schaff echoed these sentiments and developed them further. The war, they said, was a

5. *Inaugural Addresses of the Presidents of the United States* (Washington, D.C.: Government Printing Office, 1974), 127.

divine act of judgment for the collective guilt of the American people. The conflict was a sacrificial and cleansing tragedy with the potential of not only preserving the nation but regenerating it as well. This idea found its way into the rhetoric of civil and religious celebrations and provided a symbol of unity for a fractured nation, calling it back to its proper vocation and ideals.

White Protestants, the South, and the Black Church

Given the intensity of the moral and religious struggle that marked the Civil War, it was no surprise that sectional hostility was just as intense after the end of military conflict. Dominant southern churchmen and the ex-Confederate leadership in general sought to restore pre-1860 conditions, except, of course, for the institution of slavery. The presence of the occupation armies in the South all but eliminated the likelihood of the Presbyterians, Methodists, and Baptists reuniting with their northern counterparts. As a result, southern churches consolidated into a separate entity that came to be characterized by revivalism, orthodoxy, foreign missions, and an alliance with southern culture and mores, especially in regard to race relations.

There was no agreement among northern churchmen as to the punishment deserved by the South. A few, such as Henry Ward Beecher, encouraged unconditional conciliation; most, such as Theodore Tilton, Beecher's successor as editor of the *Independent* magazine, chose a more vengeful way and referred to Richmond as Babylon the Great. Pastors who identified with the Republican Party used their pulpits to advocate black suffrage, aid for the freedmen, and strict measures to deal with the "apostates" of the Confederacy. Such an approach did little to heal a fractured relationship, and southerners greeted with scorn northern missionaries who came to serve in the South.

Northern Protestant denominations provided much of the idealistic zeal and political support for the radical Reconstruction program enacted by Congress in 1867, a reform effort undergirded by the presence of an occupation army. Despite the charges of corruption and mismanagement leveled against some state regimes, the period from 1867 to 1877 was one of significant achievement. On the governmental level, enactment of the Thirteenth, Fourteenth, and Fifteenth Amendments to the Constitution, as well as numerous laws aiding the freedmen and promoting civil rights, laid the foundation for the civil rights breakthroughs of the mid-twentieth century.

A generous outpouring of northern philanthropy also flowed to the former slaves. Hundreds of home missionaries and teachers, many of them women, dispatched by the American Missionary Association (founded in Albany in 1846), and some denominational societies labored amid ridicule and economic hardship to bring education and opportunity to the blacks. Indeed, all the black colleges founded before 1900, and most of their faculties, derived from missionary efforts mounted in the North. One such teacher was Joanna P. Moore (1832–1916), a white woman who rejoiced over the liberation of the slaves but also realized how much help the freedmen needed. They did not know independence but only dependence. Although initially she had no salary, Moore went as a northern Baptist to Island 10 near Memphis to help the eleven hundred women and children there learn to read and to live independently. She labored in southern black communities until her death in 1916, focusing on interracial cooperation. Many women in the North and most in the South did not share her egalitarian views, but she commanded enormous respect among Baptists, black and white, for her untiring work.

Joanna P. Moore's (1832–1916) school. Courtesy of the American Baptist Historical Society.

Gradually, interest in the plight of the freedmen subsided, both in the churches and in Congress. Other political and economic priorities come to the forefront and weakened federal commitment to justice for the former slaves. In general, American society did not rise to the moral challenge presented by emancipation. Although Reconstruction had been a time of unparalleled advance for blacks, by 1877, the South had regained complete home rule, and by political party organization, legislation, and naked coercion soon disenfranchised the blacks and deprived them of their basic human and civil rights. The ex-slaves, however, were able to construct a self-determining institutional structure within black churches. What had necessarily been the informal practice of religion during the period of slavery was transformed into the social and belief structures of full-fledged denominations.

Black churches served important social as well as religious functions. Like the parish churches of the Middle Ages, they were community centers. There blacks could find fellowship without white intrusion and manage their affairs in their own way. As W. E. B. DuBois would later note, the black church was the first social institution in America fully controlled by black men.

Worship service in a black church. Courtesy of the Billy Graham Center Museum, Wheaton, Illinois.

Some commentators have suggested that the black church in the late nineteenth century was marked by emotionalism and primitivism. Certainly, features of African religious style were present. Yet a more important perception is this: The old spirit of evangelical revivalism flourished in African-American Christianity. Although adapted to meet their own needs, the black church cultivated the central core of the revivalistic movement: a sense of divine immediacy, spontaneity of individual response, personal holiness, and the redress of present injustices. The leaders and ministers often knew little and cared less about creedal subtleties, alien philosophies, or the conflicting claims of science. Rather, these fellowships held unswervingly to the Bible as the sole source of religious certainty, and the basics remained anchored in orthodox Christianity.

Emancipation allowed African-American men and women to emerge from the condescending tutelage of white paternalism into the trying but promising realm of independent thought and action. Despite the obstacles, the ex-slave fought hard to see himself or herself in a new light, as a person of worth, value, and potential. Some sought identity by tracing their roots and urging a return to Africa, perceived as their real home where new opportunity could be found. Others pursued education as a way to offer a uniquely black contribution to American society. The majority labored on farms or in factories and warehouses, seeking to make their peace with their adoptive country. In the midst of these struggles, the black churches became shelters, shielding their members from a hostile social climate and nurturing in them the desire for personal development as well as faith in the message of hope found in Christ.

11

Evangelical Initiatives

In the last three decades of the nineteenth century, Protestantism lost its position as the dominant influence in American culture. New economic, social, and intellectual forces reverberated through the nation. Business enterprises consolidated into ever larger units. Industrial towns and cities swelled with populations drawn from both the adjacent countryside and overseas. The Roman Catholic and Jewish faiths practiced by many of these new city dwellers enhanced religious pluralism. Unimaginable fortunes and equally generous philanthropy existed alongside working-class squalor. At the same time, the orthodox theologies that undergirded the great American denominations came under attack by new ideas, both domestic and European. In this context, the American churches adapted to changing parish circumstances while continuing the quest to serve.

Urban Parishes and City Revivalism

The concentration of upwardly mobile churchgoers in large, affluent city congregations led to a level of respectability and genteel piety that had not characterized small-town denominations such as Presbyterian, Methodist, and Baptist earlier in the century. Robed choirs performed beside robed clergymen, who were better educated and credentialed than their ministerial fathers and grandfathers. Wealthy parishioners donated vast sums of money to construct beautiful downtown churches. Whether Romanesque, neo-Gothic, or eclectic in architectural style, these imposing edifices graced the center of every city. Successful laymen assumed the direction of congregational affairs. Administrative efficiency, the professionalization of denominational leadership, and more extensive budgets and programs regularized the ebb and flow of parish life. As mentioned earlier, even the old camp meeting gave way to the summer Bible conference with its culturally uplifting lectures and comfortable latticed cottages. The emphasis on the need for evangelical Christian conversion and pious living continued, resulting in the urban evangelism personified in the ministry of Dwight Lyman Moody (1837–99), who adapted the old revivalism to the new context.

Dwight L. Moody (1837–99)

Moody had a modest childhood with a widowed mother in Northfield, Massachusetts. He moved from village to city, first to Boston and then to the vibrant Chicago of the 1850s. There he quickly prospered as a salesman of shoes. Yet a quiet but deeply felt conversion motivated him to shun personal wealth and to devote his enormous vigor to God's business. Throughout the 1860s, Moody channeled his energies into recruiting fifteen hundred impoverished youths from the Chicago streets for his Sunday school, which in 1863 grew into the nondenominational Illinois Street Church. Working for the United States Christian Commission during the war years, he tirelessly served soldiers in their camps. As the driving force behind the Chicago YMCA, he aggressively pursued a host of projects. To finance his ventures he raised astonishing amounts of money from such rich benefactors as Marshall Field, Cyrus McCormick, and George Armour.

Although Moody did not have a reputation as a preacher, he undertook an evangelistic campaign with musician Ira D. Sankey (1840–1908) throughout Britain between 1873 and 1875. This was the turning point in his career. He reached nearly three million hearers and became an international figure. Then followed five years of urban revival meetings across America from Brooklyn and Philadelphia to San Francisco. These years marked the high point of Moody's itinerant evangelistic ministry. Next he concentrated his efforts on developing the Northfield (Mass.) Seminary for girls, the nearby Mount Hermon School for boys, Moody Bible Institute in Chicago, and conferences and student work. The Student Volunteer Movement for Foreign Missions was launched at one of these conferences in 1886.

Moody's broad, nondenominational gospel message won the endorsement of practically every religious group except the Roman Catholics, Unitarians, and Universalists. He cared little for formal discussion of theological issues and claimed he had no theology. He never sought ordination or became a licensed clergyman. Yet he and Sankey were responsible for lighting the fires of revival that touched the lives of thousands who in turn joined churches in great numbers.

Finney's revivalism belonged to the age of Andrew Jackson and Lyman Beecher, whereas Moody's belonged to the age of Andrew Carnegie and P. T. Barnum. His evangelistic ministry reflected both his own sales experience and the commercial climate of Gilded Age America. Committees of prominent ministers and laymen took charge of planning the citywide meetings, but the laymen, usually successful business leaders, headed the all-important finance and executive subcommittees, leaving to the clergy lesser leadership functions. This set a pattern that Billy Sunday and Billy Graham would later follow.

Moody's own conservative attitude toward economic and social problems fit well with business leaders' concerns about urban social stability. Although Moody himself was a lifelong supporter of good causes, especially Christian education, he, like other evangelists of the day, avoided any discussion of the structural ills of society. He optimistically believed that individual conversions would effect the desired improvement of the social order.

From an alcoholic past in rural Georgia emerged Sam Jones (1847–1906), Moody's southern counterpart. Converted under his Methodist grandfather's preaching, he became a circuit rider for the North Georgia Conference of the Methodist Episcopal Church, South, in 1872. Eminently successful in winning converts in Georgia, he was then invited to conduct revivals in major southern cities and became an evangelist of national prominence, the "Moody of the South." Jones's messages, expounded in the colorful language and style of the rural southern hill country, proved highly entertaining to city audiences unaccustomed to such speech. Like Moody's, his was the simple gospel, shorn of theological elaboration and radically practical in its impact: Turn from sin, be saved, and join the crusade against urban wickedness. Jones's revivals were a significant factor in the urban recovery of the Methodist Episcopal Church, South, especially after E. O. Excell joined him as choirmaster and gospel songwriter.

Following in the pattern of Finney and Moody, a new generation of evangelists carried revival efforts across denominational and regional lines well into the twentieth century. Reuben A. Torrey (1856–1928) and J. Wilbur Chapman (1859–1918) had Moody's personal approval for their mass revival meetings. Torrey, an ordained Congregational minister, was something of an oddity among revivalists at the time. His theological conservatism belied his university education at Yale and his studies in historical criticism of the Bible at Leipzig. He ultimately became superintendent of Moody Bible Institute. Presbyterian pastor and evangelist Chapman served numerous churches in the Midwest and East before devoting himself full-time to evangelism in 1903. Author or editor of over thirty books, gospel songwriter, first director of Indiana's Winona Lake Bible Conference, and moderator of the Presbyterian General Assembly in 1917, Chapman reflected the wide leadership accomplishments and networks of these now largely forgotten preachers who exercised great influence among Protestants.

A colorful individual was Rodney (Gipsy) Smith (1860–1947), who was born of Roma (Gypsy) parents near Epping Forest, England. After a Methodist conversion, he served briefly in William Booth's Salvation Army. Reflecting the transatlantic ties of Victorian English-speaking evangelicals, Smith made fifty preaching tours to the United States between 1889 and his death on an ocean liner in 1947. He delighted in capitalizing on his origins and attracted curious crowds by appearing with his singer daughter in Gypsy costume. In a series of meetings held in Boston in 1906, he is said to have won 2,550 "decisions" for Christ. By then it was customary to judge a revivalist's success by the number of "decision cards" turned in during a campaign. The various revivals that swept across Britain and North America had repercussions in other parts of the world as well. The most important of these was the dramatic Welsh revival of 1904–5.

The best known of all early twentieth-century revivalists was the flamboyant William (Billy) Sunday (1862–1935). An Iowa farm boy who found acclaim in professional baseball, the hard-living Sunday was converted in 1883 at a Chicago rescue mission. After stints with the YMCA and J. Wilbur Chapman, Sunday launched out on his own and soon experienced success in evangelistic meetings in various Midwestern towns. Though he had only a limited education, Sunday's theatrical, direct preaching style resonated with common folks, even in urban centers such as New York City, Boston, and Chicago where large temporary wooden tabernacles were erected to accommodate the huge crowds. In 1903, he was ordained by the Presbyterian Church, despite his lack of theological training.

Billy Sunday (1862–1935). Courtesy of the Billy Graham Center Museum, Wheaton, Illinois.

The efficiency of his campaign arrangements, managed by his wife, and the talents of musician associate Homer Rodeheaver (1880–1955) added to Sunday's effectiveness. He preached to more persons in his two hundred plus campaigns than any American evangelist until Billy Graham a generation later. In spite of criticism from more liberal circles, he attained widespread popularity and influence. He supported women's rights, reached out to blacks, contributed to the achievement of the National Prohibition Amendment, and during World War I was an ardent patriot.

This new revivalism represented a departure from the theological content of the earlier revivals. Whether this was due to the urban setting or the general anti-supernatural drift of American thought is hard to say, but the change of motif was apparent. The offer of salvation from sin and eternal lostness was couched in the terms of a welcoming and loving God who was less concerned about details of dogma than forgiving and pardoning the wayward sinner. Moreover, to the lonely of America's urban centers, the revival services offered a welcome release from monotony. The thronging crowds, hymnbook vendors, rousing singing, and general excitement encouraged many to come and be warmed by an evening of participation. Although the revivalists were concerned about and worked to alleviate the evils of city life, their primary burden was to evangelize the unchurched. The Christian social vision, once pervasive throughout evangelical Protestantism, faded quietly into the background until its reassertion in the social gospel and reform movements at the century's end.

Holiness: Reviving an Old Tradition

A parallel force to the urban revivals was the wave of Holiness teaching that rippled across the denominations. With its distinctive emphasis on the work of the Holy Spirit, it created complications in evangelical theology and church alignments. John Wesley's teaching about Christian perfection, the view that it is possible for a Christian to live free from all known sin, was a factor in revivalist considerations. In fact, Wesley's unique theological contribution was his doctrine of entire sanctification or the "second blessing." Conversion, as all evangelicals consistently taught, was the first and indispensable step in salvation. However, a Christian could move on to a state of purity of life in which all temptation to sin was removed, usually through a dramatic experience that gave power to maintain a condition of sinless perfection. Wesleyan circuit riders and pastors spread these ideas.

An important step was the founding of the interdenominational National Camp Meeting Association for the Promotion of Holiness in New Jersey in 1867. Phoebe Palmer (1807–74), one of the most influential women in nineteenth-century American religion, was in the forefront of the movement. The wife of a prominent physician in New York City, she and her sister Sarah Lankford began holding their "Tuesday Meetings for the Promotion of Holiness" in 1835. She strongly advocated the right of women to preach, and through her speaking and publications, especially *The Way of Holiness* (1843), she developed an international constituency. Palmer not only epitomized the expanding role of women in the Holiness movement but in 1857 also introduced the term "baptism of the Holy Ghost" as a synonym for the experience of entire sanctification. In the twentieth century, Pentecostals appropriated this label for the experience of speaking in tongues.

Palmer also strongly influenced the Boston physician Charles Cullis, who in the 1860s introduced the idea of divine healing into the Holiness movement. In 1881, Cullis convinced A. B. Simpson, at the time a Presbyterian minister

Phoebe Palmer (1807–74). Courtesy of the Billy Graham Center Museum, Wheaton, Illinois.

in New York and eventually the founder of the Christian and Missionary Alliance, that healing was part of the atonement of Christ and made divine healing a part of his ministry. Cullis also had an impact on the distinguished Boston Baptist pastor Adoniram Judson Gordon (1836–95), who published the popular tract *The Ministry of Healing* (1882). Gordon maintained that there was a recognizable foundation in Christ's atonement for faith in bodily healing, but he avoided the more distinct Holiness tenets of eradication of sin and the second blessing. He also supported women in ministry.

These Holiness teachings were a radical departure from the Reformed and Puritan roots of evangelical theology, which denied the possibility of earthly perfection and held that the Christian life was a warfare between the old sinful nature and the new regenerated state. When combined with Arminianism, which allowed a measure of free cooperation on the part of the individual in the process of salvation, entire sanctification provided an irresistibly optimistic package to those Americans who were inclined to think rather extravagantly about both their own and their nation's possibilities. Vinson Synan, the dean of Pentecostal historians, suggests that a similarity existed between the ethical ideals of Ralph Waldo Emerson and Henry David

Thoreau and those of the early Holiness groups. In his view, Holiness was a kind of "evangelical transcendentalism" that thrived in the idealistic and growing America.[1]

Reformed circles, however, were also affected by Holiness teaching. Presbyterian minister William E. Boardman (1810–86), who was influenced by Phoebe Palmer, became a proponent of Holiness beliefs. He had ties with Robert Pearsall Smith (1827–99) and his wife, Hannah Whitall Smith (1832–1911), originally Quakers, who had become dissatisfied with their own spiritual lives. They learned about entire sanctification from the Methodists, and their lives were transformed. They then worked to spread Holiness ideas on both sides of the Atlantic. They taught that a second work of grace, namely, sanctification, needed to follow salvation, and Mrs. Smith's book, *The Christian's Secret of a Happy Life* (1875), became a classic on the subject. Yet they did not go as far as the Holiness movement in that the emphasis on a "victorious" or "higher" life did not necessarily mean the eradication of the sinful nature. Their ideas were promoted in annual conferences that took place at Keswick in the English Lake District beginning in 1875, and the resulting movement was popularly labeled "Keswick." For decades, Keswick teachings influenced American evangelical spirituality, especially through the summer Bible conference movement.

The Holiness movement drew criticism from leaders of organized Protestantism, many of whom were identified with the Methodist Church. As the century closed, moderates among the Methodists were inclined toward the "churchly" position that sanctification was a gradual process, a notion somewhat akin to Horace Bushnell's concept of Christian nurture. Those who espoused Holiness views found themselves increasingly shut out of the mainline Methodist Church (the Methodist Church South formally disavowed Holiness teachings in 1894) and other denominations as well. They gradually began to form separate denominations of their own, and some twenty-three new groups emerged over the next few years. Among these fellowships were the Church of the Nazarene, the Church of God (Anderson, Indiana), the Church of God (Cleveland, Tennessee), the Missionary Church Association, and the Christian and Missionary Alliance. Holiness teaching received additional impetus when the Salvation Army came from England to America in 1880, two years after its founding by William Booth. Led first by Ballington Booth and later by his sister Evangeline (1865–1950), children of the founder, the Army was a distinctively Wesleyan perfectionist denomination, while also carrying on extensive welfare work among the poor. Evangeline Booth in particular became a widely respected figure in American Christianity.

The piety that emerged from the Holiness movement and urban revivalism was best expressed not in formal theology but in the many published "gospel

1. Vinson Synan, *The Holiness-Pentecostal Tradition* (Grand Rapids: Eerdmans, 1997), 18–19.

Evangeline Booth (1865–1950). Courtesy of the Salvation Army National Archives.

songs" of the period that rapidly achieved popularity. Besides Sankey's compositions for the Moody meetings, the more than two thousand songs of the blind Fanny J. Crosby (1820–1915), the best-known hymn writer of the time, seemed to be on everyone's lips. In simple lyrics, her theme of consecration to the love of Jesus presented the gospel in romanticized images centering

Fanny J. Crosby (1820–1915). Courtesy of the Billy Graham Center Museum, Wheaton, Illinois.

on the emotions of the singer. In association with several collaborators, she produced such favorites as "Near the Cross," "Draw Me Nearer," "He Hideth My Soul," and "Tell Me the Story of Jesus."

Post–Civil War America saw the first signs that its spiritual foundation, once provided by a confident and aggressive Protestant majority, was shifting. After 1865, the problems of Reconstruction, immigration, urbanization, and natural science joined together to erode the evangelical consensus. The public gradually began to recognize that a nation supposedly agrarian was, in fact, becoming an urban-industrial one. The old simplicities were gone or going, and a new complexity had come. This was an age of change—change in population, economic structures, political policies, and belief. The entire process of American thought was in transition.

12

The Old Religion Reacts to New Ideas

Observers of human behavior have long recognized that ideas have consequences. Perhaps at no time in its long history did the church face such a barrage of new and unsettling intellectual formulations as in the nineteenth century, and for American Christianity, the last third of that century in particular. America had been remarkably accommodating to new ideas throughout its history. While the denominations had maintained their distinct theological traditions, they had also learned to tolerate other perspectives in a time of expanding religious pluralism. Enlightenment thought had found its initial American home in the minds of the founding fathers, but they had affirmed a generally moderate approach rather than a skeptical one, as in France.

As more radical strains of modern thought continued to flow from Europe, however, the first quarter of the nineteenth century became a watershed for theological and philosophical influences in America. Previously, British sources had been by far the most important, especially for the Unitarians, but after 1815, German influences increased, especially when many students traveled to Germany to study in its renowned universities. In all, ten thousand Americans matriculated in German schools between the War of 1812 and the First World War. The German ideal of detached, rationalistic scholarship was thus imported to American colleges and helped undercut confidence in Scripture and orthodox theology.

German romanticism, with its emphasis on subjective and intuitive truth, directly contributed to American theological liberalism. Few had previously conceived of the knowing process except in terms of the object known; now the subject or knower came into the picture. Subjectivism holds that the mind partly creates the external reality it is grasping. Consequently, truth, as reality, differs for each person perceiving it. The trends of thought articulated by German scholars Friedrich E. D. Schleiermacher (1768–1834), George W. F. Hegel (1770–1834), and Albrecht Ritschl (1822–89) reinforced the idea that true religion was based on intuition, experience, and love for others, not beliefs undergirded by an external authority such as the Bible. Such romantic ideas resonated with the ideals of American individualism and freedom. Of the many religious and idealistic American philosophers, Methodist Borden Parker Bowne (1847–1910) probably had the greatest impact on the churches. A philosopher by training, he influenced many generations of seminarians at Boston University through his religious philosophy of "transcendental empiricism," which taught that there was a reality that existed beyond the perception of the senses.

One should not assume, however, that liberal theology in America was merely a European transplant. As theologian Gary Dorrien has noted, "American Protestantism produced its own vital tradition of liberal religious thinking and piety," which "shared the same animating impulse as the German 'mediating theology' tradition with which it eventually became linked: to create a modernist Christian third way between a regnant orthodoxy and an ascending 'infidelism.'"[1]

Alongside romanticism and its variants stood faith in science as an authoritative and comprehensive worldview. Since the eighteenth century, Western science had been moving increasingly toward a rigid empiricism that closed off the universe from any spiritual realities and regarded religion as an outdated and hidebound superstition. English-born John William Draper (1811–82) early championed the claims of science over the supernatural. In 1838, he joined the scientific faculty of New York University and became a popular apologist for a unified, intelligible, altogether natural world. In his *History of the Conflict between Religion and Science,* Draper insisted that religion and science were in fundamental conflict, for religion perpetuated its power through the organized church, whereas science sought to destroy the church's pretensions by indicating the human origins of all religious institutions. Draper concluded that Christianity would disappear, as Roman paganism had done, leaving science with its "grander views of the universe, more awful views of God."[2] Of course, not all scientists were as extreme as Draper. Yet although

1. Gary Dorrien, *The Making of American Liberal Theology: Imagining Progressive Religion, 1805–1900* (Louisville: Westminster John Knox, 2001), xiv.

2. John William Draper, *History of the Conflict between Religion and Science* (New York: D. Appleton, 1874), 324.

traditional Christian vocabulary was still used by most scholars, the foundations of biblical supernaturalism were quietly being eroded.

Darwinism in American Thought

With the publication in 1859 of Charles Darwin's *Origin of Species,* a new era in scientific thinking began. The idea of development in the physical world had long been present in Western thought, but more revolutionary was the concept of organic evolution. Those who possessed a more precise and detailed theology, especially Catholics and Calvinists, soon saw the implications of the new biological theories for their time-honored doctrinal views. Protestants had long accepted the argument of design in the universe, as popularized by the English theologian William Paley (1743–1805), as proof of theism. This confidence now seemed imperiled, as did the established views of Adam's fall, man's depravity, the atonement, and immortality. Critics claimed that by undermining the fixity of concepts regarding species—plant, animal, and human—Darwin exposed mind, morals, and the entire scope of social relations to change and ultimately to naturalism.

At first, Darwin's views were of interest primarily to scientists, but soon they had a great effect on theologians and churchgoers. In the early stages of the controversy, churchmen attacked Darwinism on scientific grounds, claiming a lack of proof that species had really evolved; no record in fossils remained of the missing links. There was also no explanation for the sterility of hybrids and the inability of manmade varieties to survive in nature. According to these earnest Christians, the idea of special creation offered a more convincing explanation of natural phenomena. These critics did not accuse Darwin of furthering atheism, but soon some asserted that atheism was really implicit in Darwin's work.

In the United States, George Frederick Wright (1838–1921), Oberlin College professor of science and religion, and Asa Gray (1810–88), distinguished Harvard botanist, championed a view that harmonized Darwinism and Christian theism. This came to be called theistic evolution. They defended the compatibility of natural selection and design, and although both were deeply religious men, they disagreed that explanations of the origin of species should be left exclusively in the realm of the supernatural.

For those who put firm trust in the literal truth of the Bible, the Genesis creation story was an answer to the new theory. Some claimed that if the literal creation story was rejected, along with it would go the rest of the biblical revelation. One of the most noted theologians of the period, Charles Hodge (1797–1878) of Princeton Seminary, published a popular work that insisted that theism and natural selection could not be reconciled. *What Is Darwinism?* (1874) challenged the evolutionists by proclaiming that, according to the Bible, those who reject the Holy Scriptures are lost to reason or morals or both.

Throughout the remainder of the century, the theory of evolution held a prominent place in the debates between science and religion. Many educators and church figures, including Baptist theologian Augustus H. Strong and Princeton Seminary's B. B. Warfield, accepted the compatibility of theistic evolution and Scripture. Other church leaders and the rank and file of the laity, however, stood against the new ideas and condemned them as destructive of the truth. This opposition was markedly strong in the South, where the state legislatures of Texas, Tennessee, Arkansas, and Mississippi eventually passed statutes outlawing the teaching of evolution in public schools.

Trends in Biblical Study and the New Theology

The new methods of finding truth were soon applied to the fields of biblical and theological study. From the time of the Reformation, writers had occasionally challenged traditional views regarding certain aspects of Scripture, and modern Old Testament criticism had emerged in Germany by 1780. During the 1880s, the writings of Julius Wellhausen, a leading German Old Testament scholar, received recognition in the United States. Following the canons of the new higher criticism, Wellhausen taught that one could reconstruct the history of the development of biblical concepts by dating the books of the Bible. Using this approach, he maintained that an evolution had occurred in the Old Testament, from primitive polytheistic origins to ethical monotheism. Among other conclusions, this cast doubt on the Mosaic authorship of the Pentateuch. Other scholars asked questions about the reliability of the New Testament.

At the same time, both liberal and conservative scholars placed great emphasis on lower criticism, which dealt with the Scripture text itself. Great strides were made in determining the most reliable Hebrew and Greek texts for understanding and translating the original languages of the Bible. Extensive archaeological excavations in the area around the Mediterranean expanded knowledge of Bible times. In answer to the troubling questions higher critics were raising about the Bible, conservative scholars explained that seeming inconsistencies were the result of mistakes of copyists or translators. Only the original autographs (no longer extant) had been directly inspired and thus free from error. The writings of B. B. Warfield defended the widely held position of the plenary (full) inspiration of Scripture and the complete accuracy of the original manuscripts of the Bible. Some evangelicals, such as Scotsman James Orr, editor of the *International Standard Bible Encyclopedia* (1915), and A. H. Strong, held that the Bible is true and authoritative in all it affirms and teaches but as an ancient document is not necessarily inerrant, according to modern definition, in regard to every historical allusion.

The new emphasis on reason, biblical criticism, intuition, science, and evolutionary thought had important consequences for generally accepted ideas of God, Jesus Christ, man, and history. Familiar terms were employed, but they had new meanings. Thus, the late nineteenth century saw a growing effort on the part of some American thinkers to formulate a theology that stressed the immanence of God in the world and the progressive moral improvement of humanity. The result was an identifiably structured religious movement, even though its emphases varied from person to person. At its foundation was a favorable estimate of human nature coupled with an optimistic view of human destiny that paralleled the secular idea of progress. In line with this, the task of the churches was to promote a world-changing ethic known as the social gospel. The divine Christ of the Apostles' Creed had become the God-inspired moral guide leading humankind toward the kingdom.

Although the exponents of theological liberalism contributed to one another's thought, they by no means composed a homogeneous group. Some had no intention of breaking with inherited faith and genuinely felt they were preserving it in the context of modern knowledge. Others moved far beyond the Christian heritage. Between these extremes, theological liberals occupied a wide spectrum of viewpoints. All, however, were in some sense redefining traditional orthodox doctrines.

H. Richard Niebuhr traced the process by which the liberal movement in American theology gradually divorced itself from its roots in the Reformation tradition. The moralism of William Ellery Channing and the experientialism of Horace Bushnell remained close to traditional piety, but the next generation manifested a decline of commitment to the old spiritual expectations, and the following generation experienced an even greater loss of vitality. Niebuhr summarized the outcome in a famous line: "A God without wrath brought men without sin into a kingdom without judgment through the ministrations of a Christ without a cross."[3]

Accommodation and Dissent

As denominational leaders confronted these new viewpoints, controversy swept the churches. Issues were so hotly contested that some ministers were charged with heresy before ecclesiastical courts and disciplined by their communions. The conflict was especially severe among the Presbyterians, as illustrated by the case of Charles A. Briggs, a professor at Union Seminary in New York. Although personally devout, he was an early enthusiast of biblical

3. H. Richard Niebuhr, *The Kingdom of God in America* (Chicago: Willett, Clark, 1937), 193.

criticism and a keen student of German theology. Briggs soon clashed with conservatives over the questions of verbal inspiration of the Bible and Mosaic authorship of the Pentateuch. When he disavowed biblical inerrancy in an inaugural address delivered at Union in 1891, he was charged with heresy, tried before the General Assembly, found guilty, and suspended from the ministry. In 1899, he received ordination in the Protestant Episcopal Church. Congregationalists, Baptists, and Methodists all experienced similar incidents.

Although the penetration of higher criticism into the Roman Catholic Church caused serious problems in Europe, the effect was considerably less in the United States. Leo XIII's critique of "Americanism" in 1899, the idea of Catholic accommodations to contemporary political ideas, struck a heavy blow to the Catholic reform movement in the United States, still in its infant stage. This was followed by Pius X's encyclical *Pascendi Domini Gregis* in 1907, in which he specifically condemned "modernism" (divine immanence, evolutionary views of religious development, and the new biblical criticism) and directed that professors tainted with heresy be dismissed from their posts. Because it had to give primary attention to the tensions and demands emanating from the immigrant ethnic groups among the faithful, American Catholicism postponed coming to terms with religious modernism and individualistic pluralism in society.

A number of new religious and philosophical movements emerged in late-nineteenth-century America. Grounded in philosophical idealism and emphasizing the attainment of right states of mind, these groups were encouraged indirectly by New England Transcendentalism, with its emphasis on divine immanence and the essential goodness of human nature. The Church of Christ, Scientist is one example. In the closing years of the Civil War, Mary Baker Eddy (1821–1910) believed she had recovered from an injury through help from a faith healer, Phineas P. Quimby (1802–66). After his death, she taught this new method of religious healing. Although untrained in philosophy, she wrote *Science and Health* in 1875, to which she added *Key to the Scriptures* in 1883. Her strategy for combating individual and societal disease was that of denial. Mind was all, and matter nothing. Death and sickness were simply illusions that could be overcome, not through prayer or medicine but through *gnosis* ("knowledge"), a new method of interpreting Scripture that produced insights about the nature of the metaphysical realm and its application to human problems. A small group using *Science and Health* as a study book began to call themselves Christian Scientists, and in 1879, Eddy formed the first Church of Christ, Scientist in Lynn, Massachusetts. Two years later she moved her headquarters to Boston and in 1892 established a central organization, the Mother Church, which remains the center of the movement; other Christian Science congregations are called branches. The group carried on its work through an extensive program of literature distribution, and its professional ministers were called practitioners. By the 1930s, the church had over two hundred thousand members.

Mary Baker Eddy (1821–1910). Courtesy of the Mary Baker Eddy Library for the Betterment of Humanity.

A completely different movement, the Watch Tower Bible and Tract Society, commonly known as the Jehovah's Witnesses, was founded by Charles Taze Russell (1856–1916) in 1872. As a Bible study movement, its view of the imminence of the apocalyptic events described in the Book of Revelation (The Millennial Dawn) and of the Witnesses as the sole "righteous remnant" appealed to those marginalized or alienated by the rapid changes in society. Reorganized by J. F. "Judge" Rutherford (1869–1942) after Russell's death into a highly disciplined and structured bureaucracy, the Witnesses began engaging in vigorous recruitment efforts and eventually numbered in the millions worldwide.

The general movement away from traditional religious affiliations and beliefs also affected African-Americans. The combination of Jim Crow laws and lack of economic opportunity in the rural South resulted in a large exodus of southern blacks to the urban centers of the North and the West. The resulting sense of cultural displacement created a spiritual vacuum among migrant blacks that was filled by black churches. Many of these were storefront churches, often of the Pentecostal-Holiness variety. Pentecostalism reached across racial boundaries, and its unstructured worship, which emphasized religious experience, fit well the expressive character of black religion.

Some blacks, however, were not comfortable with Christianity. As did many American Indians, they regarded it as a "white man's religion." Accordingly, several urban movements arose, usually around charismatic figures of obscure origin, that provided non- or anti-Christian ideologies that served as a basis for racial identity and pride. The best known was the Father Divine Peace Mission Movement. Its founder was born George Baker, probably around 1880, on a rice plantation in South Carolina. Arriving in New York City in 1915, he gradually began to acquire a following. He eventually relocated the center of the movement to Philadelphia. Never modest, Father Divine claimed to be God and demanded total loyalty from his disciples (including some well-to-do whites). In many ways, the movement constituted a withdrawal from everyday American life into a separate world with a communitarian economy. In another sense, however, it was a powerful (if eccentric) political protest against white racism, and the life of its members in interracial community was a literal expression of the "kingdom beyond caste."

In the West, Protestant and Catholic missionaries had brought the Christian faith to various Indian tribes, and their churches and mission stations dotted the reservations. The northern Baptists even founded a training school for Native Americans in Oklahoma, Bacone College. However, some were dissatisfied with these efforts at evangelization and the ensuing detachment from their people's indigenous traditions.

One noteworthy group of Native Americans sought to reclaim their land, build racial solidarity, and develop a religion of hope foreign to but influenced by Christian imagery. The prophet Wovoka, who was raised as Jack Wilson and instructed in Christianity in a white home, claimed to be a new Indian messiah. Wovoka borrowed religious symbols from Christianity, Mormonism, and traditional Shamanism and set out to lead Indians to a new paradise devoid of whites. A rite that whites dubbed "Ghost Dance" solidified and energized the devout and provided a sense of solidarity. When the idea spread that bullets could not pierce the dancers' shirts, the stage was set for tragedy. In 1890, at Wounded Knee in South Dakota, the U.S. Seventh Cavalry killed at least 123 men, women, and children as Wovoka's followers were herded back to the reservation. Wovoka felt these deaths resulted from a violation of his message of nonresistance. The movement soon collapsed, but it was yet another example of the varied nature of the late-nineteenth-century American religious landscape.

Pentecostalism and Early Fundamentalism

Two other religious currents began to take shape during this period, Pentecostalism and fundamentalism. Whereas nineteenth-century revivalism and even the early Methodist Holiness movement took a relatively optimistic view of a believer's place in the world, Pentecostals and fundamentalists were, in considerable measure, otherworldly in their orientation and often pessimistic about the course of their own times.

Pentecostalism, in many ways the successor to the enthusiastic religion of the first two Awakenings, attracted its largest number of adherents from among the urban and rural poor. The more direct source was Methodism and the Holiness movements. Throughout church history, experiences of intense religious fervor have been interpreted by those involved as fulfillments of Peter's message on the day of Pentecost (Acts 2:1–21). On January 1, 1901, the "gift of the Spirit" came to Agnes Ozman, a student at Bethel Bible College, recently founded in Topeka, Kansas. Soon other Bethel students were speaking in tongues they could not understand, and the phenomenon spread rapidly among other Holiness groups. Whether this was the beginning of Pentecostalism or one of many "Pentecostalisms" is debated by historians.

An even more important figure was William J. Seymour, a black Holiness preacher and son of former slaves. He attended a Bible school in 1905 that Charles Parham operated in Houston, and then a small Holiness group in Los Angeles that had begun a house church mission called him to assist in the work. After some of the members had experienced tongues, they decided to rent a building at 312 Azusa Street and hold public meetings. Under Seymour's inspired ministry, a Pentecostal revival broke out in April 1906 at this Azusa Street mission. The interracial services there continued for weeks, and the revival quickly spread as the events received press coverage and itinerant ministers went out to other places. Soon independent centers

Azusa Street mission. Courtesy of the Flower Pentecostal Heritage Center.

of Pentecostalism sprang up all over the United States and Canada, with similar movements arising in Europe as well. Although the black roots of Pentecostalism were an embarrassment to some whites (including Parham himself), they proved to be a major source of strength. In Pentecostal circles, interracial fellowships and worship styles existed that many white Protestants found difficult to comprehend, but the movement's emphasis on experiential religion and appeal to all peoples, regardless of race, were major factors in its spread throughout the world.

However, Pentecostalism soon split along racial lines. Seymour's lack of formal education and the social pressures of Jim Crow society unraveled the interracial quality of the Azusa Street congregation and early Pentecostalism as a whole. The two largest denominations, the white Assemblies of God and the black Church of God in Christ emerged from these divisions. A number of other African-American and white denominational fellowships came into existence as well, some of which continued to affirm their Holiness roots.

Fundamentalism is an amorphous term used to designate the early twentieth-century antimodernist movement. Its hallmark was the affirmation of the traditional tenets, or "fundamentals," of the Christian faith in the face of an eroding supernaturalism. The term itself, however, was not used until the editor of an independent Baptist weekly, the *Watchman-Examiner,* coined it in 1920.

This reaffirmation of orthodox Christianity arose out of an interdenominational movement of evangelicals who were troubled by the advance of theological liberalism and the decline of traditional morality. During the 1870s and 1880s, various northern ministers, predominantly Congregationalist, Presbyterian, and Baptist, assembled at annual meetings for Bible study. From these grew widely publicized summer prophecy conferences, most notably the Niagara Conferences, which flourished in the 1880s and 1890s. Convinced that the last days were approaching, the present church was apostate, and scriptural preaching was sorely needed, the participants searched for God's "pattern for the ages." They were attracted to a system of biblical interpretation known as dispensational premillennialism, which had been formulated by J. N. Darby (1800–1882), an English Plymouth Brethren Bible teacher. His prophetic emphasis on the personal and premillennial advent of Christ was well received and popularized by such notables as D. L. Moody; James H. Brookes (1830–97), president of the Niagara Bible Conference; and W. E. Blackstone (1841–1935), author of the popular book *Jesus Is Coming* (1908).

Darbyism's most significant exponent was C. I. Scofield (1843–1921). After serving in the Confederate army and working as a lawyer, Scofield, who lived in St. Louis, experienced an evangelical conversion in 1879. He was mentored by J. H. Brookes and then moved to Dallas to serve as a Congregationalist minister. There he developed and propagated his own scheme of dispensationalism through public lectures, a Bible correspondence course, the book *Rightly Dividing the Word of Truth* (1888), and most notably the *Scofield Reference Bible* (1909, revised 1917). The notes to his study Bible expounded the basic form of American dispensationalism, and for millions of churchgoers, these forthright comments were an authoritative guide to Scripture. According to this scheme of interpretation, the sacred history of both Jews and Gentiles can be divided into a number of distinct periods, or dispensations, each of which was determined by a separate covenant, handed down by God, through which people would relate to him. The last dispensation, which is yet to come, is that of the kingdom, in which Christ will restore the Davidic monarchy and rule from its throne for a thousand years. Subsequent preachers elaborately explicated this theological scenario in charts and innumerable books, and acceptance of it was a mark of many fundamentalists, especially in areas outside the South. For earnest laypersons, the approach of the Scofield Bible seemed to make sense and refuted the criticisms of Scripture posed by liberal scholars.

C. I. Scofield (1843–1921). Courtesy of the Billy Graham Center Museum, Wheaton, Illinois.

However, not all who came to be known as fundamentalists adopted the dispensational approach. Also, many ministers and scholars in North America and Britain, who considered themselves evangelical in faith, were not involved with either dispensationalism or the growing fundamentalist coalition. Although dispensationalism was considered orthodoxy by many sincere believers, many other equally devout evangelicals rejected all or part of this approach.

The desire to thwart the advance of theological liberalism led to another major event in the early history of fundamentalism. With the encouragement and financial support of Lyman and Milton Stewart, two wealthy Los Angeles oilmen, a series of twelve booklets called *The Fundamentals,* containing essays by approximately ninety Bible teachers from both sides of the Atlantic, was compiled. The booklets were distributed, it was claimed, to every pastor, evangelist, minister, theological professor, theological student, Sunday school superintendent, and YMCA and YWCA secretary in the English-speaking world. These booklets, published between 1910 and 1915, addressed the theological issues of the day from a conservative Protestant viewpoint, and eventually, three million copies were produced. The tone of *The Fundamentals* was primarily scholarly, nonconfrontational, and traditionally biblical. The project provided links between evangelical scholars and pastors in the denominations and the emerging Bible institute movement, which often had a dispensational orientation.

Fundamentalism as a movement eventually reflected cultural values as much as it did theological propositions. The fundamentalists regarded themselves as a "saving remnant" who was loyal to traditional American Christian values and rejected modernism in theological thought and churchly practice. The movement endeavored to maintain boundaries that would resist all efforts to erode the historic Christian faith. Some historians accused them of being rigid in their attitudes toward both "religious" and "secular" life and suggested that this was rooted in the clash between urban and rural values that polarized Americans in the early twentieth century. Other interpreters maintained that, on the contrary, fundamentalism was a valid religious movement in its own right. It attracted a wide variety of supporters who rejected the truth claims of the new psychology, the new theology, and Darwinian science. Its adherents, many of whom were reputable scholars and highly regarded preachers, emphasized biblical piety and orthodox doctrines as the proper course for American Christianity to follow.

13

Churches in the Gilded Age

A founding father returning to America in 1860 would have easily recognized the country he had helped to create. That would not be so in the America of 1918. In 1890, the Department of the Census announced the official end to the frontier; no longer was there a significant amount of arable land left to be settled. The new era thus was one of a large-scale confrontation with industrial and urban conditions, and it must be seen as both a backdrop to the history of the churches at the turn of the twentieth century and as an example of a society undergoing change. The result was a crisis of values. At the same time, America faced the challenge of assimilating the masses of new ethnic and religious immigrants arriving on its shores.

Industrialism and Urbanization

Although America's industrial revolution was already underway prior to the Civil War, the postwar years were marked by astounding economic growth. Older industries expanded, and new ones—especially oil, electricity, and steel—reached gigantic proportions by the early twentieth century. Manufacturing, mainly concentrated in the Northeast, rapidly spread westward after 1865. Heavy industry and mass production came to dominate American output, which surpassed that of Britain by 1900. The huge corporation became a familiar American institution, and this had profound results. A large working class and middle class of professionals thronged to the growing cities, and the number of rural Americans declined relative to the urban population. In 1860, only 20 percent of people lived in cities of more than twenty-five hundred inhabitants. In 1900, the figure was 40 percent and increasing. In addition, almost thirty-nine million people immigrated to the United States between 1820 and 1920. Few nations could have absorbed such a staggering influx, and America handled it only with difficulty. African-Americans, who migrated in large numbers from southern farms to northern cities, suffered additionally because of racism.

In this new societal context, "business thinking" was the dominant mode of American thought and praxis. In government, university education, and fields far removed from the sphere of the marketplace, efficiency and "scientific management" became the criteria of sound judgment. During the "gilded age," as writer Mark Twain dubbed the times, money made the national pulse beat faster, and the businessman led the way. This frenzied quest for wealth received legitimation in the theory of social Darwinism, which applied the biological ideas of Darwin to the socioeconomic culture. This view rationalized the harsh conditions of industrial society and justified unfettered competition and consolidation of business firms into monopolies and trusts. Social evolution was seen as an automatic and beneficent process, and any effort to tamper with it would only do more harm than good. Although some sensitive thinkers challenged the theory, it nevertheless cast its spell throughout these years.

The new wave of immigration increasingly eroded the Protestant establishment. As the American population grew more ethnically diverse, the attitudes of many "older" Americans to newcomers grew less friendly. Not surprisingly, the post–Civil War generation that out of prejudice had failed to protect and provide for the millions of emancipated slaves attempted to exclude specific immigrant groups. First Chinese and then Japanese immigration was legally banned, and those of Asian ancestry were treated as second-class citizens wherever they lived. Anti-Catholicism prevailed, often accompanied by anti-Semitism. In the 1890s, the American Protective Association crusaded against Roman Catholic, Jewish, and non-Anglo-Saxon ideas and immigrants.

For many Americans, the changes opened doors to expanded horizons. Employment opportunities multiplied; railroad and steamship travel countered provincialism; telephones and transoceanic telegraph cables linked places near and far; mass-circulation newspapers and magazines widened access to information; art museums and symphony orchestras, financed by business philanthropy, brought "high" culture to thousands; modern medicine added to life expectancy; laborsaving devices entered the home, illuminated first by gaslights and later by electricity; and canned and prepared foods added variety to diets.

The dramatic changes resulting from urbanization and industrialization particularly affected the role of women. Middle- and upper-class women obtained more access to educational, professional, and political participation outside the home, while women on society's lower levels competed with men and boys for employment, often unsuccessfully when times were difficult.

The Churches and the New Social Climate

The American churches, both Protestant and Catholic, were unprepared to deal with the moral dilemmas of the new industrial era. Protestantism had enjoyed the status of a virtually established faith in the pre–Civil War era. Its values infused the culture even as the churches themselves enjoyed complete freedom from state regulation. In many ways, it was part and parcel of the national character. Because of the frontier ethos and the heritage of revivalism, it was a highly individualistic faith, which had little understanding of corporate responsibility for the well-being of society as a whole. Even when Protestants confronted social evils, they did so through the approach of individual initiative and influence. Although Catholics were heirs to the medieval ideal of a Christian society under the influence of the church, they belonged to a body that in America as well as other parts of the world had its own vested interests to protect.

For millions of immigrants from southern and eastern Europe, the Roman Catholic Church was the one familiar landmark in a strange and alien land. In the parishes and religious societies of Catholicism, they found both a link with Europe and a bond with America. Besides Italian and Polish Catholics, whose numbers were the largest, there were Czech, Slovak, Slovene, Croatian, Magyar (Hungarian), Portuguese, Lithuanian, and western Ukrainian Catholics. In the church, they found help in adjusting to their new life. Yet in another sense, the ethnic churches impeded Americanization by preserving the diverse cultures brought to the New World. The Catholic presence was now vast, and Protestants were forced to accommodate themselves to it.

An influx of immigrants also came from lands where varieties of Eastern Orthodoxy prevailed, such as Greece, Serbia, Bulgaria, Rumania, Russia, and Syria. The earliest Orthodox parishes in the United States were founded in New Orleans, San Francisco, and New York between 1864 and 1870, and within the next fifty years, roughly 150 congregations were formed in the cities where immigrants had settled. The same pattern of development occurred among the Jewish immigrants from Eastern Europe who came in massive numbers in the three decades prior to World War I. In the West, Christian churches developed among the Chinese and Japanese immigrants and gave them spiritual sustenance in the face of racial discrimination. For example, the pioneer missionary work of the Baptist pastor Dong Gong (c. 1850–1917) in Portland, Oregon, and Seattle led to the formation of several schools and congregations that ministered to Chinese immigrants. As Asian migrants moved eastward, their churches went with them.

Dong Gong (c. 1850–1917).
Courtesy of the American
Baptist Historical Society.

Religious diversity was further enhanced by the arrival of ethnic Protestants, many of whom perpetuated native-language worship in their respective parishes well into the twentieth century. The variety of denominational groups that drew from both state-church and pietistic free church traditions is quite extensive. The Midwest, especially the St. Louis area, received a large number of German-speaking Lutherans. The conservative German Evangelical Lutheran Synod of Missouri, Ohio, and Other States (now the Lutheran Church-Missouri Synod) settled there after its formation in 1847. It grew under the leadership of Carl F. W. Walther (1811–87), who upheld Old World confessional and ecclesiastical standards against the more Americanized Lutheran parishes dating from the colonial period. Further concentrations of German Lutherans in Iowa, Wisconsin, and other Midwestern states founded their own synods. Prussian United Church (Lutheran-Reformed) immigrants formed the Evangelical Synod in 1849. Norwegian, Swedish, Danish, and Finnish Lutherans established separate ethnic churches as well.

The Christian Reformed Church, organized in 1889 on the basis of the earlier True Reformed Church, attracted Dutch Calvinist immigrants who were dissatisfied with the Americanized Dutch Reformed Church (since 1867 the Reformed Church in America). The German-speaking Evangelical Association and United Brethren in Christ promoted Methodist and pietistic holiness. German and Swedish Baptists planted congregations in the upper Mississippi Valley, and German Mennonites settled in Kansas and the northern plains. Swedish Lutheran pietists formed the Evangelical Mission Covenant

Church and the Evangelical Free Church of America, both centered in Chicago and the upper Midwest.

In the large industrial communities, many in the laboring classes were impervious to the ministry and message of the churches, and this group of people constituted a continuing challenge. How were they to be reached? How could those who held middle-class values deal with the squalor of the poor?

Christians were anything but united in their approach to contemporary social problems. Many adhered to the old pattern of ameliorating social evils by fighting sin and dispensing charity; a few advocated socialism; still others were dissatisfied with the present social structure but were more conservative in their approach to change. The first of these predominated in the thirty years following the Civil War. Many "skid row" missions were founded, along with shelters for indigent women. Prosperous urban churches built gymnasiums and sponsored neighborhood social programs. In spite of the efforts of earnest churchmen, however, large numbers of Americans were mercilessly squeezed: blacks in the southern fields, immigrants in the northern slums, farmers on their western homesteads, children in eastern factories, and laborers everywhere. They were trapped without protection between the harsh realities of the new order and the inadequate social theories of the old.

The southern and western farmers, mostly evangelical Protestants, politically and morally challenged the new industrial society. They demanded that the United States abandon the monetary gold standard because its deflationary nature prevented them from receiving fair prices for their products. They also urged the institution of a federal income tax, government ownership of railroads and telephone service, direct election of senators, postal savings banks, legislation requiring an eight-hour workday, and other actions to offset the concentrated power of the industrial and banking communities. A devout Presbyterian layman from Nebraska, William Jennings Bryan (1860–1926), championed their cause as leader of the agrarian Populist Party, which joined with the Democrats in 1896 to nominate him for the presidency. Destined to run for president twice more, Bryan, more than any other person, represented the aspirations of rural Protestant America during the era when it was losing influence in the larger economic and social order.

In contrast, some prestigious urban preachers reflected a conservative social outlook and sometimes a puzzling naivete. Boston's Phillips Brooks (1835–93), born into social and economic security, claimed that excessive poverty and suffering were comparatively rare. Henry Ward Beecher (1813–87), who enjoyed a large salary from Plymouth Church in Brooklyn and revenues from publishing royalties, pointed out to strikers in 1877 that a dollar a day was enough for a wife and five or six children unless the man smoked or drank beer. Underlying such callous statements was the firm belief that the American system was basically sound and that urban and industrial problems were the result of personal moral relapses.

Henry Ward Beecher
(1813–87)

Gradually, however, the religious press took a more favorable attitude toward industrial workers and unions. Stirring books by an optimistic Congregational clergyman, Josiah Strong (1847–1916), stressed the possibility of social regeneration. Written in a spirit of fervent evangelicalism, his best-selling *Our Country* (1885) became an *Uncle Tom's Cabin* of city reform. The details of terrible conditions in urban life, described in books such as Jacob Riis's *How the Other Half Lives* (1890), shocked Christians. Such disclosures pricked the conscience of churchgoing America and stimulated the expansion of missions in the slums, support for the Salvation Army (which as mentioned earlier had arrived from Great Britain in 1880), and the building of more recreational facilities and social settlement homes.

Before long, clergymen who were dissatisfied with moderate, piecemeal changes called for significant change in the social order itself. To them, it was not enough to advocate individual regeneration; they looked for specific actions that would improve the life of organized society. Basically Victorian in outlook, they were optimistic and retained much of the traditional American individualism. Especially congenial to the growth of this progressive type of Christianity were three emphases of liberal theology: the immanence of God, the organic character of nature and human life, and the ideal of the kingdom of God on earth. This new outlook soon came to be known as the social gospel.

The social gospel was not a revolutionary attack on capitalistic society from the outside but a reforming effort from within. Its ideal of the kingdom of God resonated with the bourgeois idealism of post–Civil War Victorian America and its confidence in Anglo-Saxon institutions. Theologians in the 1930s charged that this form of social Christianity, with its confidence in the rationality and selflessness of human conduct, was less realistic than either Marxist-style proletarian radicalism or prophetic biblical religion. But proponents of the social gospel did reveal a keen awareness that society is more than the sum total of individuals comprising it. They realized that Christianity has ethical obligations to the community in which it is rooted, and they stated them in terms of their own theology.

Among the most influential was Washington Gladden (1836–1918), who starting in 1882 served for more than thirty years as pastor of the First Congregational Church of Columbus, Ohio. Influenced deeply by Horace Bushnell, he affirmed the validity of Christian principles for the whole of life. Gladden insisted on labor's right to collective bargaining and advocated an adequate form of profit sharing to help resolve tensions between capital and labor. Finding no ultimate solution for the problem either in the older individualism or in socialism, he recognized the need for greater governmental intervention. His plain speech and genuine religious spirit won him wide respect.

Also significant was Walter Rauschenbusch (1861–1918), who as a young Baptist clergyman in 1886 accepted the pastorate of a German immigrant church in a poverty-stricken area in New York City. While serving for eleven

Walter Rauschenbusch (1861–1918). Courtesy of the American Baptist Historical Society.

years in this desperate environment, he gained a real understanding of the importance of meeting human needs. Through study of the Bible and the works of various contemporary social critics, he discovered the ideal of the kingdom of God on earth. He saw the kingdom as the key to the teachings and work of Christ and maintained that carrying out its demands would lead to "Christianizing of the social order." This was the "very aim with which Christianity set out."[1] Although he never abandoned his evangelical emphasis on the life-changing gospel of Christ, he felt that churches needed to devote more attention to economic and social problems and less to merely theological matters as a way of offering greater service to Christ.

In 1897, Rauschenbusch was called to a professorship at Rochester Theological Seminary. There over the next two decades he exercised wide influence as he formulated the theory associated with the social gospel in several books, beginning with the landmark *Christianity and the Social Order* (1907). After Pope Leo XIII issued his famous encyclical *Rerum Novarum* in 1891, many Catholics in America also became interested in social problems and taught the social relevance of Catholic doctrine. An outstanding example of the practical outworking of the social gospel was Presbyterian Jane Addams (1860–1935). In 1890, she founded Hull House to aid the urban poor in Chicago, and in twenty years it grew into a highly regarded social service enterprise. She was also distinguished for her labors on behalf of world peace and women's rights.

However, the social gospel's vision, conceived in terms of social redemption, lacked broad appeal because of its liberal stance, both theologically and socially. Although the social gospel of Rauschenbusch and Gladden had a considerable impact on seminary education and denominational bureaucracies, it failed to become the stuff of popular Protestantism for most neighborhood congregations. Representative of social gospel principles was the "Social Creed of the Churches," a statement adopted by the Federal Council of Churches in 1912 that encouraged engagement among its member denominations. Although a few leaders of the social gospel movement were becoming aware of the plight of African-Americans, especially Willis D. Weatherford in his pioneering *Negro Life in the South* (1910), others were less sure about such matters and in some cases harbored doubts about women's rights as well.

Some activists were attracted to Christian socialism, a highly diverse movement that appealed to more liberal intellectuals. A common tie among its adherents was a commitment to some type of non-Marxian democratic socialism. William D. P. Bliss (1856–1926), an Episcopalian rector in Boston who was influenced by Anglican Christian socialism, founded the Society of Christian Socialists, which lasted from 1889 to 1896. George D. Herron (1862–1925), a Congregationalist minister and spellbinding prophet of social-

---

1. Walter Rauschenbusch, *Christianizing the Social Order* (New York: Macmillan, 1912), viii.

ism, cofounded the American Socialist Party. Methodist minister Edward Ellis Carr edited the magazine the *Christian Socialist* (1906–17), which at its height had fifteen hundred subscribers and was a major force in Eugene V. Debs's presidential campaigns on the Socialist ticket. Christian socialism lost most of its momentum during World War I, but its banner was carried for many years by Presbyterian minister Norman Thomas (1884–1968), who ran for president six times on the Socialist ticket.

Reflective of more traditional sentiments was the best-selling novel *In His Steps,* which Charles M. Sheldon, a Congregational minister from Kansas, published in 1897 to sensitize the Christian masses to social concerns. The book revolves around a conscientious minister's attempts to rouse his comfortable parishioners by asking them to consider what Jesus would do if he were confronted with the moral decisions they had to make. Although the book is often labeled the great social gospel novel of the era, in reality Sheldon's vision of reform simply merged evangelical morality and conservative political progressivism. He did not make the radical calls for social legislation that other social gospel spokesmen were making.

It is difficult to generalize about the role of churches in the attempt to address social problems. Sincere efforts occurred across the theological spectrum. The liberal social gospel proponents were, however, the most prominent, and their objectives seemed to be directly in line with those of the Progressive reform movements that animated American politics in the early twentieth century. At the same time, their wide vision of a "modernized Christian America" that would serve as a model for all the world's peoples was far too optimistic and unrealistic.

Many Protestants, however, were hostile to the idea of confronting social justice issues. Although evangelicals had inherited a glowing tradition of social reform in the nineteenth century, their changed attitudes by the early twentieth century reflected what historian Timothy L. Smith called the "Great Reversal" in social orientation by evangelical conservatives.[2] They linked rejection of the social gospel with their opposition to theological liberalism. Moreover, the appeal of dispensationalism, with its emphasis on worsening societal conditions in the end times, worked against political involvement beyond individual charitable acts and public opposition to vice and liquor.

The church has always lived in tension with the surrounding social order. It responds to the gospel call, urging people to look heavenward and to live redeemed lives marked by just and unselfish behavior. Yet the churches are human organizations subject to the economic and social values of earthly culture. Whenever Christians adopt a hands-off policy toward social problems, they unconsciously affirm the injustices of the moment and sanctify

2. As cited in David O. Moberg, *The Great Reversal: Evangelism versus Social Concern* (Philadelphia: Lippincott, 1972), 11.

the status quo as God's will, thus compromising their own ideals and losing moral credibility. On the other hand, if Christians challenge the prevailing economic and social forces too strongly, they may be forced into sectarian withdrawal and lose the opportunity to have a genuine cultural and social influence.

While the American churches faced many dilemmas amid the swirling tides of the late nineteenth century, most Christian believers were still confident that honest efforts by government and individuals of goodwill would eventually correct social problems, and both the nation and the churches would fulfill their destinies. In fact, this confidence and hope helped launch the missionary movement that reached to the earth's remotest corners. The churches were entering an era of dynamic international outreach.

14

International Engagement and Mission

The Ecumenical Missionary Conference that met at Carnegie Hall in New York from April 21 to May 1, 1900, symbolized the new era for American Christianity and the nation as well. With nearly 200,000 people taking part in over 60 sessions, this conclave was the largest religious event in the country to that time and possibly the best-attended missionary conference in history. Some 2,500 official delegates from 162 mission boards worldwide were present; the word *ecumenical* signified that it was a global enterprise. Indicative of how important foreign missions were in church life and even the popular imagination of that generation, former president Benjamin Harrison, a Presbyterian elder, presided over the gathering, and New York governor (and future president) Theodore Roosevelt and President William McKinley were featured speakers. The foreign missions effort not only influenced congregations but also contributed to a broader international awareness. As historian Sydney Ahlstrom observed, "The missionary on furlough was the great American window on the non-Western world."[1]

America's international involvement soared to new heights after the brief war with Spain in 1898. As a result of the war, ostensibly fought to free Cuba from what the media portrayed as Spanish misrule, the United

1. Sydney E. Ahlstrom, *A Religious History of the American People* (New Haven: Yale University Press, 1972), 865. For a full discussion of the gathering, see Thomas A. Askew, "The New York Ecumenical Missionary Conference: A Centennial Reflection," *International Bulletin of Missionary Research* 24, no. 4 (October 2000): 146–54.

States acquired an empire, including Puerto Rico, Guam, and the Philippine Islands. America had already acquired the territory of Alaska in 1867 and part of the Samoan Islands in 1889, and it was in the process of taking over Hawaii. Thus, expansion abroad was not a sudden, unprecedented action. But many felt that annexing the Philippines, which was too distant and such a large territory, was going too far, especially since many Filipinos expected to receive independence, as Cuba had. Still, majorities in Congress supported the action, and despite a strong anti-imperialist minority, which included William Jennings Bryan and numerous churchmen, most Americans regarded the expansionist actions as appropriate ventures for a great and powerful country.

Some expansionists appealed to the notions of national mission and manifest destiny to justify the move on the world stage. Typical of such thinking was the statement Albert Beveridge made on the floor of the U.S. Senate on January 9, 1900, defending the acquisition of the Philippines:

> God has not been preparing the English speaking and Teutonic peoples for a thousand years for nothing but vain and idle self-contemplation and admiration. No! He made us the master organizers of the world to establish system where chaos reigns. . . . He has marked the American people as his chosen nation to lead in the regeneration of the world.[2]

This sort of imperialistic nationalism rested heavily on the academically respectable view that the Anglo-Saxon peoples, defined as the British, Germans, and Americans, were morally and racially superior to others, especially Latin Americans, Asians, and Africans. The Anglo-Saxons were, as Josiah Strong put it, the great representatives of "a pure, spiritual Christianity" and civil liberty.[3] Accompanying such feelings of cultural superiority was the obligation, popularized by Rudyard Kipling as "the white man's burden," to bring Christianity, civilization, and commerce to the lesser peoples.

American Christians often reflected this larger national ethos as they vigorously promoted the cause of overseas missions. The extent of lay support for missionary causes reached record levels as the denominations sought to engage every member in the effort. The dynamic concept of the church-as-mission channeled denominational energy and resources into the effort of conveying to the entire world the saving grace of the Christian gospel. In the nineteenth century, Christianity became more widespread geographically than it or any other faith had ever been before,

2. The text of the entire speech is in the *Congressional Record,* 1899–1900, vol. 3, pt. 1, 704–12.

3. Josiah Strong, *Our Country,* ed. Juergen Herbst (Cambridge: Harvard University Press, 1963), 201–2.

and it "entered as a transforming agency into more cultures than in all the preceding centuries."[4]

The Extension of World Missions

While denominational missionary agencies greatly expanded their work throughout the nineteenth century, new developments also occurred that significantly affected the course of Christian work overseas: the heightened role of female missionaries, the beginning of faith missions and Bible institutes, and the Student Volunteer Movement for Foreign Missions. All originated in the latter part of the nineteenth century and achieved their full importance in the 1900s.

The largest functioning women's organizations (including temperance and women's suffrage groups) during this era were the female mission societies and committees scattered throughout the denominations. Outstanding national leaders such as Congregationalist Abbie Child (1840–1902) and Northern Baptists Helen Barrett Montgomery (1861–1934) and Lucy Peabody (1861–1949) set a new pace for mission mobilization. Heroic women such as Southern Baptist Lottie Moon (1840–1912) in China engaged in extraordinary labors that few males could match.

Helen Barrett Montgomery (1861–1934). Courtesy of the American Baptist Historical Society.

4. Kenneth Scott Latourette, *A History of the Expansion of Christianity,* vol. 4 (New York: Harper, 1941), 7.

Lottie Moon (1840–1912). Courtesy of the International Mission Board, SBC.

The faith missions were largely interdenominational agencies that, because they lacked guaranteed income from a specific denominational constituency, had to rely on the gifts of individuals and congregations to support their work. They viewed their relationships with the existing denominations as cooperative and complementary rather than competitive, although mainline churches sometimes regarded the movement as sectarian. Over time these missions succeeded remarkably. All of the major nineteenth-century societies still exist, and several are today among the largest in the world. Among these are the China Inland Mission (now Overseas Missionary Fellowship), Africa Inland Mission, and Sudan Interior Mission (now SIM International).

The Bible institute movement, born in the 1880s, remained primarily a North American phenomenon. Initially created to increase the number of candidates available for home and foreign ministries when the volume of seminary graduates became inadequate, the institutes paralleled the creation of specialized schools for teachers and nurses taking place at the same time. The institutes attracted many female students and emphasized the study of Scripture and "practical" subjects such as conducting Sunday schools and missionary methods. As many colleges and seminaries moved away from their nineteenth-century evangelical roots, the Bible institutes replaced them as centers of ministerial preparation. This was especially the case during the years of fundamentalist growth (1920s–30s). The institutes provided educational opportunities for devout evangelical youths who often lacked the financial means to attend regular colleges or seminaries.

The earliest Bible institutes were the Missionary Training Institute of Nyack (1882), now Nyack College (New York); Chicago's Moody Bible Institute (1886); and the Boston Missionary Training School (1889), which evolved into Gordon College and Gordon-Conwell Theological Seminary, named after its Baptist founder, Adoniram Judson Gordon (1836–95), one of the foremost advocates for foreign missions of the time. At the height of the movement there were more than three hundred Bible institutes and Bible colleges in the United States and Canada, and they produced well over half of the North American Protestant missionary recruits. Although these Bible institutes and colleges were nondenominational in character, many smaller and separatist denominations, such as the Christian Churches-Church of Christ, also founded such schools.

Adoniram Judson Gordon (1836–95). Courtesy of the Archives of Gordon College.

The individuals responsible for the formation of the Student Volunteer Movement for Foreign Missions, the largest organization that sponsored the recruitment of missionaries, were Robert Wilder (1863–1938), a graduate of Princeton University; John Mott (1865–1955), a student at Cornell University; and the evangelist Dwight L. Moody. At a student conference held at Moody's Mount Hermon, Massachusetts, home in 1886, an enthusiastic group of missionary-minded students challenged the 250 college-aged men and women present to consider foreign service, and 100 responded. Following this groundbreaking meeting, Wilder toured American colleges, urging students to sign the pledge, "It is my purpose, God permitting, to become a foreign missionary." In 1888, the three men formally organized the SVM, with Mott as chairman and Robert Speer as traveling secretary. It adopted as its motto "The Evangelization of the World in This Generation,"[5] a phrase coined by Presbyterian Arthur T. Pierson (1837–1911), the foremost missions theorist and promoter in the late nineteenth century. In 1891, the first of the quadrennial conventions that distinguished the group's activities over the next forty years took place. Soon over two thousand volunteers were enrolled, of whom roughly five hundred were women, a significant indication of the increasing role they were coming to play in the Protestant missionary enterprise.

John Mott (1865–1955). Courtesy of the Day Missions Library, Yale University Divinity School.

Eventually, more than twenty thousand volunteers served overseas as a direct result of the SVM's call. The group was able to bridge the gap between conservatives and liberals in the mainline churches, and it influenced thousands of congregants who engaged in all sorts of international ministries and peace efforts throughout World War I and the 1920s. Thus, an important aspect of the foreign missions impulse was its effect on the lives and church activities of Christians at home. In addition, as historian Dana Robert points out, "The internationalist discourse within the missionary movement in the 1920s and 1930s . . . of a cooperative, worldwide, peaceful community of

5. C. Howard Hopkins, *John R. Mott, 1865–1955: A Biography* (Grand Rapids: Eerdmans, 1979), 68. For Wilder's pledge, see page 26.

Arthur T. Pierson
(1837–1911)

different races and cultures" contributed to the broader, even global, orientation of that era.[6]

Ecumenical Beginnings

The twentieth-century ecumenical movement was the direct result of the missionary enterprise of the nineteenth century. It could be defined as the process whereby Christian communions in every part of the world strove to discover and express a common faith and life centered in commitment to Jesus Christ.

Protestant leaders in America and Europe realized that interdenominational teamwork was necessary if the worldwide missionary enterprise was to be effective, and, in fact, the first examples of ecumenical effort were the various cooperative ventures that took place on the mission fields. The challenge was particularly relevant in America, with its array of Protestant styles of church life. Because American believers found it difficult to cooper-

6. Dana L. Robert, "The First Globalization: The Internationalization of the Protestant Missionary Movement between the World Wars," *International Bulletin of Missionary Research* 26 (April 2002): 50–56.

ate across denominational lines, they sensed the need for a mechanism that would enable those within the same "confessional family" to come together on a worldwide basis.

To this end, interdenominational meetings were convened in large cities in Europe and America from 1854 onward, the largest being those in London in 1888 and New York in 1900. These were inter-ecclesiastical exchanges, in contrast to the Evangelical Alliance, formed in England in 1846 and in America in 1867, which was comprised of individual believers. The most significant ecumenical gathering was the World Missionary Conference of 1910 held in Edinburgh. Attended by roughly one thousand delegates appointed by missionary societies, it enjoyed a more official character than had previous assemblies. The major outcome was the formation of a Continuation Committee, presided over by American Methodist Mott, to coordinate overseas endeavors. Unfortunately, World War I shattered the Edinburgh unity, and the Continuation Committee became largely ineffective. After the return of peace, strenuous effort was made to bring the Christian leaders from both warring sides together again, resulting in the creation of the International Missionary Council in 1921.

One of the prominent delegates to the 1910 World Missionary Conference, Charles Brent, Protestant Episcopal missionary bishop in the Philippines, along with other leaders, called for a world conference on faith and order. The war delayed effective action until 1920, when Brent and those who shared his views worked out the details for the meeting and invited all churches that "accept our Lord Jesus Christ as God and Saviour" to send delegates to a conference in 1927 in Lausanne, Switzerland.[7] All the major Protestant denominations as well as the Eastern Orthodox Church responded favorably. Pope Pius XI, however, in the interest of doctrinal orthodoxy and church authority, forbade Roman Catholic participation in this groundbreaking ecumenical event. A refusal to participate in any meaningful way in the ecumenical movement was papal policy until the radical shift in outlook toward interchurch cooperation that occurred under John XXIII (1881–1963) and the Second Vatican Council in the 1960s.

Although theological differences repeatedly surfaced at Lausanne, a spirit of Christian charity prevailed, and noteworthy agreements emerged. First, the faith of the church universal was that expressed by the Apostles' and Nicene Creeds, and second, congregational, episcopal, and presbyterian forms of government all had appropriate places in a reunited church. A second meeting at Edinburgh in 1937 joined with the Life and Work movement (founded in 1925) to begin planning for a World Council of Churches, which its proponents expected would eventually achieve Christian unity throughout the world. At the same time, however, most evangelical and fundamentalist

---

7. H. N. Bate, ed., *Faith and Order: Proceedings of the World Conference, Lausanne, August 3–21, 1927* (London: SCM, 1927), vii.

church leaders, fearful of theological dilution or bureaucratic control, opted out of the ecumenical movement.

The ecumenical meetings, the rise of councils of churches on local, state, and national levels, especially the Federal Council of Churches of Christ, founded in 1908 with thirty-three denominations participating, and cooperative agencies such as the Commission on Church and Social Services (1912) revealed the desire of American Protestant leaders to deal with the fracturing pressures of modern life. In fact, the Federal Council's constitution affirmed that its purpose was "to manifest the essential oneness of the Christian churches of America in Jesus Christ as their divine Lord and Saviour."[8] The councils undoubtedly contributed to the lowering of old barriers between church communions and fostered a genuine spirit of ecumenicity. At the same time, all too often Western pride was implicit in the ecumenical efforts, which may help to explain why so many non-Westerners were hostile to the Christian faith later in the century. In their minds, it was difficult to separate Christianity from other expressions of Western power and hegemony.

The Peace Movement

In the late nineteenth century, a resurgence of the American movement for world peace took place. The so-called historic peace churches—the Quakers, the Mennonites, the pietistic German Baptist Brethren, later known as the Church of the Brethren, and the Brethren in Christ (which had both pietist and Mennonite roots)—had already distinguished themselves in early America for their commitment to a simple lifestyle and nonviolence. They would continue to uphold these principles throughout the next two centuries. In the early nineteenth century, many saw the incompatibility of Christianity and war, and by 1826, there were roughly fifty peace organizations in the country, including the American Peace Society, which thrived with the aid of the churches. The peace movement ceased during the Civil War but revived in the 1890s, and its period of greatest vitality was between the Spanish-American War and the outbreak of World War I. The campaign for peace was closely identified with that against American imperial expansion. Churchmen joined hands with other anti-imperialists such as William Graham Sumner, Mark Twain, and William James to advance their mutual interests.

The Department of Peace and Arbitration of the Women's Christian Temperance Union (WCTU), formed in 1889, supplemented the activities of the American Peace Society. The Conference of Friends, convened by Quakers in Philadelphia in 1901, had as its sole purpose the discussion of ways to promote

8. Elias B. Sanford, ed., *Federal Council of the Churches of Christ in America: Report of the First Meeting* (New York: Revell, 1909), 512.

peace. On the international level, representatives of twenty-six nations met in the Hague in 1899 to discuss plans for the promotion of peace. This was followed by a second conference in 1907 with even more delegates. In 1902, a group of clergymen in New York City organized the American Association of Ministers for the Advancement of Peace. Thereafter, the peace movement in the United States took the offensive. The American Peace Society more than doubled its membership and took on new vigor as it reestablished its headquarters in Washington, D.C., in 1912. One of the ideas international peace activists promoted most vigorously was the negotiation of arbitration treaties, which required the signatories to submit conflicts to an arbitration commission and to resolve their differences in a peaceful manner. When William Jennings Bryan became the U.S. Secretary of State in 1913, he negotiated many such agreements with various countries.

Steel maker Andrew Carnegie contributed a large sum of money to an endowment for world peace and to found the Church Peace Union in 1914, one of the earliest expressions of interfaith cooperation among American Protestants, Jews, and Catholics. (It still exists today as the Carnegie Council on Ethics and International Affairs.) The general secretary of the Federal Council of Churches, Charles McFarland, played a key role in this effort and in working for closer cooperation among American and European churches, which in turn led to the creation of the World Alliance for Promoting International Friendship Through the Churches in 1914. In the interwar years, this was the foremost ecumenical peace organization.

While peace enthusiasts in the American churches were optimistic about their cause, the European political scene turned toward disaster. Although initially committed to neutrality at the outbreak of war in 1914, many Americans soon found themselves favoring the Western Allies as allegations spread of German atrocities and resentment mounted over their use of submarines to counter the British blockade. The change in religious thinking is perhaps best illustrated by evangelist Billy Sunday. At first he opposed American involvement in European affairs, but his attitude shifted following the sinking of the *Lusitania* in 1915. Then Sunday became an outspoken interventionist, and after the United States entered the war in 1917, he helped to raise thousands of dollars in Liberty bonds to aid the crusade against "the Hun." In a more bitter mood, he once declared, "If you turn hell upside down, you will find 'Made in Germany' stamped there."[9] Americans were persuaded that, in the phrase of their president, Woodrow Wilson, "the world must be made safe for democracy" and that the war was not an imperialistic conflict but a just crusade for the triumph of good over evil. Therefore, when the United States entered the international struggle, animated by a sense of divine calling, the peace movement was again forced to submerge.

9. Ray H. Abrams, *Preachers Present Arms* (New York: Round Table Press, 1933), 79.

PART 5

THE CHURCHES IN A PLURALISTIC SOCIETY (1917–PRESENT)

15

War, Prosperity, and Depression

Few American Christians would have taken issue when evangelist Billy Sunday prayed the following prayer before the House of Representatives on January 10, 1918:

> Thou knowest, O Lord, we are in a life-and-death struggle with one of the most infamous, vile, greedy, avaricious, bloodthirsty nations that has ever disgraced the pages of history. . . . Make bare thy mighty arm, O Lord, and beat back that great pack of hungry, wolfish Huns, whose fangs drip with blood and gore. We will forever raise our voice to thy praise.[1]

The nation had plunged into a holy war to punish evil and bring a final end to war itself. It was a "Great Crusade" in which the churches overwhelmingly enlisted. The contemporary reader can scarcely perceive the idealism, even naiveté, that characterized the rapid change of churchly opinion from the neutrality of 1914–16 to the enthusiasm for military combat in 1917–18.

The American Churches and World War I

Although not all ministers employed Sunday's graphic language, most denominations passed resolutions condemning the German "Hunish Hordes" and endorsing America's fight for world freedom. Presbyterian liberal Henry

1. *Congressional Record,* vol. 56, pt. 1 (1918), 762.

van Dyke even advocated hanging "everybody who lifts his voice against America's entering the war."[2] Such anti-German sentiment extended even to the German language: Several states passed legislation banning the use of the language in public services, resulting in a rapid shift to English among German-speaking Lutherans and Methodists.

With the nation focusing all its energies on winning the war, churches bordered on becoming government agencies. Local Red Cross units met in church sanctuaries, as did other wartime agencies; religious periodicals urged the purchase of Liberty bonds; and ministers preached from outlines supplied by the government propaganda office. The large denominations formed social service committees to carry out their efforts, while the Federal Council of Churches created the General War-Time Commission of the Churches, which coordinated the activities of the denominations and such agencies as the YMCA, appointed and trained Protestant chaplains for the armed forces, and distributed Bibles and religious tracts in the camps. The YMCA, Salvation Army, Red Cross, and Knights of Columbus provided medical assistance,

James Cardinal Gibbons (1834–1921). Courtesy of the Archives of the Archdiocese of Boston.

2. Mark Sullivan, *Our Times: The United States, 1900–1925,* vol. 5 (New York: Scribners, 1935), 467–68.

recreation, entertainment, and education, while individual congregations were beehives of support activity.

Roman Catholic archbishop James Cardinal Gibbons (1834–1921), who earlier had praised the benefits of the American doctrine of the separation of church and state for Catholicism and had secured Vatican approval for organized labor in America, placed his church firmly behind the war effort. In August 1917, the National Catholic War Council was formed, which provided support to Catholic chaplains and servicemen and cooperated with Protestant and Jewish groups in home front activities. In 1919, it was reorganized on a permanent basis as the National Catholic Welfare Conference to be an informational clearinghouse for American Catholic leaders and a political lobby to protect Catholic interests. This intensive wartime involvement decisively marked the emergence of Roman Catholicism as a mainline American faith.

Unfortunately, there was also widespread contempt for members of the historic peace churches and conscientious objectors who belonged to other churches. In 1918, Congress passed legislation allowing alternative (non-combatant) service for objectors, but before then they were badly treated, and some were even imprisoned or killed by overzealous patriots. Pacifist ministers were often mistreated as well.

In the midst of the campaign to defeat the Kaiser, church leaders seized the opportunity to subdue John Barleycorn as well, a reform championed by women and long sought by many Christians. One of the spearheads of this move was the aforementioned Women's Christian Temperance Union, led by the dynamic Frances Willard. Another was the Anti-Saloon League, arguably one of the most effective political pressure groups in American history, which was heavily supported by Methodists. The Prohibition Party fielded candidates dedicated to the elimination of the sale and use of alcoholic beverages. Adoption of a prohibitionist stance enabled the hitherto marginal Church of the Brethren (formerly the Dunker or German Baptist Brethren Church) to enter the mainstream of American denominational life. Although backing for national Prohibition was strongest among Methodists and Baptists, Protestant groups of every theological stripe (with the exception of some Lutherans and Episcopalians) supported the anti-saloon effort. Catholics, however, were much less enthusiastic about the reform. At the time of the U.S. entry into the war, Prohibition was already law in twenty-six states.

The necessity to conserve alcohol and grain for the war effort as well as the alleged German origins of the brewing and distilling industries provided justification for the Eighteenth Amendment banning the manufacture and sale of intoxicating beverages. Ratified by the states in October 1919, the Amendment went into effect on January 16, 1920. For the next dozen years, a Protestant coalition labored valiantly to make a success of the "noble experiment," as some political leaders called it.

America entered the war to achieve two righteous aims: to defeat Germany and to outlaw war permanently. The armistice signed on November 11, 1918, represented the fulfillment of the first, but its justness rested squarely on the commitment to the second. Protestant churchmen, drawing on the momentum of wartime enthusiasm, launched a vast fund-raising scheme called the Interchurch World Movement, which they expected would bring in a new world order of peace and democracy. They did not foresee the postwar letdown and disillusionment that would limit America's involvement in the international order. In fact, the war and its aftermath marked the passage from nineteenth-century optimism and the vision of a glorious future to twentieth-century pessimism and political realism.

The intensity of the war ideology helped unleash the latent nativist tendencies that repressed thoughtful dissent and demanded conformity, as reflected in the so-called Red Scare of 1919–20. Fearful of worldwide communist revolution and the dilution of Anglo-Saxon democratic institutions, many Americans, both in and out of the churches, harbored deep prejudices against blacks, Jews, Catholics, and the new immigrants. Congress passed laws severely limiting immigration, and only a handful of churches opposed them. The result was a resurgence of nativism, reflected in the actions of the Ku Klux Klan in the 1920s (in both the North and the South), whose program was the defense of Protestant America against alien peoples and ideas. In short, the tendency to regard Christian and American ways as identical led to an idealized picture of America that did not fit the experience of black Christians, Native Americans, and ethnic victims of prejudice.

The Retreat to "Normalcy"

The mutually supportive merger of church and state in the Great Crusade gave no hint of its transitory quality. What followed the war was a decade of steady decline (in spite of financial prosperity) in all aspects of church life. Peacetime "normalcy," a term coined by President Warren G. Harding, was a time of accelerating secularization in American public life. Intellectuals in their writing and common people in their behavior reflected the new mood of skepticism. H. L. Mencken and Clarence Darrow charged that the churches were behind the times, and religion as a subject of serious and intelligent discussion all but disappeared from the literary monthlies. The nature of urban life, with its emphasis on mobility and anonymity, contributed to a casual attitude toward church attendance, and Sunday took on the character of a recreational holiday.

The overwhelming confidence in the power of science to solve human problems, as well as Freudian psychology and pragmatism in philosophy, intensified the drift toward relativism and the naturalistic approach to all things. Scores of books popularized the new psychology with its emphasis on human irrationality. Pragmatism, a view generally associated with John Dewey (1859–1952), declared that the sense, or the truthfulness, of an idea derives from its consequences or uses. Put simply, that which works is what is true. More a methodology than a systematic philosophy, pragmatism was concerned with immediate results rather than ultimate ends. As such, it heavily influenced teaching methodology and the curriculum in schools.

On a more practical level, new merchandising, mass media, leisure industries, and automobiles dramatically shaped people's lives. Installment buying and wild business speculation, traditionally frowned upon in religious circles, offered an avenue to enjoyment, extravagance, and status. Sophisticated advertising techniques created desires for consumer products, and movies and radio created a new celebrity class that set the trends for both clothing and behavior.

Except in rural regions, especially in the South, churches no longer provided the unique formative role in community, family, and individual life that had been so evident in nineteenth-century America. At the beginning of the twentieth century, Protestants supplied the broad evangelical ideals and rhetoric from which the progressive social reformers drew much of their inspiration. The same was true of Woodrow Wilson, whose wartime appeals reflected his Presbyterian faith and worldview. During the 1920s, however, the forces of controversy tore at the soul of Protestantism at the very time when pluralism and secularization in America took on new intensity. The fundamentalist controversy was a debate over foundational theological and social issues, but the resulting polarization of positions and the acrimonious debates and church splits marked the end of Protestant hegemony in the United States. In 1933, Alfred North Whitehead observed that Protestantism and its institutions no longer directed the patterns of life.[3] A Judeo-Christian tradition, however, still provided the value base that determined public and private morality. The full impact of pluralism and secularism would not be felt for another generation.

The Fundamentalist-Modernist Controversy

Many historians have caricatured fundamentalism as the last gasp of a bigoted Protestant establishment. Unaware of the diverse nature of the fundamentalist movement, such scholars have presented it as a monolith of defensive religious fanaticism. To be sure, there were episodes that betrayed the parochialism, divisiveness, and arrogance of some fundamentalists,

3. A. N. Whitehead, *Adventures of Ideas* (Cambridge: Cambridge University Press, 1933), 205.

but thoughtful leaders such as the urbane and erudite J. Gresham Machen (1881–1937) also revealed the considerable intellectual depth found in the movement. Commentators also tend to minimize the sincerity of lay adherents of fundamentalism and fail to appreciate the dilemma they faced in confronting the decline of what they believed to be the foundational value structure of both society and the church.

J. Gresham Machen (1881–1937). Courtesy of the Archives, Westminster Theological Seminary, Philadelphia, Pennsylvania.

During the 1920s, the underlying theological differences between conservatives and liberals erupted into open confrontation. Before World War I, churchmen in the various communions, whether liberal or conservative, had cooperated in the task of reaching the world for Christ. They wrote for the same journals, prayed for the same causes, and shared similar hopes for the Christianization of humankind. After the war, the uneasy consensus collapsed as the theological debate intensified and a conservative coalition determined to uphold orthodoxy dug in its heels.

The issues dividing the two factions were hardly minor ones: the authority and infallibility of the Bible, the virgin birth of Jesus, his bodily resurrection, the personal salvation of the believer through Christ's substitutionary atonement, and the second coming of Christ. Conservatives insisted that these "fundamentals" were the foundation of historic Christianity. Such a debate did not occur in American Catholicism because the aforementioned papal decrees condemning "Americanism" and "modernism" ensured that liberalism as such was not tolerated in Catholic intellectual life.

Among the defenders of orthodoxy, Princeton Seminary professor Machen stands out. In *The Origin of Paul's Religion* (1921), *Christianity and Liberalism* (1923), and *The Virgin Birth of Christ* (1930), he charged that liberalism (or modernism, terms used interchangeably by both sides) was not essentially

Christian because it denied the historic creeds that all believers had traditionally affirmed, especially those sections regarding Christ's death to save sinners and his physical resurrection. He and others insisted that the modernists leave the denominations and found new ones that accepted their novel theology with its faith in humankind and science.

Although the best-known popular spokesperson for liberalism in the 1920s was New York City clergyman Harry Emerson Fosdick (1878–1969), who preached in the famous Riverside Church from 1930 to 1946, the most cohesive statement of liberal theology was made by Shailer Mathews (1863–1941), dean of the University of Chicago Divinity School. In his widely read *The Faith of Modernism* (1924), Mathews maintained that Christianity is life, not doctrine. It is more a matter of experience and practical morality, revealed in the example of Christ, than adherence to doctrinal formulations in confessions that represented the faith needs of a past era.

The struggle between the fundamentalist and liberal parties reached the most serious levels in the Northern Baptist Convention and the Presbyterian Church in the U.S.A. during 1924 and 1925. While other denominations experienced flurries of activity that restricted the inroads of liberalism in their ranks, the most intense debate and denominational splits occurred among the Presbyterians and the Baptists with their Calvinistic emphasis on precise theological definitions.

Recent studies of the controversy have revealed that complete polarization did not take place. The balance of political influence resided with a moderate middle party, generally evangelical in viewpoint but not militant enough to join with the more determined fundamentalists to root out liberalism when doing so carried the risk of division. In the long run, the reluctance of the moderates to vote with their fundamentalist colleagues prevented the expulsion of liberal ministers from the denominations.

As an indication of the vital place that missions held in American Protestantism, when Baptist and Presbyterian schisms did occur, they centered on the presence of perceived liberals in the missionary force. Adding fuel to the controversy was the Laymen's Foreign Missions Inquiry, a massive study of the missionary enterprise financed by John D. Rockefeller. The summary report, *Rethinking Missions* (1932), authored by Harvard philosopher of religion William Ernest Hocking (1873–1966), called for more cooperation among the world's religions and downplayed evangelization and church planting. Conservatives felt strongly that this undermined the Great Commission. Rather than submitting to the denominational demand to cease supporting an alternate mission board he had helped to create, an action the church regarded as a violation of its laws, Machen left both Princeton Seminary and the Presbyterian Church in the U.S.A. With his followers he founded Westminster Theological Seminary (Philadelphia) in 1929 and a separate denomination that became known as the Orthodox Presbyterian Church in 1939. Dissident

Baptist fundamentalists withdrew from the Northern Baptist Convention in 1932 and created the General Association of Regular Baptists in 1933. The distinctives of this group were a strong commitment to foreign missions to be carried on by independent Baptist societies and separation from both modernists and evangelicals who cooperated with them. Continuing dissatisfaction with the Northern Baptist standards for missionaries led a second group to form a separate mission board in 1943 and a new denomination, the Conservative Baptist Association, four years later.

On the whole, during the 1920s, southern denominations did not undergo the same type of wrenching controversy. The major exception involved J. Frank Norris (1877–1952), a militantly fundamentalist pastor in Texas who alleged that there was liberalism in the Southern Baptist Convention. After his ouster from the SBC, he formed a separate denomination, eventually named the World Baptist Fellowship. In 1950, a group broke off from Norris's group and organized the Baptist Bible Fellowship, which historian Leon McBeth argues was the moderate wing of Southern Baptist fundamentalism, just as the Conservative Baptist Association was the moderate wing of Northern Baptist fundamentalism.[4]

Nevertheless, the regional divisions in American Christianity and the denominations emanating from the Civil War era still persisted. In the South, evangelical Protestantism was thoroughly intertwined with southern cultural conservatism. Compared to their northern counterparts, members of the southern Presbyterian church (Presbyterian Church in the U.S.) and the Southern Baptist Convention had no difficulty affirming orthodox doctrine. Penetration of the region's public schools by evolutionary theories of human origins, however, became a rallying cry for southern fundamentalists. The contest for control of the school curriculum reached its zenith in the sensational Scopes trial.

In Tennessee, as in other southern states, the political influence of fundamentalists was quite strong, and they pressured the state legislature to make it unlawful to "teach any theory that denies the Story of Divine Creation of man as taught in the Bible, and to teach instead that man has descended from a lower order of animal."[5] In the town of Dayton, a high school biology teacher, John Scopes, continued to teach evolutionary views. He was arrested and brought to trial in 1925.

The details of this sensational trial, one of the first great media events, have become part of American legend. The defense lawyer, religious skeptic Clarence Darrow, ridiculed the fundamentalist spokesman William Jennings Bryan, who, although the prosecuting attorney, allowed himself to be ques-

4. H. Leon McBeth, *The Baptist Heritage: Four Centuries of Baptist Witness* (Nashville: Broadman, 1987), 766–67.

5. 1925 Tenn. House Bill 185, quoted in Edward J. Larson, *Summer for the Gods: The Scopes Trial and America's Continuing Debate over Science and Religion* (New York: Basic Books, 1997), 50.

tioned about his anti-evolution views. For many fundamentalists and liberals, it was an apocalyptic confrontation. The issues raised remained touchstones in the unresolved struggle of fundamentalists to maintain influence on the general culture, or at least to approve the worldview and values encountered by their children in public schools.

In the end, Scopes was convicted but later acquitted on a technicality. Bryan died a few days later of a stroke, and fundamentalism became increasingly associated in the popular mind with ignorance, backwardness, and reaction. In short, the term that originally had referred to an orthodox ministerial effort to oppose theological liberalism in the northern denominations came to connote hostility to modern culture and social change.

Unable to achieve orthodox uniformity in the mainline denominations or to halt the drift of American society away from traditional Protestant values, the fundamentalists developed a life, an identity, and ultimately a subculture of their own. Although the vision of a great national campaign coordinated through the World Christian Fundamentals Association (founded in 1919 and led by Baptist William Bell Riley [1861–1947]), had largely dissipated by 1930, fundamentalism as a religious force was sustained by an institutional network of Bible institutes, small colleges and seminaries, Bible conferences, itinerant evangelists, religious periodicals, faith missions societies, radio preachers, publishing houses, and a host of small denominations and independent congregations. Particularly significant were ministries that used the new medium of radio. From this network developed an institutional base for evangelical advances later in the century.

As historian George Marsden has shown in *Fundamentalism and American Culture* (1980), religious fundamentalism must be seen as a peculiarly American response by evangelicals to the social and intellectual challenges of the times. Unfortunately, in the name of pure Christianity and loyal Americanism, fundamentalists retreated from exercising significant influence in the cultural and intellectual centers of society. The dispensational theology many of them held further encouraged societal withdrawal. Nevertheless, fundamentalists perpetuated the evangelical dynamic of a Bible-based Christianity and the gospel call for personal commitment to a risen Christ.

The fundamentalist-modernist controversy of the 1920s has frequently been described in simplistic terms as a rural-urban conflict between traditional agrarian religionists and progressive urban liberals. However, cities such as Philadelphia, Dallas-Fort Worth, Minneapolis, Chicago, Denver, and Los Angeles were all centers of fundamentalist strength. On a more symbolic level, the conflict can perhaps be seen as a clash between two mentalities: the one more comfortable in a preindustrial, homogeneous environment in which religious faith is central and traditional authority structures are honored, the other more oriented to the technology and diversity of the modern urban world with its emphasis on individual autonomy, open-ended search for truth, and pluralistic culture.

It should not be assumed, however, that all Protestant America was divided into two camps, the liberals or the fundamentalists. As historian D. G. Hart argues in *The Lost Soul of American Protestantism* (2002), various denominations, sometimes called confessionalists, were not caught up in the theological controversies of the 1920s and following period. Two of these denominations, the Lutheran Church-Missouri Synod and the Christian Reformed, were ethnic churches that had recently become Americanized, and these "Confessional Protestants" emphasized the Apostles' Creed and the Reformation creeds, traditional liturgies, a high significance of the Lord's Supper, and the pastoral ministry of an educated clergy. Their tone of congregational life as a community of faith was corporate and doctrinal rather than pietistic, revivalistic, or social reconstructionist. As such, they represented a middle way in twentieth-century American Protestantism. To some extent this was also true of the Mennonites and other peace churches and the many Holiness and Pentecostal groups.

The Churches and the Economic Crisis

The stock market crash of October 1929, which ended the precarious "normalcy" of the Harding-Coolidge era, shook American society even more deeply than had World War I, and the churches did not escape the economic upheaval that had begun to sweep the world even before the Wall Street debacle. The decade marked by an upwardly spiraling economy and unlimited opportunity ended. Ahead lay the threat of permanent economic class divisions such as those of the Old World. While most Protestants lived far above the lowest level of destitution, they were confronted on all sides by human suffering, confusion, and social anxiety.

No revival took place in the major denominations, such as had often accompanied previous economic crises. But those evangelistic churches that stressed a better life in heaven and espoused premillennial views of history, particularly the Pentecostal and the Holiness communions, experienced substantial growth during the lean years of the 1930s. They, as well as black churches, attracted Americans from the lower economic classes, whose numbers were increasing rapidly as hard times set in. Particularly noteworthy among these denominations was the International Church of the Foursquare Gospel, founded in 1927 by Aimee Semple McPherson (1890–1944), the most widely known female evangelist of the time, who ministered at the Angelus Temple in Los Angeles.

In most mainline churches, budgets were slashed, membership dwindled, and missionary enterprises were curtailed. In some cases, ministers were dis-

Aimee Semple McPherson (1890–1944). Courtesy of the Billy Graham Center Museum, Wheaton, Illinois.

missed and the churches closed. It was a difficult, disheartening period, and churches struggled along as best they could, as did their individual members. In the midst of this, the Prohibition experiment, for which so many church people had campaigned, came to an end with the repeal of the Eighteenth Amendment. The *Christian Century* grimly stated in 1935 that the Christian

The Salvation Army sponsored a variety of programs to meet the needs of people during the depression. Courtesy of the Salvation Army National Archives.

church was wholly unprepared for the depression and unable to minister to the deepest human need that it produced.

Churches did what they could to alleviate the pain of their parishioners but without notable success. The suffering was too pervasive, and workable solutions eluded those earnest pastors who tried to exercise charity. Manifesting something of the spirit of the social gospel, Franklin Roosevelt's New Deal became the substitute for traditional church charity. The modern world called for big solutions, and most of the traditional churches, sapped by secularism and the perplexities of the depression, easily succumbed to the agenda of the larger society and culture. As historian Winthrop Hudson observed, "With its basic theological insights largely emasculated, Protestantism was robbed of any independently grounded vision of life and became more and more the creature of American culture rather than its creator."[6] The times called for a renewed emphasis on well-articulated social and theological criticism from within the churches.

6. Winthrop S. Hudson, *Religion in America* (New York: Scribners, 1973), 371.

16

World War II and Religious Change

By the 1930s, the process of theological redefinition was well under way in America. Its origins could be traced to the writings of Karl Barth (1886–1968), a sensitive minister who served a small parish in Switzerland during World War I. As the horrors of war enveloped Europe, he lost confidence in optimistic liberal theology. For him, its emphasis on human rationality and scientifically induced progress did not square with either reality or the crucial themes of the New Testament.

The Post-liberal Theological Mind

Barth saw that liberalism had brushed aside the Pauline insistence on the sovereignty of a righteous God, the sinfulness of humans, and God's initiative in salvation through grace. Barth spelled out these ideas in his *Commentary on the Epistle to the Romans* (1919), which resoundingly called for the rediscovery of biblical theology and a renewed emphasis on the views of the Protestant Reformers of the sixteenth century. Barth stressed the "infinite qualitative difference" between God and humans—a phrase borrowed from Søren Kierkegaard (1813–55), the Danish religious thinker—and rejected natural theology (arguments for theism based on the observation of nature). Barth argued that if man reaches God by the light of his reason, he will find only an idol of his own creation, not the self-revealing God, who is transcendent, wholly other, always subject, and never object. Barth in essence said that humans are sinners and cannot achieve "utopia" by their own efforts. The human race stands under judgment and requires the spiritual healing that can come only through the grace of God through faith in the Christ revealed in the Scriptures. The Bible is not a "mechanically" inspired and "infallible" book but a humanly formed record of the "true Word of God," Jesus Christ. The Bible is a fallible record because it is a human book, but it becomes the Word of God as God speaks to humans through it and uses it to bring people to him.

Zurich's Emil Brunner (1889–1966), who lectured at Princeton Seminary in 1938–39, did much to introduce Barth's views to the United States, although Brunner himself differed with Barth on some points. Disillusioned by depression at home and the spread of totalitarian regimes abroad, some American theologians welcomed this fresh theological realism with its emphasis on human sinfulness and the need for divine redeeming grace.

The leading American spokesperson for these convictions was Reinhold Niebuhr (1892–1971). The son of a German immigrant pastor in the Evangelical Synod of North America, a body that in 1934 united with the Reformed Church in the United States (before 1863 the German Reformed Church) to form the Evangelical and Reformed Church, Niebuhr was trained in his denomination's college and seminary and Yale Divinity School. He then served as pastor in a

Reinhold Niebuhr
(1892–1971). Courtesy of
the Burke Library, Union
Theological Seminary.

poor industrial parish in Detroit for thirteen years, which provided him with an insider's understanding of urban social conditions. In 1928, he accepted a professorship at New York's Union Theological Seminary, where he spent the remainder of his career. In 1932, Niebuhr published the most influential theological polemic of its time, *Moral Man and Immoral Society*, which criticized liberalism for lacking the realism to meet the problems of modern society. In particular, the book castigated the romantic moralists in education, sociology, and religion. Eventually, other Protestant liberals recognized that their theology was inadequate and reformulated their views under such labels as neo-orthodoxy, desperation theology, realistic theology, and neo-supernaturalism. Such terms fail to capture the great diversity of ideas in the writings of these theologians, including H. Richard Niebuhr (1894–1963), Reinhold's younger brother, who had a brilliant career as professor of Christian ethics at Yale Divinity School. Nevertheless, a distinctive pattern of traits can be identified that marked the evolution of what some have called the post-liberal theological mind.

First, it placed God's sovereignty (theocentrism) and transcendence over against any attempt to make humans central (anthropocentrism) in articulating theology. Second, it emphasized the Bible as the bearer of divine revelation, although even the so-called neo-orthodox theologians accepted higher criticism and generally shied away from the traditional view of the Bible as the objective, historical Word of God. Third, it recognized humanity's moral predicament and saw sin as rooted in human pride and selfishness. Only when encountered by God is humankind able to seek relative good in a complex and sinful society. On the other hand, in *The Social Sources of Denominationalism* (1929) and *The Kingdom of God in America* (1937), H. Richard Niebuhr pointed out the susceptibility of the churches to being overtaken by societal values and warned of the dangers of taking direction from contemporary culture.

A revived interest in Christology was a fourth trend. One of the most influential works in this field was *Existence and the Christ* (1957) by Paul Tillich (1886–1965), who left Nazi Germany in 1933 for a post at Union Theological Seminary. Though to the left of Barth's theology, Tillich's writings, including his three-volume *Systematic Theology* (1951–63), contributed to the renewal of theological thought in mainline circles. Finally, post-liberal thinking explored the nature of the church. In the 1920s, Catholics began to stress the Pauline metaphor of the church as the body of Christ rather than the traditional idea of the church as the kingdom of God. Although the notion was initially greeted with disfavor, Pope Pius XII endorsed it in his 1943 encyclical, *Mystici Corporis Christi*. Renewed interest in the church also led to a liturgical renewal, especially among Roman Catholics, Lutherans, and Episcopalians.

Considered in their totality, these tendencies revealed that the old liberal theology had undergone substantial revision. They did not signify the rejection of all elements of historic liberalism but only its demise as a coherent system.

Neo-orthodoxy's emphasis on divine sovereignty, sin, revelation, and redemption shifted the focus of theological debate back to the central biblical themes of historic Christianity, but it would be a long time before the implications of the new theology would filter down to the parishioners in the pews of mainline churches. For them, the growing international tensions were of much greater concern. Conservative critics, while they appreciated neo-orthodoxy's return to biblical themes, insisted that the movement was far too subjective and selective in its use of Scripture. They also condemned the neo-orthodox rejection of the Bible as the objective Word of God and affirmed plenary inspiration as an antidote to this approach to Scripture.

World War II

Although liberal clerics were involved in various internationalist and peace causes during the interwar years, they did not speak for the mass of the people. They could not direct their parishioners away from isolationist neutrality, a reaction to the way people had been drawn into World War I as a crusade for international righteousness. In fact, many peace activists themselves believed the Great War had really been a conspiracy by the munitions industry, the "merchants of death," to enhance their profits, and thus they had ignored the deteriorating world situation. At the same time, fundamentalist leaders distanced themselves from peace activism because of their political conservatism and opposition to modernism. Some such as Kansas preacher Gerald Winrod even admired Adolf Hitler's Germany for cleaning up public morality and for its opposition to atheistic communism.

The issue of participation in war became clearer after Hitler overran Poland and then Western Europe in 1939–40. The brutal actions of the Japanese in Asia and the German persecution of the Jews undermined the pacifist cause, and the advocates of neutrality, as exemplified by the America First group, were increasingly ineffective. Reinhold Niebuhr argued that in a sinful world the only way to advance justice was to engage in armed conflict to protect lives and halt the spread of tyranny. Unhappy with the continuing pacifism of the liberal-oriented magazine *Christian Century,* in early 1941 he helped to launch the journal *Christianity and Crisis* as the voice of those who wanted to prevent a German victory. They insisted that such a victory would mean the annihilation of the Jewish people, subjection of the world to the domination of a master race, elimination of the Christian religion, and destruction of Western civilization. Another ecumenical leader, Presbyterian layperson John Foster Dulles (1888–1959), chaired the Commission on a Just and Durable Peace, formed by the Federal Council of Churches in 1941 to mobilize support for a postwar peace in line with Christian principles. It had a major influence on the formation of the United Nations in 1945.

After the attack on Pearl Harbor, the peace movement collapsed, and churches, both Protestant and Catholic, enthusiastically supported the war effort with salvage drives, bond sales, patriotic sermons, and prominently displayed banners. What occurred this time, however, was not the crusading enthusiasm of 1917 but a more reasoned and sober understanding of the task that lay ahead. The number of chaplains on active duty quickly rose from 200 to roughly 11,000, and they were 3.7 percent Jewish, 30.5 percent Roman Catholic, and 65.8 percent Protestant, a catchall category that included Eastern Orthodox, Mormons, and others. Chapels were built on posts and provided on ships, and chaplains functioned in an ecumenical fashion, ministering to all who were in need. The Federal Council's General Committee on Army and Navy Chaplains and the National Association of Evangelicals assisted the denominations in accrediting ministers for placement. As clergy in uniform, they were firmly committed to the war effort.

Of the ten million males who were ordered to report for induction into the armed forces, approximately 43,000 were classified as conscientious objectors (CO). Roughly 25,000 engaged in noncombatant service, 11,887 accepted alternative service (in special camps created for this purpose), and 6,086 were imprisoned for refusing to serve at all. The latter included Jehovah's Witnesses and those who objected to war on political or philosophical grounds. Three-fifths of Mennonite young men opted for CO status; the number of Quaker and Church of the Brethren men to do so was much smaller.

The denominations not only took part in the chaplaincy and alternative service programs but also fostered new church development in the wartime boom towns, took part in USO (United Service Organization for National Defense) programs to assist service people, provided spiritual help for German war prisoners, and assisted in resettling Japanese-Americans. The Church Committee on Overseas Relief and Reconstruction coordinated Protestant efforts in war-torn areas, while the American Council of Voluntary Agencies for Foreign Service (formed in October 1943) brought the various Protestant, Catholic, and Jewish relief agencies under one umbrella. It worked in partnership with the government and ensured that the "three faiths" policy would dominate American religious philanthropy abroad.

Franklin Roosevelt, himself a liberal Episcopalian, did much to advance interfaith relations during his presidency. He saw idealism, patriotism, and faith as inseparable, and he promoted a public faith characterized by brotherhood and civility among the three great faiths, Protestant, Catholic, and Jewish. He regarded the defense of religion and democracy as the same fight, and in 1941, he identified freedom of worship as one of the four essential human freedoms, which were the antithesis of the new order the dictators wished to create. During the war, he frequently appealed to the public's faith in God and sense of national purpose and called on people to pray, most notably on the evening of the D-Day invasion in 1944.

A product of the war effort was a surging tide of religious interest. The deep human needs that were magnified by war's fears, separations, and devastation contributed to this interest. The tide began in battlefield foxholes, ship chapels, military hospitals, homes, and churches well before the end of the conflict, and it eventually culminated in a revival.

The Postwar Religious Revival

America experienced a resurgence of religious engagement in the decade and a half following World War II. Membership in religious groups increased twice as fast as the population. A host of new church buildings, sanctuaries, and synagogues were constructed, especially in the expanding suburbs. Religious books topped best-seller lists, and purchases of the Revised Standard Version of the Bible (1950) broke all records for Bible sales—two million in its first year alone. Mass evangelism reached more people than ever before, aided by the new parachurch youth ministries. Religion departments were founded in many colleges and universities, and several new theological seminaries were established. President Dwight Eisenhower personally spoke about the importance of faith, and the prayer breakfast movement enlisted and encouraged government leaders in the cause of morality and Christian faith. Legislation was adopted in 1954 to add the phrase "under God" to the national pledge of allegiance and in 1956 to make "In God We Trust," a phrase that had appeared on coins since 1864, the official national motto.

This upsurge in religious activity came as a surprise to secular journalists and scholars, who offered various explanations for it. One was that the war experience had heightened spiritual concerns. Another was that the peace was marked by anxieties over the threat of atomic warfare and the developing Cold War with the Soviets. When conflict broke out in Korea in June 1950, which brought Americans back into combat, a third world war seemed imminent. Americans also feared domestic communism. During these years, the investigations of the House Un-American Activities Committee and Senator Joseph McCarthy, who became the discredited denouncer of "reds" and "pinks" in government, reached their zenith, while such conservative religious figures as Carl McIntire (1906–2002), Billy James Hargis (1925–), and Fred Schwarz (1912–) sounded the alarm that communists had infiltrated the mainline denominations and ecumenical bodies.

At the same time, American society was very much in flux. Whites were leaving large cities for homes in the burgeoning bedroom suburbs, while blacks and Hispanics were replacing them in the old urban neighborhoods. Professional and managerial types often did not put down roots but moved every few years as they followed careers. Air travel and the influence of television broke down regional barriers and accelerated the pace of change. For many, the postwar period marked a return to personal security and economic prosperity after years of depression and war, and people flooded into the churches, an act that reflected prevailing social and religious values. In 1955, almost half the population attended a religious service once a week. By 1960, 70 percent held membership in a religious body. In the same year, more than one billion dollars was spent on religious buildings of all kinds.

Like periods of renewal in the past, the new surge of mass evangelism was traditional in its message of personal salvation but contemporary in its upbeat presentation, use of media, and application of the gospel message to the unique anxieties of the age. Leading this movement was a number of youthful evangelistic preachers and musicians who circulated among the interdenominational Saturday night Youth for Christ rallies that took place beginning in 1943 in American and Canadian cities. On Saturday night, many thousands discovered the liveliness and joy of a new kind of old-time religion that often contrasted with the formalism of their Sunday morning church experience.

From among the magnetic personalities on the Youth for Christ circuit emerged one person who would become the most widely heard Christian evangelist of all time: William Franklin (Billy) Graham. Born in 1918 in Charlotte, North Carolina, he was converted at age sixteen in an evangelistic meeting in his hometown, went away to college to become a preacher, and eventually ended up at Wheaton College in Illinois, where he received a liberal arts bachelor's degree in 1943. This handsome young man with the dashing smile and disarming southern drawl exuded quiet sincerity and a deep desire to preach the gospel. Ordained a Baptist minister, he quickly gained fame as an evangelist.

A tent-meeting revival campaign launched Graham as a national figure. Newspaperman William Randolph Hearst sensed significance in Graham's 1949 Los Angeles evangelistic meetings and sent his reporters to cover them. They found crowds flocking to the big tent for eight weeks, and many, even a few celebrities, made decisions to accept Christ as their Savior. As the news filtered across America, Christians began to envision similar revivals in their own cities. For this purpose, in 1950, Graham and a small group of friends formed the Billy Graham Evangelistic Association. They did not plan a campaign in a city unless invited by a majority of the Protestant clergy, and soon highly successful evangelistic meetings took place in several cities. Often overlooked yet highly significant for the churches in New England was the far-reaching Boston campaign of 1950. Historian Garth Rosell's research on the Boston meetings reveals that they were a turning point in Graham's ministry; it had become a national, not merely a regional, phenomenon.[1]

1. Rosell makes this point in his forthcoming book on Harold J. Ockenga and the rise of the new evangelical movement.

Billy Graham revival, Los Angeles, 1949. Courtesy of the Archives of the Billy Graham Center, Wheaton, Illinois.

Graham received a remarkably positive response from the three-month Greater London Crusade of 1954, despite British reserve and skepticism. After that his ministry became global, with campaigns in Asia, Africa, and Australia by the end of the decade. Eventually, Graham preached to over one hundred million listeners in countries on six continents, often in the presence of monarchs, archbishops, presidents, and dignitaries of all kinds. He always offered the simple gospel call to repentance, saving faith, and hope for the individual and society.

Graham's ministry impacted American churches in numerous ways. While holding to orthodox doctrine, he rose above intolerance and sectarianism to unite Christians of all stripes in the task of evangelism. He also refused to adopt an anti-Catholic stance, for which he was strongly criticized by separatistic fundamentalists. Graham's personal winsomeness, increasing cosmopolitanism, restrained lifestyle, and accountability in his business affairs enhanced the credibility of evangelicals in general. His utilization of the media and presentation of testimonies by entertainers and athletes helped to ease the traditional evangelical taboos regarding cinema, theater, and professional sports. Finally, his growing sensitivity to the issues surrounding the social application of the gospel reflected increasing insight. In 1967, he testified in Washington to support President Lyndon Johnson's War on Poverty, claiming biblical mandate for such a program. From the early 1950s, he spoke out against racism and refused to allow a segregated audience at his meetings either in the United States or in apartheid-ruled South Africa. In the late 1970s, he began raising questions about nuclear armament and calling for disarmament negotiations.

Simultaneous with the upsurge of mass evangelism was the quest for inner peace. The year 1946 saw the publication of Rabbi Joshua Liebman's popular *Peace of Mind,* a book about religious psychology that pointed toward newness of life. Similar themes followed from Roman Catholic Fulton Sheen (1895–1979) (*Peace of Soul,* 1949) and Protestant Graham (*Peace with God,* 1953). But among the peace of mind advocates, none surpassed Norman Vincent Peale (1898–1993), pastor of Marble Collegiate Church in New York City. Through his syndicated radio and television shows and magazine *(Guideposts),* he reached an audience of perhaps thirty million in the 1950s. In his books, especially the best-selling *Power of Positive Thinking* (1952), he advocated a big-thinking, success-oriented Christianity that drew criticism from liberals for its social conservatism, from fundamentalists for diluting the gospel, and from neo-orthodox for its optimism. Nevertheless, Peale influenced millions in what had become a depersonalized society dominated by large institutional structures.

Fulton Sheen (1895–1979).
Courtesy of the Archives of the
Archdiocese of Boston. Fabian
Bachrach, photographer.

Historians and sociologists noticed the shallowness of personal commitment and insight that accompanied much of the postwar religious resurgence. For some people, church membership easily meant little more than respectability and belief in the American way of life. President-elect Eisenhower summed it up in 1952: "Our government has no sense unless it is founded on a deeply felt religious faith, and I don't care what it is."[2] In *Protestant, Catholic, Jew* (1955), Will Herberg suggested that confidence in the American way (democracy, free enterprise, humanitarianism, and optimism) was the real integrating force for people of all faiths, although the book did ignore non-Western religions and other Christian traditions such as Eastern Orthodoxy. In spite of the plight of minorities and other social problems, the status quo was sanctified.

In an era of conflict with "godless communism," it was understandable that many linked American interests with God's eternal purposes and identified the churches with the larger society. This was a manifestation of American civil religion. Church historian Martin Marty asked why so much overlap existed between Christianity and secularism during these years. His answer: "A non-existent God and a completely captive God are very much alike: Under the one or under the other 'all things are permissible.'"[3] The social turmoil of the 1960s swept away the more superficial elements of the religious upswing. Still, many people remained whose lives were deeply altered by the revival and who moved beyond their own personal security to carry forward the legacy of spirituality and piety in American churches as well as the commitment to evangelism in a rapidly changing world.

Evangelical Advance

The intellectual and institutional base for the renewal of conservative Protestantism was laid during the 1940s and 1950s. Most significant was the break with 1930s-style fundamentalism by those who adopted the label "neo-evangelical." These "new evangelicals" were orthodox in doctrine but rejected what they felt were the cultural and theological excesses in fundamentalism: sectarianism, judgmentalism, anti-intellectualism, and cultural isolation.

Spearheading the neo-evangelical thrust was a cluster of preachers, writers, organizations, and educational institutions who had been involved in the fundamentalist movement. The pacesetter was the National Association of Evangelicals, whose origins lay in the New England Fellowship, founded in 1929 by J. Elwin Wright (1890–1973). Within the NEF arose the vision of a nationwide cooperative organization of orthodox Protestants, one that would be an alternative to the more liberal Federal Council of Churches. Its leaders called a meeting of prominent fundamentalists in St. Louis in 1942 to explore the possibility. The following year the NAE was formally constituted in Chicago, and Boston pastor Harold John Ockenga (1905–85) was chosen as its first president. Meanwhile, Carl McIntire, a follower of J. G. Machen

2. *New York Times,* 23 December 1952, 16.
3. Martin E. Marty, *The New Shape of American Religion* (New York: Harper, 1959), 40.

who had broken with his mentor in 1937 and had started a new and even more separatist denomination known as the Bible Presbyterian Church, created his own national association in 1941, the American Council of Christian Churches. McIntire invited the NAE group to join forces with the ACCC, but they saw it as too divisive and rejected his offer. Although the NAE itself represented only a minority of the evangelicals in the country, its subsidiary organizations, the National Religious Broadcasters and the World Relief Commission, highlighted significant forces in the evangelical advance.

Another important step in the emergence of the new evangelicalism was the publication in 1947 of *The Uneasy Conscience of Fundamentalism* by Carl F. H. Henry (1913–2003), a journalist and theologian. The book called for Christians to develop a comprehensive worldview that included the social and political dimensions of life. That same year radio evangelist Charles E. Fuller (1887–1968) recruited Ockenga to head up a new theological seminary in Pasadena, California, that would engage modern scholarship and biblical criticism. With its faculty of reputable evangelical scholars, Fuller Seminary became the flagship of the new evangelicalism. The conservative Christian liberal arts colleges upgraded their programs, while many Bible institutes achieved collegiate status, and several publishing houses propagated the literature of the renewed fundamentalism.

Carl F. H. Henry (1913–2003).
Courtesy of Carl F. H. Henry.

Further enhancing the scholarly base of the movement were the founding of the American Scientific Affiliation in 1941 and the Evangelical Theological Society in 1949 and the launching of the magazine *Christianity Today* in 1956 with the backing of the Billy Graham organization. Its editor, Carl

Henry, recruited top evangelical figures in America and abroad as writers, and his intention was to make it a respectable counterpart to the *Christian Century*. Also contributing to the development of neo-evangelicalism were the large number of parachurch ministries such as Youth for Christ, Young Life, InterVarsity Christian Fellowship, and Campus Crusade for Christ that evangelized and discipled young people, and the many denominational and independent foreign missionary agencies that provided a vocational outlet for the newly awakened believers.

Neo-evangelicalism endeavored to draw boundaries between itself and the older fundamentalism, but the line between them was quite fluid. Many fundamentalists viewed the evangelical renewal with a jaundiced eye, feeling that it compromised too much with modernism, and some rejected it completely. At the same time, the new evangelicalism owed as much to the parachurch enterprises as to resurgent denominational life. Leadership and opinion setting came from the network of college and seminary presidents, theological educators, writers, and prominent preachers, several of whom had radio or television ministries. The parachurch organizations, with their efficiency, centralized decision making, and task-oriented character, were able to mobilize people across denominational lines, utilize laypeople (especially women), and provide specialized services for target groups. Critics of the parachurch agencies argued, however, that their entrepreneurial spirit, ability to shield their finances and internal operations, and strong leaders made them vulnerable to empire building. There were also questions about their relationship with the church itself. The parachurch bodies were structured like business corporations, whereas churches were voluntary fellowships that were more responsive to local lay control and needs.

Another component in the resurgence of evangelical religion was the growth of smaller denominations that were Holiness or Pentecostal in orientation such as the Christian and Missionary Alliance, Church of God (both the Anderson, Indiana, and Cleveland, Tennessee, branches), Church of the Nazarene, Free Methodists, Wesleyan Methodists (the Wesleyan Church after a merger with the Pilgrim Holiness in 1968), Pentecostal Holiness Church, Church of the Foursquare Gospel, Pentecostal Church of God, and that unique combination of Holiness doctrine and intense Christian social action, the Salvation Army. A major thrust in Pentecostalism was a renewed emphasis on healing, beginning with William Branham in 1946 and Oral Roberts in 1942. The latter became the nation's foremost healing evangelist. A number of other luminaries, including Kathryn Kuhlman, T. L. Osborn, A. A. Allen, and Gordon Lindsay, also had well-received ministries. The unnoticed but rapidly growing Holiness and Pentecostal movement first received national recognition in 1958 when President Henry Pitney Van Dusen of Union Theological Seminary affirmed in a widely read *Life* magazine article that it was the "Third Force" in American Protestantism.

Another factor contributing to the conservative advance was the large Seventh-day Adventist Church moving from sectarian isolation to closer relations with the evangelical community. The North American Christian Convention, a conservative group formed within the Christian Church–Disciples of Christ in 1927, gradually evolved into a million-member denomination particularly noted for its Bible colleges and foreign missionary work. Also influential were large independent churches such as Moody Memorial Church in Chicago, the People's Church in Toronto, and Church of the Open Door in Los Angeles. In the South, phenomenal growth took place among the Southern Baptists and Churches of Christ, and the smaller, highly decentralized "Landmark" groups, such as the American Baptist Association and the Baptist Missionary Association of America, had a continuing presence. In the early stages of the new evangelical movement, the southern groups had little association with their northern brethren, but the Billy Graham enterprise helped to bridge the gap and to bring the two sections closer together.

Evangelically inclined congregations in the traditional or mainline denominations contributed to the resurgence as well. Park Street Congregational Church in Boston, First Baptist Church in Minneapolis, Tenth Presbyterian Church in Philadelphia, and Hollywood Presbyterian Church in California all became centers of strong preaching and exemplary Christian education programs in urban settings. In spite of the deep tensions caused by the fundamentalist-modernist controversy, American Protestantism never completely polarized into hostile right and left theological camps. Hosts of pastors and parishioners followed a moderate, biblically oriented way as they sought to live out their faith. In spite of fundamentalist criticisms, the foreign missionary personnel of the mainline denominations also remained largely evangelical in their orientation.

The Racial Crisis

As the 1950s drew to a close, Americans faced an unresolved social justice crisis. Too presumptively had they equated the ideals of American society with reality. The tensions surrounding school desegregation after the 1954 Supreme Court decision ordering an end to racially segregated schools revealed the ambivalence of many white Christians regarding the matters of race relations and civil rights. With the initiation of the Montgomery, Alabama, bus boycott in 1955 and the use of National Guard troops to protect black students at Central High School in Little Rock, Arkansas, in 1957, the question of racial justice could no longer be ignored.

During the 1950s, the National Council of Churches, the successor to the Federal Council, passed antisegregation and antidiscrimination resolutions, but implementation of them in local situations proved to be difficult if not impossible. Among those evangelicals who linked conservative social views with their conservative religion, the mounting outcry for civil rights produced unease as the injustices of discrimination in both the North and the South demanded immediate attention and action. Most white American churchgoers were unprepared theologically or personally for a rapid change in race relations. Nor could they have anticipated the dislocation, disarray, and disaffection about to confront the society and its churches in the 1960s. The historians who suggested that the postwar religious revival reflected not the opening of a new era but the close of an older one soon were proven to be correct.

17

Unity and Service at Home and Abroad

The United States emerged from World War II as the most formidable economic and military power in history, and many Americans who had served overseas in the military sought to find ways to minister to a disrupted world. Although the emerging Cold War undermined efforts to create a peaceful international order led by the newly formed United Nations, the relative stability and prosperity of the postwar years enabled the church to engage in renewed mission and relief efforts. Many of these took place in the ecumenical context of the greater body of Christ.

The Flowering of Ecumenism

One force prompting the ecumenical movement was the desire for unity in various ecclesiastical circles around the world. The churches in India, China, and Japan were troubled by the denominational divisions in the West, a situation the "home" churches essentially regarded as normal. These distinctions and rivalries, which had originated often centuries before, were being perpetuated around the globe. Many earnest church leaders in the West recognized such divisions as a hindrance to the effectiveness of Christian mission, and to alleviate them they made comity agreements on the mission fields that allocated various geographical areas to the different missionary agencies—thus forestalling rivalry and competition—and formed national

Christian councils to foster missionary and indigenous church cooperation. This in turn led to church unity movements, beginning with the creation of the Church of South India in 1947. The postwar period saw a flowering of ecumenism, and in a global sense, this was the most significant development in mid-twentieth-century Protestantism.

The culminating ecumenical event was the founding of the World Council of Churches (WCC) at Amsterdam in 1948 as "a fellowship of churches which accept our Lord Jesus Christ as God and Saviour." The statement was amended in 1961, largely at the urging of the Eastern Orthodox, resulting in its present form: "The World Council of Churches is a fellowship of churches which confess the Lord Jesus Christ as God and Saviour according to the scriptures and therefore seek to fulfill their common calling to the glory of the one God, Father, Son and Holy Spirit."[1] Of the 147 church bodies from 44 countries that were charter members, 29 were American. The organization represented the fulfillment of decades of effort by American missionary leaders to bring about worldwide cooperation among the churches. The second assembly of the WCC, which met at Evanston, Illinois, in 1954, was America's first major ecumenical gathering and a strong force in heightening American interest in ecumenism.

The various strains of cooperative Christianity in the United States, reflected in the Federal Council of Churches (1908) and the Foreign Missions Conference of North America (1911), converged into the National Council of the Churches of Christ in the U.S.A. (NCC), officially chartered in Cleveland, Ohio, in November 1950. Under the umbrella of the NCC, a number of denominational and interdenominational agencies and committees merged into unified agencies to foster ministry at home and mission abroad. Most of the original members were mainline churches; a few years later some Orthodox bodies joined.

Denominational leaders learned through their ecumenical endeavors that the range of doctrinal differences among them was smaller than many had assumed. Members of the NCC actually found a high level of agreement on such charged subjects as "gospel" and "grace"—doctrines that had splintered churches since the sixteenth century. Yet the depth of disagreement on particular doctrines such as the nature of the church, the character of the ministry, and the theory and practice of the sacraments was still substantial. As a result, the NCC focused more on bringing the implications of the gospel to bear on the problems of church and society. These included questions of social justice, international understanding, and peace; pastoral relations with Christians in the communist bloc countries; and combating racism both in the United States, where the NCC was heavily involved in the Civil Rights

1. "World Council of Churches," in *Dictionary of the Ecumenical Movement,* ed. Nicholas Lossky et al. (Geneva: WCC Publications, 1994), 1084.

movement, and in southern Africa. These interests contributed to the deep gulf between the NCC and Protestant evangelicals who were largely politically and socially conservative. Among the NCC's major achievements were the publication of the Revised Standard Version of the Bible in 1952 and the widely acclaimed relief programs of Church World Service.

The other side of ecumenism was specific church unions. Several significant unions within denominational families had occurred before the NCC appeared on the scene. The Old and New School Presbyterians joined in 1870 to form the Presbyterian Church in the U.S.A., and in 1918, three Lutheran synods merged as the United Lutheran Church. In 1939, the Methodist Episcopal Church, the Methodist Episcopal Church, South, and the Methodist Protestant Church came together to create the Methodist Church. Later mergers, however, coincided with the age of ecumenism. The United Church of Christ, formed in 1957, encompassed four denominational traditions (Congregational, restorationist Christian, Lutheran, and Reformed) and two types of church polity (congregational and presbyterian). In 1961, the Unitarian and Universalist churches created the Unitarian-Universalist Association, while in 1968, the Evangelical United Brethren (itself a 1946 merger of two churches of German revivalist origins) joined with the Methodist Church to become the United Methodist Church.

The most complex mergers occurred in the Presbyterian and Lutheran churches. In 1958, the moderate Scottish Covenanter United Presbyterian Church joined hands with the Presbyterian Church in the U.S.A., and in 1983, the southern and northern Presbyterians ended their Civil War era schism by reuniting as the Presbyterian Church (U.S.A.) to become the nation's fifth largest denomination. In 1973, those southerners who had theological misgivings about the impending merger organized the Presbyterian Church in America, which is now the largest of the smaller Presbyterian denominations. In 1962, the American Lutheran bodies that had come together in 1918 united with the Swedish Augustana Synod and a Danish and Finnish synod to form the Lutheran Church in America. Meanwhile, four essentially pietistic synods in the Midwest and the South that had merged in 1930 to become the "old" American Lutheran Church joined with two largely Norwegian synods in 1960 to become the "new" American Lutheran Church, which was smaller but theologically more conservative than the Lutheran Church in America. Standing apart were the Lutheran Church-Missouri Synod and Wisconsin Evangelical Lutheran Synod, who saw such "unionism" as unacceptable compromises that went against the historic Lutheran confessions. A schism occurred in the LCMS in 1976, and the breakaway group joined with the LCA and the ALC in 1988 to create the Evangelical Lutheran Church in America, whose membership encompassed two-thirds of all American Lutherans. It is now the sixth largest communion in the United States.

A more controversial and less successful effort at denominational ecumenism was the Consultation on Church Union. The idea for a united church—"truly catholic, truly evangelical, and truly reformed"—was advanced by the prominent Presbyterian ecumenist Eugene Carson Blake (1906–85) in 1960. His proposal resulted in a series of meetings that brought together representatives from several mainline white denominations as well as the black Methodist bodies. At these meetings, various drafts of documents detailing the vision of a united church were discussed. In recent years, the COCU focus shifted to finding commonalities in "sacred things" and working to overcome racism, sexism, and nationalism rather than trying to merge existing church organizations.

Despite the leaders' ideals, the ecumenical movement from its inception was the target of criticism. Some faulted it for a vision that was too limited; others thought such church union would be too bureaucratized. Southern Baptists and Missouri Synod Lutherans rejected it because their understanding of the nature of the church did not permit unqualified recognition of other Christian bodies as "true" churches. Other conservatives found ecumenism theologically too latitudinarian or politically too activistic. The most vigorous criticism came from the fundamentalists, who labeled the World and National Councils instruments of modernism. Carl McIntire was a prominent exponent of this view. He founded not only the American Council of Christian Churches to counter ecumenism at home but also the International Council of Christian Churches to challenge the WCC.

The Roman Catholic Church also stood apart from ecumenical involvement. In 1928, Pope Pius XI issued the encyclical *Mortalium Animos* (Fostering True Religious Unity), which forbade Catholics to give "countenance to a false Christianity quite alien to the one Church of Christ." A later statement in 1949, however, allowed concerned Catholics to participate unofficially in

Pope John XXIII (1881–1963). Courtesy of the Archives of the Archdiocese of Boston and Brunner and Co., Rome.

world ecumenical endeavors. With the accession to the papal throne in 1958 of the innovative John XXIII, the church's attitude toward non-Catholics underwent far-reaching change.

Postwar Trends on the Mission Field

For Christian missions, the demise of the Western colonial system was the decisive development of the mid-twentieth century. First, the image of Christianity shifted in the minds of many so-called third world peoples. Missionaries had come to those lands along with the colonialists, and many nationals considered the Christian gospel foreign by association. Reinforcing this view were the Western cultural accretions that too often were part of the missionaries' message. Nevertheless, when the colonial powers withdrew, most missionaries remained, thereby demonstrating that their motives transcended political interests. Gradually, the Christian faith came to be understood as a truly transcultural faith, one that beckoned to "Jew and Greek, slave and free," in the words of St. Paul.

Second, the demise of imperialism allowed the process of self-definition to take place among the local congregations. They were now free to recognize and affirm their own potentials and talents in working out what it meant to be part of the body of Christ in a particular culture. A third consequence was the changed role of the missionary from leader and spiritual parent to partner and servant.

The new national freedoms also produced complications for Christian mission. Traditional ethnic religions resurfaced and in many instances were aggressively militant. In some new countries, missionaries were expelled and anti-conversion laws passed. Some countries experienced an ethnic religious offensive and sent missionaries to the West, where secularizing forces had created fertile soil for mysticism, transcendental meditation, and varieties of Buddhism. In the latter half of the twentieth century, however, churches in the non-Western world flourished, especially in Africa and Asia. Nourished by indigenous pastors, evangelists, priests, and bishops and despite persecution, Christianity increased among non-European peoples. In Latin America, Pentecostalism spread rapidly and became a major religious force. By the turn of the twenty-first century, approximately two-thirds of the world's Christians were non-Westerners, a reality that had dramatic implications for the future of the faith,[2] which for fifteen hundred years had been dominated by European culture and personnel.

2. This is brought out in the latest edition of David B. Barrett, George T. Kurian, and Todd M. Johnson, eds., *World Christian Encyclopedia: A Comparative Survey of Churches and Religions in the Modern World,* 2d ed. (New York: Oxford University Press, 2001).

The Roman Catholic Church for centuries had been the leader in foreign missionary outreach, and in America, a renewed effort followed a decline in immigration after World War I. (Attending to immigrants had required much attention from the church.) With their practices of celibacy and an austere lifestyle, Catholic missionaries often outdid their Protestant brethren. Particularly noteworthy was the Catholic Foreign Missionary Society of America, with its headquarters in Maryknoll, New York. The group sent its first missionaries in 1918 and by 1950 was at work in Asia, Africa, Central and South America, and the Pacific islands. The Maryknoll Missioners became major interpreters and disseminators of third world theological thought through their publishing house, Orbis Books. The endeavors of the Jesuits, the Franciscans, and the Society of the Divine Word also enhanced the growth of Catholic missions. In 1970, Roman Catholic missionaries numbered roughly one hundred thousand worldwide and were more numerous than those of all the non-Roman churches put together.[3] Of these workers more than 10 percent were Americans.

On the Protestant side, missionary interest and activity in the mainline denominations reached their highest levels in the 1920s and by the 1950s had sharply declined. Between 1958 and 1971, the number of missionaries from America's six largest church bodies further declined from 4,548 to 3,160. Partially responsible for this reduction was the theological shift of their leadership. The trend in mission work was away from evangelization and toward social service, institutional work, and justice concerns. In contrast, the more conservative groups (e.g., Southern Baptists, General Association of Regular Baptists, Conservative Baptists, Assemblies of God, and Christian and Missionary Alliance) along with the faith missions (e.g., Wycliffe Bible Translators, Africa Inland Mission, Send International, New Tribes Mission [now NTMI], and Overseas Missionary Fellowship) held their own, and the number of personnel engaged in foreign outreach actually increased. An important stimulus for evangelical missions was the vision of servicemen and women whose overseas experiences gave them the desire to return to minister among the peoples there. For example, the World War II pilot Betty Greene (1920–97) was the genius behind the Missionary Aviation Fellowship. Another factor was the murder of five missionaries by Auca Indians in Ecuador in January 1956, an event that electrified the evangelical community and was immortalized by one of the widows, Elisabeth Elliot, in *Through Gates of Splendor* (1957).

Evangelical and other conservative missions agencies pioneered various innovative methods that have become standard practice. The most notable were the short-term mission experiences of one summer to one year that

---

3. Peter J. Dirven, "Roman Catholic Religious Orders," in *Concise Dictionary of the Christian World Mission,* ed. Stephen Neill et al. (Nashville: Abingdon, 1971), 532.

Missionary Aviation Fellowship's first plane, Betty Greene (1920–97) in center. Courtesy of the Archives of the Billy Graham Center, Wheaton, Illinois.

served as a time of experimentation for youth and aspiring missionaries and the utilization of retired persons or specialists who could not make a lifetime commitment. Both short-term and career missionaries traveled to more remote locations by means of airplane transport offered by Missionary Aviation Fellowship and similar agencies. Also, radio allowed penetration of areas closed to overt gospel presentation. Over sixty international stations, such as HCJB (Ecuador) and Trans-World Radio, used powerful transmitters to broadcast thousands of program hours in scores of languages and dialects. Bible correspondence courses also took advantage of increasing literacy to nurture young Christians in non-Western countries.

Other evangelical-inspired programs included the church growth movement, spearheaded by Donald McGavran (1897–1990), with the credo "Making Converts, Discipling the Nations, Multiplying Churches"; Evangelism-in-Depth (also called saturation evangelism), the process of conveying the gospel in verbal form to every family in a given region; and Theological Education by Extension, an educational outreach to pastors in remote areas. Specialized agencies, which originally worked only in the United States, became international in their outreach (e.g., Campus Crusade for Christ, Young Life, and Navigators). In 1950, World Vision mobilized widespread support for meeting the plight of children and eventually became one of the largest Christian relief agencies in the world.

Major factors in the effectiveness of postwar missions were cultural anthropology and linguistics. Fostered by the American Bible Society, along with the Summer Institute of Linguistics and its affiliate, Wycliffe Bible Translators (founded in 1942), great advances occurred in transforming oral tribal languages into written form and providing Scripture translations. Ac-

cording to the noted African scholar Lamin Sanneh, this emphasis on culturally sensitive preservation of tribal languages proved pivotal in perpetuating
and honoring indigenous cultures that would have otherwise been lost in
the modern world.[4] Of particular importance were achievements of female
missionaries in linguistic and scriptural translation who often worked in very
remote settings. Cross-cultural and inter-ecclesiastical understanding of the
Christian world mission has been enhanced by the work of the Overseas
Ministries Study Center in New Haven, Connecticut, which publishes the
International Bulletin of Missionary Research. Concomitant developments were
the emergence of missiology as an academic discipline, the establishment
of schools of world mission in theological seminaries, and the founding of
professional societies such as the International Association of Mission Studies
and the American Society of Missiology.

Also noteworthy was the quest by key evangelical leaders for greater
understanding and definition of the mission task. Conferences, consultations, and publications sought to address the larger implications of Christ's
Great Commission. Contributing to this multilevel dialogue were the triennial missionary conferences conducted by InterVarsity Christian Fellowship
in Urbana, Illinois, and attended by thousands of students. In 1966, two
evangelism and inter-mission congresses took place in Wheaton, Illinois, and
Berlin, Germany. Although not all participants came to agreement, out of
these deliberations emerged a broadening vision. Evangelization and church
planting were emphasized as the primary tasks of missions, but the conferees
also recognized that the alleviation of suffering and political injustice flowed
directly from the gospel message. At these gatherings, church leaders from
the non-Western world cautioned against the dangers of Western cultural
chauvinism, American religious individualism, and Christian triumphalism,
which they showed were counterproductive to mission efforts.

Changing Roles for the Protestant Clergy

In the late 1950s, it was clear that pastoral roles were shifting. Although the
vast majority of conservative pastors ministered in traditional ways, others
across the denominations began, in the opinion of historian Winthrop Hudson, to lose a sense of vocation.[5] This paralleled Protestantism's diminished
influence on the larger culture and the increasing privatization of religion.
Some well-educated ministers entered the popular fields of psychology and
counseling. Others, discontented with the status quo in their communions,
plunged into urban social work, desiring to become agents of change in a

4. See Lamin Sanneh, *Translating the Message: The Missionary Impact on Culture* (Maryknoll,
N.Y.: Orbis, 1991).

5. Winthrop S. Hudson, *Religion in America* (New York: Scribners, 1973), 409.

society marred by poverty and discrimination. For females, acceptance into ordained ministry remained difficult, as many church people saw it as unbiblical at worst and unworkable at best. Women served sacrificially, however, as Christian education directors, religious social workers, and missionaries. Few anticipated how significant the issue of female ordination would become later in the century.

18

Tradition under Fire

On an album about growing up in the early 1960s, pop recording artist Donald Fagen opened with a song entitled "I.G.Y." (International Geophysical Year, 1958):

> Standing tough under stars and stripes
> We can tell,
> This dream's in sight;
> You've got to admit it,
> At this point in time that it's clear,
> The future looks bright.
> On that train all graphite and glitter,
> Undersea by rail,
> Ninety minutes from New York to Paris—
> Well by '76 we'll be A.O.K.

Looking back from the perspective of the twenty-first century, the irony of the lyrics is bitterly clear. But for those embarking on the new decade, the dream seemed real and the times bright. In the words of the youthful President John F. Kennedy, Americans were entering a "new frontier."

The Age of Uncertainty

The country developed momentum just as Kennedy promised, but it was not in the anticipated direction. The Cold War heated up, resulting in several trying events: the Bay of Pigs fiasco (April 1961), the building of the Berlin Wall (August 1961), and most importantly, the Cuban missile crisis (October 1962). Only after this threat of nuclear war was a modicum of accommodation with the Soviets reached with the signing of a nuclear test-ban treaty. Civil Rights confrontations occurred across the South, culminating in the 1963 march on Washington, where Martin Luther King Jr. delivered his immortal "I Have a Dream" address. Tensions escalated rapidly over the unending war in Vietnam, and beginning with the 1964 "Free Speech" movement in Berkeley, student protests and demonstrations became a way of life on the nation's campuses.

Because the events influenced students in particular, some observers suggested that simple generational dynamics lay behind much of the decade's tumult. In the years between 1945 and 1959, as Americans wiped out economic traces of the depression years and created an affluent society without precedent in their history, they produced children by the tens of millions. The result of this baby boom was a national population surge from 150 to 180 million people. The annual rate of increase (19 percent) was higher than that of the year of heaviest immigration earlier in the century. By the mid-1960s, these youths with their boundless energy had grown into a virtual army: idealistic, restless, searching, unacquainted with suffering, accustomed to the spoils of a materialistic and television-oriented culture. The generational clash was not surprising, and it occurred in other Western societies as well, reaching a crisis point overseas in 1968.

Few areas of American life remained untouched by the ferment of these buoyant years, when the national consensus of the postwar era came unraveled. The detached social criticism of the previous decade gave way to passionate tracts such as Michael Harrington's *Other America* (1962), which was credited with inspiring President Lyndon Johnson to launch his War on Poverty. Betty Friedan's *Feminine Mystique* (1963) explored the attitudes and structures of American culture that kept women "in their place" and prevented them from having full equality with men. She helped launch the National Organization for Women in 1966, which worked to raise the consciousness of women and society as a whole regarding issues of women's rights. Soon even more radical feminists appeared on the scene demanding an end to what they labeled "patriarchy." A new realism and a depth of social commentary were reflected in the films and novels of the times, signaling an erosion of the old social restraints. Novels such as Joseph Heller's *Catch 22* (1961) and Ken Kesey's *One Flew Over the Cuckoo's Nest* (1962) and movies such as *Dr. Strangelove* (1963) and *The Graduate* (1967) popularized relativism and existentialism while exposing the shallowness of American society.

As the sixties progressed, the cultural rift widened, and the nation encountered dissension and upheaval comparable in magnitude to that of 1861. Racial tensions, political assassinations, radical theological currents, widespread disenchantment among the youth, an increasingly unpopular foreign war, political corruption at the highest level, and strident demands for social and economic equality were forces that together created a social climate in which traditional answers, including those offered by institutional religion, appeared both anemic and irrelevant. For American churches, it was a time of testing never experienced before.

Radical Theology in the Age of Aquarius

As the uniformity of the 1950s was displaced by dissent and diversity in the 1960s, radical intellectual currents burst from beneath the surface with intense vitality. The more liberal American theologians assumed the cause, and rationalistic theological trends born earlier in the century expanded in new and even more controversial directions. Although not subject to wide public discussion, these tendencies nevertheless exerted a strong influence on the shape of theological discourse.

Paralleling the religious sources such as Scripture, ecclesiastical forms, and theological traditions were the secular sources that nourished the radical theology of the 1960s. Foundational was the scientific mood, which assumed facts to be determined exclusively by empirical scientific inquiry, be it natural, historical, or social. This orientation intensified as military and space technology pointed optimistically to science as the answer to human dilemmas. Another factor was the notion that all human experience is historical or developmental and thus relative to time and place. Religious ideas accordingly were seen as culture-bound reflections of humanity's evolving experience rather than timeless truths or the products of divine revelation.

The this-worldly focus of modern culture also nurtured radical theology. It shifted religious concerns from matters of salvation to the usefulness of religion for this life, be it for self-fulfillment, establishing ethical norms, or simply peace of mind. Psychology, sociology, and anthropology recognized only naturalistic explanations of human behavior. An important stimulus for radical theology was the shift in ethical concern from personal holiness to loving relationships. Social community became more important than condemning personal vices, except as they directly affected other people. Situation ethics, usually defined as "loving actions," replaced conformity to moral absolutes as the basis for human choices.

A catalyst for the new theological radicalism were the writings of Dietrich Bonhoeffer (1906–45), a man executed by the Nazi regime for his part in the conspiracy to assassinate Adolf Hitler. His *Letters and Papers from Prison* (1953) summoned Christians to rethink the demands of their faith in a "world come of age." He set the tone for radical theology when he affirmed:

Our relationship to God is not a religious relation to a supreme Being, absolute in power and goodness . . . but a new life for others, through participation in the Being of God.[1]

God, said Bonhoeffer, is encountered in the horizontal relations common to humanity's worldly existence.

H. Richard Niebuhr responded to Bonhoeffer's concerns in his provocative *Radical Monotheism and Western Culture* (1960), which grappled with questions of religious experience in the modern secular world. Harvey Cox (1929–) sought in *The Secular City* (1965) to make Christianity acceptable to "modern man" and boldly challenged churches to adopt a more secular approach to reaching people. A number of theologians picked up the phrase "God is dead" from the late-nineteenth-century German philosopher Friedrich Nietzsche and provided an entirely "secular" interpretation of the gospel. Thomas J. J. Altizer (1927–) maintained that God had become fully human in Christ and thereby had lost his divine existence. William Hamilton (1924–) declared that the divine is absent from the world, and one must embrace the secular existence and reject otherworldliness and the return of Christ. Modern people were no longer able to believe in God, and the church had to seek to do without him as well. Death of God theologians even gave their system the pompous title "theothanotology," but it proved to be little more than radical chic. Three decades later cynics justifiably quipped, "God is dead is dead."

Paul van Buren (1924–) drew on logical positivism to argue that the traditional language used to describe God and his ways ("God-talk") was "cognitively meaningless," since God's existence and nature could not be verified by the methods of science. The gospel would become significant for people in the contemporary world only when it was translated into the empirical terms of a scientific, technological society. From another quarter, John Cobb (1925–) and other process theologians asserted that theology must present God as evolving rather than static and that both Christ and the church represent higher stages of human evolution. As the various radical attempts to "modernize" Christianity ran their course, however, they created a context for the eventual numerical decline in the mainline denominations.

Maturation in Roman Catholicism

The relationship between Roman Catholicism and American society had always been ambivalent. From the beginning, Catholics had been a minority in a Protestant America, while the legal separation of church and state had added to their difficulties in adjusting to the post-Reformation world.

1. Dietrich Bonhoeffer, *Prisoner for God: Letters and Papers from Prison* (New York: Macmillan, 1953), 179.

Anti-Catholic hostility in the nineteenth century and the formidable task of assimilating millions of immigrants had further aggravated the situation. For Roman Catholicism, the 1960s also proved to be a time of trial.

Three major events affected American Catholics during the late 1950s and early 1960s: the elevation of the visionary John XXIII to the papacy in 1958, the election of the first Roman Catholic to the presidency of the United States in 1960 (John F. Kennedy), and the extensive changes implemented by the Second Vatican Council of 1962–65. Of these the third had the most far-reaching impact on the Catholic tradition as a whole, an influence whose significance cannot be overemphasized. It was the first such meeting since Vatican I (1869–70), and before that a period of three hundred years had elapsed since the Council of Trent, which defined the post-Reformation church.

The council, like Pope John, was a blend of tradition and forward-looking attitudes, and this mix appeared throughout the Vatican II documents. While they addressed twentieth-century concerns and bore the marks of new theological departures, they also remained in the mainstream of Catholic orthodoxy and reaffirmed many of the positions of the two previous councils.

Meeting of Pope John XXIII and Southern Baptist leader Brooks Hays at the Vatican in 1963. Courtesy of the Baptist Joint Committee, Washington, D.C.

Notwithstanding, Vatican II touched every feature of church life in fresh ways. Among the developments emanating from it were a greater emphasis on interfaith contact and collaboration (many non-Catholics attended the council); more participation by laity, especially women, in the church's mission; attention to social and economic trends as indicators of directions for ministry; sweeping innovations in liturgy; more sharing of responsibility among different levels of the hierarchy and with lay councils; and significant changes in theology without modification of "official" doctrine. Several members of the American hierarchy, especially Joseph Cardinal Ritter of St. Louis and Albert Cardinal Meyer of Chicago, were prominent reform leaders at the council.

Most American bishops responded cautiously to Vatican II, although few denied that the church was in trouble. Catholic magazines lamented the plight of parochial schools. Declining numbers of seminarians and women entering religious orders, combined with an increasing number of men leaving the priesthood, forced the hiring of more lay teachers, which in turn created heavier financial burdens. Migrations to the suburbs left many inner-city parishes with small congregations who were unable to maintain church properties. Eager young priests, with the support of like-minded youthful parishioners, launched enthusiastically into uncharted waters in their quest for relevance. Various changes occurred at the parish level. English replaced Latin in the mass; the priest said mass facing the congregation; hymns, often Protestant ones, were sung with guitar and percussion accompaniment during services; abstinence from meat on Fridays was no longer required; and experimental communities and "people's altars" added variety to the worship experience.

Both the right and the left reacted to the new situation in the church. Some conservatives rejected the vernacular mass, a movement led in part by the Catholic Traditionalist Movement. Other rightist groups, such as Catholics United for the Faith, organized to combat abortion and secular influence in parochial schools. Those on the left sought more extensive changes in areas such as birth control, priestly celibacy, and papal infallibility. A 1967 study of the life and ministry of priests reported a decline in traditional devotional practices among clergy and a tendency to question church authority on such "decided" issues as abortion, divorce, and contraception. The Vatican II decrees on ecumenism gave priests and nuns the flexibility to collaborate with those of other religious persuasions, resulting in their active participation in the Civil Rights movement and protest actions against the Vietnam War. Fathers Daniel and Philip Berrigan and others risked their reputations in acts of civil disobedience. Nuns also stood in the front lines in the Civil Rights demonstrations. While calling for equal rights for blacks, they also demanded greater recognition of their personhood and expressed their desire for full ministerial equality with men.

American Catholics did not openly rebel during the sixties. Many, especially the young, simply ignored church teaching. Others continued in their traditional beliefs and practices despite the unprecedented changes going on around them. The conservative wing identified itself with leaders such as Fulton Sheen and Francis Cardinal Spellman; liberals turned to Pope John and his reformist council decrees. John's successor, Paul VI (1963–78), found the situation so unsettling that he sought to undo some of the more "extreme" measures of Vatican II. Subsequent debate merely widened the divide. These controversies and their consequences were inseparable from the tumult tearing at the larger society.

New Wineskins: The Churches Experiment

The new directions in theological discourse and liturgical practice of both Protestants and Catholics reflected the larger quest for social and institutional relevance. Ecclesiastical leaders worked to show that "the church as institution" and "the church as community of the Spirit" were not mutually exclusive concepts. Various factors complicated the churches' situation, especially toward the close of the decade, when the protest movement became most acute. Even when confronted with the pervasive secularization of American society, many church leaders recognized only slowly that Christianity no longer commanded an automatic hearing and acceptance. The long-term alliance between reason and moral-religious faith no longer existed.

Particularly for youth, intellectuals, and shapers of the media, pluralism meant that there was no single, final truth in issues of religion, art, morals, and politics. Pluralism stood for subjectivism, relativism, and privatism in these matters. Because the nation had become so religiously diverse, the Supreme Court by necessity had to rule that overt religious observances in public schools that favored one faith over another, or discriminated against those who practiced no faith, could no longer take place. Government was thus excluded from the business of sponsoring religious activity; it was now completely the responsibility of individual citizens in their homes and churches.

Conflicts also occurred in local congregations across America. Progressive young Protestant ministers in the South clashed with reluctant deacons and vestrymen over church segregation. Inner-city pastors were frustrated in their attempts to acquaint affluent, suburban Christians with the blight of poverty. Priests and Catholic laity desiring immediate implementation of the Vatican II decrees struggled with bishops who feared rapid shifts from traditional patterns. Most Christians affirmed that the churches should dedicate themselves to the social good; how they should achieve this was the source of deep disagreement.

Nonetheless, the 1960s witnessed a resurgence, however controversial and disjointed, of that socially active style of faith that had been such a vital force in American Christianity. Originally a product of the Second Awakening and enhanced by the social gospel movement, it now resurfaced. Like their predecessors, the new generation of Christian activists quested after the kingdom of God on earth, but with a more realistic sense of the nature of evil and the functions of power. They organized welfare unions, tenants' councils, rent strikes, and school boycotts. Some joined Civil Rights demonstrations, led open-housing marches, and faced arrest, fines, and imprisonment. Even so, for most clergy and laity, such drastic actions were the exception rather than the rule. A substantial gap existed between many church professionals and their parishioners. Political and religious conservatives challenged much of the social activism and questioned the spiritual implications of the radical theologies.

A unique movement for religious reformation was the Jesus People. Their youthful adherents possessed an intense albeit simplistic faith, and many engaged in communal living experiments. They drew their ideas mainly from fundamentalism and Pentecostalism, but their ideology and style were geared to the tastes of the new generation. The movement originated in San Francisco and spread rapidly throughout the country. Some groups experimented with the new ideas and moved away from theological orthodoxy, while others demanded complete and disciplined separation from the world, including one's family. Many formed "house churches" or carried on a campus-oriented ministry, such as the Christian World Liberation Front in Berkeley. Although a few Jesus People related to evangelical organizations such as InterVarsity Christian Fellowship and Campus Crusade for Christ, the movement on the whole was sharply critical of institutional Christianity. It was a vigorous protest against traditional religious structures, which in the minds of the Jesus People had compromised with the dominant values of middle-class America. Like many similar efforts in the past, it was an attempt to return to basic New Testament Christianity, unencumbered by ecclesiastical machinery and open to the promptings of the Holy Spirit.

The Legacy of the 1960s

A changed America resulted from the revolutionary ferment of the 1960s. Public pressure brought an inglorious end to the Vietnam War in 1975, further eroding American optimism, which already had been weakened by unsettling assassinations, the Watergate scandal, and embarrassing failures in foreign policy.

Civil Rights legislation provided blacks with new status and voting power, which inspired other minorities to seek justice. Women of all ages pursued further education, turning to the marketplace, and often the divorce court, as they moved to claim the equality secured for them by legislation and court decisions. They emerged as a potent political force, but many accused them of abandoning the home and family life. A tidal wave of pop psychology focused attention on the autonomous self and its fulfillment as the only things in life, rejecting traditional religion as an oppressive, moral authority.

Religion was portrayed as the tyrant parent whose rule the liberated adult should cast aside.

This erosion of authority of all kinds, especially in the moral realm, most troubled earnestly religious people, both Christians and Jews. Disrespect of elders, drug and alcohol abuse, easy divorce, soaring crime rates, and sexual promiscuity were the daily manifestations of a void that seemed to exist at the core of American life. Many conservative Christians were also unhappy that the Supreme Court had restricted religious practices in schools.

The decade of the 1960s was a watershed in American history and values, and it marked a fundamental transition in Western culture itself. The term *post-Christian* was used to describe its legacy. Going even further, in *The Future of Christianity* (2001), theologian Alister McGrath labeled the intellectual, moral, and spiritual shifts of the 1960s one of the great reversals for Christianity in the twentieth century. He saw them as comparable to the failure of churches to respond adequately to the 1915 Armenian genocide and to confront Nazi and communist policies and persecutions.

Other disillusionments added to the feeling of drift. President Johnson's highly vaunted War on Poverty had accomplished little in overcoming poverty, urban blight, malnutrition, and inferior schools. Galloping inflation was accompanied by worldwide recession and high unemployment. Those religious leaders who had embraced the reform causes of the 1960s and had closely identified with a remade secular order saw their efforts fade into nothingness as students gradually returned to career preparation and the public retreated to private concerns. The kind of religion that represented the focus of life's commitments had not disappeared from American society, but it was in the process of relocating itself outside churchly institutions. The only standard of choice seemed to be individual tastes and felt needs. Eastern religions, transcendental meditation, and exotic cults began to enjoy an appeal never seen before, and even Satanism and witchcraft claimed the right to religious recognition.

It is against this backdrop that a renewal of evangelical Protestantism took place in America in the 1970s that infused new vitality into the term *born again*. The anything-goes public attitude had to allow a measure of respect for those personally energized by this kind of Christianity, and statistics quickly revealed that there were many more born-again believers than the media had supposed. While the more liberal mainline denominations continued to decline in membership, conservative evangelical groups experienced significant growth. This recovery of evangelical faith would have an enormous impact on American religion and politics in the later 1970s and 1980s.

19

Urban Migration and Civil Rights

The progress of African-Americans toward racial and economic equality has been slow, to say the least. From the very beginning of their forced arrival on America's shores, the oppressive forces confronting them perpetuated an extraordinary level of prejudice that essentially denied their existence as human beings. The Thirteenth Amendment of 1865 abolishing involuntary servitude did not greatly alter their status. The four million liberated slaves were cast into an alien and hostile society where they experienced the full effects of three centuries of prejudice. Because they did not receive title to the land on which they had worked for generations, they became tenant farmers or were forced into sharecropping, which differed little from medieval serfdom. The infamous Jim Crow laws limited their mobility and political participation. Because the North had depended very little on black labor, and the smaller number of blacks in the North made them less threatening to white hegemony, the legal restrictions there were less severe, though discrimination was strong.

The most important institution for post–Civil War blacks was the church. The freedmen established their own independent churches, which enabled them to avoid the imposed segregation in white churches and to fulfill the desire for their own community and religious expression. The years 1865 to 1900 witnessed the fusion of these visible churches with the invisible institution of black Christianity that had earlier taken root among the slaves. What resulted was a structured religious community that was the chief social organization of the African-American masses. From these churches emanated aid societies, schools, distinctive forms of music and dance, and, perhaps most important, opportunities for development of black leadership. Booker T. Washington (1856–1915), who founded the renowned Tuskegee Institute in Alabama in 1881, was a product of the black church and a promoter of African-American self-reliance.

Booker T. Washington (1856–1915)

Sunday morning in the Virginia Pines. Courtesy of the Billy Graham Center Museum, Wheaton, Illinois.

African-American Church Life in Flux

The combination of Jim Crow laws and lack of economic opportunity in the rural South encouraged a mass exodus of southern blacks from plantations to the urban centers of the North during and following World War I. Previously, nine-tenths of all blacks lived in the South, with four-fifths of them in rural areas. So many left rural life for new homes in cities that by 1960 nearly two-thirds of the African-American population had become urban dwellers. The story of the black church in the twentieth century is one of responding to the challenges of urbanization and of activism to change the deplorable conditions under which their people were living.

The most significant factors in their new urban experience were the opportunity for education and the possibility of upward mobility. Consequently, occupational differentiation increased among African-Americans in northern cities. For example, preachers accounted for roughly half of the black professional class in the South; in northern cities, only one black professional in ten was a minister. As new socioeconomic classes came into existence, the church had to adapt to the needs of these groups.

A minority of blacks, freedmen of long standing who had risen to the middle class, were acclimated to mainstream American life and more or less assimilated into white churches. About two-thirds of these were Baptists; another third was Methodist, with a sprinkling of Episcopalians, Presbyterians, and Catholics. Much more numerous were those of middle-class and lower-middle-class economic and social standing who remained in the existing black churches. The largest were the African Methodist Episcopal Church (1816), the African Methodist Episcopal Zion Church (1821), the Christian Methodist Episcopal Church (1870), and the National Baptist Convention, U.S.A., Inc. (1886). All of these rapidly moved beyond the otherworldly quality that had marked the early indigenous black expressions of Christian faith in America. Their association with the middle-class white population and their emphasis on educational achievement fostered a more this-worldly posture toward social and economic life. This paralleled the dynamics seen in early Methodism and other religious bodies that originated among marginal classes and then merged with the mainstream. One example of the new black Christian elite was William J. Simmons (1849–90). An escaped slave who obtained an education in the North, he returned to the South as an educational missionary. He helped to form the National Baptist Convention and served as its first president.

The large numbers of African-American Christians who migrated to northern cities, however, were for all practical purposes excluded from this development. Poor, often illiterate, these new arrivals felt alienated from their middle-class brethren. Their need for familiar "down-home" religion helped give rise to the phenomenon of the storefront church. These churches owed their existence to a forceful preacher, often of limited education, who gathered a congregation of people seeking a religious leader and teacher. Services were conducted in rented or abandoned inner-city stores or occasionally in private. In a 1933 survey of black churches in twelve cities, 777 out of 2,104 church buildings were storefronts. These churches provided intimacy and affirmed identity, and they became preserves of black folk tradition through which, by means of spiritual songs and recitations, blacks recounted their burdensome history. Worship involved the body and emotions, and hearers responded spontaneously to sermons with interjections of "Amen!" and "That's right!" Singing was often accompanied by dancing and other forms of free spiritual expression and participation. These same traits quickly found their way into the worship experience of the traditional black denominations.

Many blacks, like the Native Americans, were not comfortable with American Christianity, the "white man's religion." Unlike the Indians, however, blacks lacked a substantial memory of their traditional religions, to which they could turn as an alternative. This void invited the rise of new non- (or anti-) Christian movements that claimed to provide a basis for racial identity and pride. Because of their contribution to the development of black consciousness, two urban religious developments merit special comment.

The first was the Universal Negro Improvement Association founded by Marcus Garvey (1887–1940) in New York City. Garvey was a widely traveled Jamaican who eventually arrived in New York. His program called for a literal rather than a mythological return to the African homeland, and he self-consciously borrowed the Jewish interpretation of a people in diaspora awaiting a return to the place of their origin.

Before he was jailed in 1925 on the trumped-up charge of mail fraud and deported two years later, Garvey's organization operated two steamship lines, created a nurses' corps and a manufacturing firm, and produced numerous publications. Although the more "respectable" community leaders turned against the movement, to the masses of alienated blacks, even those who were not fully involved, Garvey's message of a new day was quite attractive. He coined the phrase "black is beautiful," which in the 1960s became a powerful slogan for African-American activists.

A more durable ideology, which drew inspiration from earlier expressions of black nationalism, arose in Detroit in the 1930s. Inspired by W. D. Fard, Elijah Muhammad (originally Elijah Poole [1897–1975], the son of a Baptist minister), organized the Nation of Islam, or Black Muslims. Like other extra-ecclesiastical black religious movements, the Nation of Islam appealed to alienated urban African-Americans and stressed the nurture of pride. The Black Muslims developed a successful network of cooperative business institutions and required adherents to repudiate their former lives and confine their associations solely to the religious community. In their recruitment efforts, they focused especially on the black prison population. The most vivid introduction to the Black Muslims is the *Autobiography of Malcolm X* (1965), the life story of the movement's fiery spokesman who was eventually murdered by men who once had been his associates.

When the business slowdown began in the late 1920s, blacks were among the first to lose their jobs, and by October 1933, roughly 33 percent of African-Americans were being supported by public welfare. Similar to white Protestantism, the fastest-growing churches among blacks during these difficult years were the smaller ones of independent and Pentecostal-Holiness background. But in the African-American communities, suffering was endemic despite the availability of religious comfort, and in few places were public welfare funds administered on an equal basis. As distress and pessimism increasingly gripped blacks, many began to feel that they could improve their situation only through aggressive political action.

With the implementation of Franklin Roosevelt's ambitious recovery programs, a large majority of blacks switched their political allegiance from the Republican Party of Abraham Lincoln to the Democratic Party. The New Deal president captured the imaginations of the oppressed population. As some blacks found their way into governmental departments, they began pressing for economic and political equality and fair employment practices. But the forces they challenged would not yield easily. In fact, in the early years of World War II, military service boards discriminated against black volunteers. Army and navy units were segregated, and no black officer was allowed to outrank or command a white person. Conscription and the rapid influx of African-Americans into the services, however, made it increasingly difficult to maintain all the old racial barriers. Blacks began serving in combat, but in platoons assigned to white companies, and the navy began integrating its ships after May 1944.

Civil Rights Efforts

World War II unleashed a desire for human rights that could no longer be held back. Black women, formerly limited to domestic service, found new independence by engaging in war work. Returning servicemen who had demonstrated not only courage in combat but also competence in handling the machines of a technological society were unwilling to accept the traditional roles assigned to them. Groups such as the National Association for the Advancement of Colored People and the National Urban League launched concerted efforts to combat the social discrimination enshrined in law. They worked through the federal courts and appealed to white consciences and soon achieved important breakthroughs.

President Harry Truman abolished segregation in the armed forces through an executive order on July 26, 1948. He also ordered an end to discrimination in federal employment and created a committee to combat job discrimination in private industries. In 1957, Congress passed the first civil rights law since 1875, providing some modest federal protection for black voting rights and creating the Civil Rights Commission. The Supreme Court's historic decision on May 12, 1954, *Brown v. Board of Education,* overturned the "separate but equal" doctrine it had asserted in 1896, in effect ordering the end of public school segregation.

Although national opinion was receptive to such changes, dominant elements in southern white society remained hostile. Segregationist White Citizens' Councils spread throughout the region. Eight states vowed to ignore the Brown decision, and some whites resorted to violence. Such resistance to integration, combined with heightened expectations among African-Americans, resulted in an upsurge of militancy.

The black churches had traditionally not engaged much in interracial activities, but within their walls a ferment was in process. Some of the younger ministers, trained in integrated northern institutions, spoke in measured tones about the churches' responsibility in seeking freedom from social oppression. Educated laypersons, especially in the cities, sought ways to move against segregation. Older church members who were passive but not unmoved did not obstruct the rising new forces.

A new phase of the struggle began in 1955 when blacks in Montgomery, Alabama, launched a boycott to end segregated seating in the city's public transportation. The key figure in this successful campaign was the young pastor of the Dexter Avenue Baptist Church, Martin Luther King Jr. (1929–68). Born in Atlanta, King was educated at Morehouse College, Crozer Theological Seminary, and Boston University, from which he received a Ph.D. degree in 1955. Following the Montgomery achievement, King in 1957 became the first president of the Southern Christian Leadership Conference (SCLC), which endeavored to extend the drive for integration throughout the South.

In a 1960 article in the *Christian Century,* he described his view of the Christian gospel and its contemporary demands:

> The gospel at its best deals with the whole man, not only his soul but his body, not only his spiritual well-being, but his material well-being. Any religion that professes to be concerned about the souls of men and is not concerned about the slums that damn them, the economic conditions that strangle them, and the social conditions that cripple them is a spiritually moribund religion awaiting burial.[1]

King's approach was that of nonviolent resistance, learned from the life and teachings of the Indian leader Mahatma Gandhi. His passion succeeded in translating religious fervor into political action, and he attracted supporters among black clergy, college students, and some northern white clergy. Their commitment to nonviolence grew stronger in proportion to the violence they met. The brutal actions received much exposure in the media, resulting in widespread public revulsion. Millions of white Americans who otherwise

1. Martin Luther King Jr., "Pilgrimage to Nonviolence," *Christian Century* 77 (13 April 1960): 439.

might have remained indifferent became sympathetic, and many northern denominational leaders advocated the cause. The wide support for the movement was dramatized in August 1963, when more than two hundred thousand black and white Americans marched in Washington, D.C., in a demonstration calling for complete equality in citizenship. The following year Congress passed a sweeping civil rights law that committed the federal government to positive action on behalf of minorities. This was followed by the Voting Rights Act in 1965. Through the impact of black migrations and the struggle of the Civil Rights movement, the black church was transformed from refuge to social/cultural religious force, which profoundly affected the religious thought and behavior of blacks and of many whites as well.

Black Power and Christ's Power

The very successes of the Civil Rights movement led some militant young activists, most notably Stokely Carmichael and H. Rap Brown (as they were then called), to question its methods and goals. They claimed that the laws and court decisions did not really defeat racism or do anything to help the poor in the ghettos. They also said that the philosophy of nonviolence was degrading to blacks, and they proclaimed a form of black nationalism based on racial pride and exaltation of the African heritage. Under the slogan "black power," they called for a new, much more aggressive movement comprised only of blacks. They no longer saw a need for white allies.

Although King and his followers rejected such an approach, the militant message struck a responsive chord in the urban neighborhoods, where anger at discrimination and lack of economic opportunity had reached the boiling point. Riots in Los Angeles, Detroit, Newark, and elsewhere resulted in dozens of deaths and the destruction of entire sections of the inner cities. In April 1968, the assassination of thirty-nine-year-old King sparked even more riots in over one hundred cities, including the nation's capital, and opened the way for militant groups such as the Black Panthers and the Black Muslims to exercise greater influence.

Many of these vigorous advocates for black equality had grown up in the black evangelical and fundamentalist churches. They turned their backs on their spiritual upbringing and adopted a pragmatic or secular approach that was often anti-Christian in character. The extremists viewed conservative churches as a hindrance to the movement's progress and accused the two largest black Baptist denominations and the black Methodists of inaction. Such sentiments challenged African-American Christians to rethink their faith in this new era of heightened racial consciousness and emerging identity.

Black theology, which paralleled and drew ideas from other radical theologies devoted to the liberation of the oppressed, was expressed by such thinkers as Albert Cleage, Major J. Jones, J. Deotis Roberts, James Washington, and James Cone. Among the most significant works were Cone's *Black Theology and Black Power* (1969) and *A Black Theology of Liberation* (1970). Evangelicals, who had been on the sidelines during the early stages of the Civil Rights movement and had even founded Christian schools in the South ("segregation academies") to avoid court-mandated school desegregation measures, now began to stir. As mentioned earlier (chap. 16), Billy Graham had taken the lead in desegregating his meetings and in 1957 appointed a black associate evangelist to his staff, Howard Jones. A National Negro (now Black) Association of Evangelicals was formed in 1963 as a counterpart to the white-dominated NAE and pushed it in the direction of confronting social issues.

In 1965, a white fundamentalist Baptist urban missionary in Cleveland, Fred Alexander, began the magazine *Freedom Now* (now *The Other Side*) to explain the plight of blacks to white evangelicals. Quickly, other evangelicals, both white and black, joined the rising chorus of those demanding racial and social justice. These were, however, tensions between black Christians and the emerging white evangelical social activists. Such figures as Ronald Sider, Jim Wallis, and Tony Campolo called for a much greater level of involvement by white evangelicals in racial issues, while black evangelicals such as William Bentley, William Pannell, Tom Skinner, and John Perkins looked for clearer signs of repentance among their white allies and a greater acceptance of black leadership in their cooperative ventures.

As the activism of the 1960s receded, some African-American militants moved toward more moderate positions. However, the demand for positive social action continued unabated, particularly among church leaders. Jesse Jackson organized People United to Save Humanity (PUSH) in 1971, which offered a comprehensive program to upgrade the quality of life in black communities. Ministers from the major African-American Protestant denominations came together to find ways to combat white racism and enhance black leadership, while the National Office for Black Catholics encouraged similar trends in their church. Although their roles shifted in the 1960s and their actions were often not understood by white churchgoers, the black churches continued to be a center of community structure as well as the communicators of hope to their millions of adherents.

As the bicentennial of the American Revolution approached, the ideals of the Declaration of Independence that affirmed human rights and equality had not yet been realized in American society. But progress had been made, and the drive toward the achievement of full equality would not be halted in the coming years.

20

From the Bicentennial to the New Millennium

The 1976 bicentennial of the American Revolution was the occasion for memorializing America's spiritual heritage. Many churches highlighted the privileges of religious liberty and honored individuals involved in establishing the republic that apparently had a Christian identity. Numerous writers examined the links among religion, morality, and the public order. They rediscovered the importance of religious faith for understanding contemporary society and as a guide for people as they faced the remaining years of the century.

A Gallup poll taken in August 1976 revealed a rising level of religious consciousness in the United States. For the first time in two decades, an increase in worship attendance was recorded. During a typical week of the bicentennial year, approximately 42 percent of Americans attended a church or synagogue. Six out of ten affirmed religion as "very important" in their personal lives, and seven out of ten claimed to hold church membership. Most notably, one-third of those interviewed attested to a "born-again" experience, a conversion wherein one made a commitment to Jesus Christ. Almost half (48 percent) of the Protestants surveyed offered such a testimony, as well as 18 percent of Catholics.[1] Drawing on these statistics and Southern Baptist presidential candidate Jimmy Carter's acknowledgment that he was born

1. *Religion in America 1976: Gallup Opinion Index,* no. 130 (Princeton, N.J.: American Institute of Public Opinion, 1976).

Billy Graham with Jimmy and Rosalynn Carter, 1973. Courtesy of the Archives of the Billy Graham Center, Wheaton, Illinois.

again, both *Newsweek* magazine and George Gallup Jr. dubbed 1976 "the year of the evangelical."

Gallup's delineation of "evangelical" was straightforward: An evangelical has experienced a personal conversion to Christ, holds to a literal, authoritative interpretation of the Bible, and seeks to witness to others about his or her faith. He then suggested reasons for the upsurge in religious awareness, clearly a surprise to secular analysts. Among these were Carter's candid witness to his faith; a general tarnishing of the American dream and disillusionment with materialism; a looking inward as a response to the uncertainties of an age of technology and mass organization; the creative communication of biblical ideas by many clergy, especially to the youth; and a cyclic upswing after a period of decline. Gallup underscored the view long held by casual observers that the United States had the most religious populace of any of the industrialized nations. Yet he found it difficult to account for such a high level of religiosity while simultaneously the rates of violent crime and drug addiction were rising, social turmoil and racial prejudice were plaguing the nation, and moral erosion and secularism were advancing. Although religious sentiment was pervasive, it rapidly was becoming clear, as sociologist Peter Berger observed in various writings, that the ability of American religious institutions to shape society was eroding.

The Evangelical Coalition and Varieties of Religious Experience

The new visibility of evangelicals raised questions about the nature of this heritage. An outside observer might have said that those who called themselves evangelicals were all alike, but in fact substantial differences existed. As a result of this diversity, the most suitable description might have been "coalition" or "mosaic."

A number of perspectives conditioned the soil from which the renewed American evangelicalism sprang. One was Calvinism with its emphasis on precise theological formulations and biblically oriented worldviews; another was the Wesleyan/Arminian impulse with its stress on free will, holiness, and vitality; and a third was the Anabaptist legacy of the believers' church. Other identifiable influences came from Lutheran pietism and Episcopalianism. The latter was reflected in the deep interest in the British writer C. S. Lewis and the Anglican liturgical tradition. Complicating the situation was the way in which these broad traditions were channeled into contemporary denominational (or nondenominational) communions by means that cut across educational and economic levels yet allowed the groups to retain their historic theological characters.

Three transdenominational waves that swept across geographical and ecclesiastical boundaries further shaped evangelical convictions. First was revivalism with its individualistic thrust and simple Bible message and of which television evangelists and gospel music were versions. Historian Grant Wacker suggested that the increasing contemporary emphasis on experiential conversion-centered faith represented the "Southernization" of American religion.[2] While revivalism was a common American practice, it was in southern Methodist and Baptist circles that it flourished most greatly and came to influence national church life after World War II. Second was the stress on doctrinal purity and strict behavioral practices of twentieth-century fundamentalism. Always concerned with clear boundary setting, the fundamentalists continued to emphasize detailed doctrinal statements, separation from ecumenical efforts, and opposition to worldliness as exemplified by dancing, alcohol, card playing, smoking, and swimming with both sexes present.

Third was the charismatic phenomenon, about which it is difficult to generalize given its diverse and complex manifestations. Many charismatics highlight speaking in tongues as a prayer language flowing from an intimate experience of God's presence. Some emphasize the gifts of healing and prophecy or demonstrative signs such as collapsing in a trance (being slain in the Spirit) and holy laughter (the Toronto blessing). All practice a free, open, and unstructured style of worship. The exercise of spiritual gifts spread beyond the traditional Pentecostal denominations with the formation of the Full Gospel Businessmen's Fellowship in 1951 and the contacts its members had with other evangelicals. Within a decade the charismatic

2. Grant Wacker, "Uneasy in Zion: Evangelicals in Postmodern Society," in *Evangelicalism and Modern America, 1930–1980,* ed. George M. Marsden (Grand Rapids: Eerdmans, 1984), 17–28.

approach had begun to penetrate mainline denominations and even Roman Catholicism. With their distinctive style of caring, fellowship, and worship, the charismatics were a variant of Christian spirituality. The movement had extensive interdenominational networks, and it also gave rise to groups such as Vineyard and Rock Churches and Calvary Chapels, which for all practical purposes took on a denominational character.

A prominent feature of modern evangelicalism was the galaxy of parachurch organizations and agencies it spawned—evangelistic associations, student ministries, academic and professional fellowships, home and foreign mission societies, independent primary and secondary schools, Bible institutes, liberal arts colleges, theological seminaries, publishing houses, Christian bookstores, motion picture companies, summer camps and conference grounds, radio and television programs, charitable and relief agencies—that reflected the evangelical vision and enabled the mobilization of its constituency. Of course, voluntary societies had been a key factor in American religious life from the early days of the republic. Reaching across denominational lines, they provided opportunities for laypeople, women in particular, to exercise leadership and to contribute to the spreading of the gospel.

By the 1970s, the meaning of the evangelical heritage was a topic of vigorous debate in theological, biblical, and historical scholarship. Books and articles poured from the presses, and numerous consultations took place seeking to explain evangelicalism both to outsiders and to evangelicals themselves. The most difficult issue was that of defining biblical inspiration and inerrancy, and the quest for unanimity of thinking on this was never fully realized. A new generation of Christian scholars worked to integrate a biblical worldview with their academic disciplines. Theologian Carl Henry hoped to create a "truly great interdenominational university" that would influence public policy through positions developed out of a Christian consensus, but the enormous diversity within the evangelical movement made this increasingly impossible.

Many believed they could find scriptural warrant to link conservative religion, conservative politics, and laissez-faire economics, while others developed equally biblically based reformist and even radical stances on social issues that diverged widely from the social and political values of middle-class America. A noteworthy challenge to the status quo was that of the Evangelicals for Social Action in their landmark Chicago Declaration (1973). It called for application of the gospel and political efforts to promote civil rights and economic justice for the powerless. Another was the establishment of the periodical *Sojourners* by Jim Wallis and the community of the same name in Washington, D.C. Working from a somewhat different perspective in the Calvinist tradition, that of the well-known Dutch theologian and political leader Abraham Kuyper, the Association for Public Justice formulated a variety of Christian positions on public issues and functioned as a voice of Christian political concern in the nation's capital.

The Gospel and the Media

Ben Armstrong, a leader of the influential National Religious Broadcasters, affirmed in 1979, "God has raised up this powerful technology of radio and television expressly to reach every man, woman, boy and girl on earth with the even more powerful message of the Gospel."[3] This belief underlay the work of radio and television evangelists from the beginning of religious programming in 1921 and reflected the ability of American Christianity to adopt the latest in communications technology. In the 1920s and 1930s, evangelists such as Paul Rader, Aimee Semple McPherson, Charles Fuller *(The Old Fashioned Revival Hour),* and William "Bible Bill" Aberhart preached the old-time religion by means of the new-time technology of radio. In 1935, theologian Walter Maier (1893–1950) became the regular speaker on *The Lutheran Hour,* which in the 1940s became the world's largest radio broadcast enterprise of its time and introduced the Confessionalist Lutheran Church-Missouri Synod to the American Protestant mainstream. The leading mainline radio personality was Methodist bishop Ralph Sockman (1889–1970), who for twenty-five years was the voice of the National Radio Pulpit. The pioneering Catholic radio priest was Father Charles Coughlin (1891–1979), who began a radio ministry from suburban Detroit in 1926. During the 1930s, one-third of the population heard his increasing political message. Because of his pro-German views, he was ordered off the air by church authorities when the United States entered World War II. By the 1980s, 20 percent of all American radio stations were religiously oriented, and the airwaves also became the means for global evangelical outreach. In the 1950s, television attracted a new generation of electronic preachers whose messages eventually were carried around the world by satellite and cable television.

The high visibility and immense clientele of the televangelists and the electronic church were the result of several factors, some social and some technical. As a medium, television offered an illusion of intimacy. Especially for shut-ins, who lacked other outside connections, a continuing contact with a television personality led to extraordinary feelings of trust. The success of the television preachers, although often exaggerated, suggests that they struck a responsive chord with listeners.

The numerical support for the electronic church and its impact on local congregational life are still matters of debate. Critics charge that it is an "armchair religion" that fosters privatism and siphons off resources from local churches and that the message is too upbeat, simplified, and geared toward quick solutions. Because of the huge amounts of money raised by the television ministries, the chances for misuse of funds is great. In an effort to reduce the rising level of criticism, the Evangelical Council for Financial

3. Ben Armstrong, *The Electric Church* (Nashville: Nelson, 1979), 7.

Accountability was formed in 1979. Ministries wishing to receive its seal of approval must meet strict organizational and accounting standards. Especially controversial has been the involvement of television preachers in conservative political causes. The desire to bring Americans "back to God" and to link moral and public policy issues lay behind their efforts to organize those who previously had been politically inactive.

Serving a Society in Flux

It was evident by the mid-1980s that the United States was a nation in transition, gripped by a sweeping cultural revolution that was transforming the rules that had once guided American life. Affluence and the unprecedented availability of consumer goods led to materialism, a depletion of resources, and an unlimited number of choices that drew attention away from spiritual and moral spheres. Mass communications, rapid mobility, and centralized political administrations contributed to the decline of the so-called mediating institutions—the home, parish, synagogue, school, neighborhood—where previous generations had found their meaning, values, and personhood. Individuals were free to fashion new identities and religious beliefs outside the framework of traditional religion and the family. The continuing impact of the sexual revolution of the 1960s and 1970s and the political and ideological influences of feminism were also significant forces for change.

Among the American intellectual elite, steeped in secular Enlightenment rationalism, confidence in scientific and political solutions to the human condition persisted. At the same time, postmodernist theory in the humanities and the social sciences challenged all concepts of universal truth and reliable knowledge, while cultural relativism undermined traditional beliefs and understandings of reality. Politically, the erosion of a common ethical framework seemed to reduce domestic politics to a conflict of competing interests and moralities. The Civil Rights struggle, the Vietnam War debates, and the Nixon scandals eroded confidence in governmental institutions. The ongoing Cold War tensions and fear of nuclear warfare lingered in the public consciousness. In this context, churches searched for ways to serve people, provide a framework of meaning, and have a positive impact on society.

Political Action

From the earliest days of the republic, religious people utilized biblical ideas to bolster their political arguments. The debates over slavery, prohibition, civil rights, and communism were emotionally charged because foundational values were at stake. The nation was accustomed to the theologically pluralistic mainline denominations being involved in political debates. Similarly, the National Conference of Catholic Bishops frequently addressed political, economic, and social issues. Supreme Court decisions affirmed that the First Amendment right of free speech included religious expression. The creation of what the media labeled the "New Christian Right," however, revealed the explosive potential of a group claiming theological certainty. In the democratic process, the goal is to achieve compromise among the competing positions or at least a temporary consensus so that people can get along with one another. But the tough question posed by this foray of conservative Christians into politics was how persons and groups with strong religious faith and convictions can cooperate or work with others who hold different moral or spiritual principles.

The Christian Right appealed to those who wanted to protect "family values" from the perceived threats of gay rights, equal rights for women, and Supreme Court rulings permitting abortions and forbidding officially sanctioned public school prayers. Others claimed that threats to the family included the teaching of evolution instead of divine creation in public schools. The Christian Right also expressed concern over the expansion of the federal government.

The publicists of the new conservatism argued that the primary reason for the "national malaise" during the Carter administration was secular humanism, the relativistic, materialistic ideology of a small liberal elite who controlled the media, education, the government bureaucracies, and the courts. To counter this force, Jerry Falwell in 1979 formed the Moral Majority, and a number of evangelical figures lent their support. After the Moral Majority faded from the scene, televangelist Pat Robertson made an unsuccessful presidential bid in 1988 and formed a new Christian Right group called the Christian Coalition.

Worth noting is that the initiative for greater involvement by evangelicals in politics drew heavily on southern ministerial leadership. The Moral Majority, the Christian Coalition, and other Christian Right efforts had large lay constituencies in the South that reached out to like-minded persons in the North and the West. The evangelical churches in the former Confederate states had continued to exert a role as cultural custodians of public life that the northern churches had not realized for decades. Thus, when public policy and court decisions moved in more secular and pluralistic directions after 1950, the South felt the change most acutely, but it was also where evangelical believers were most experienced in engaging in the political process.

The reaction of the secular press to the Christian Right was soon shown to be excessive. The accusations of fascist or totalitarian intentions were exaggerated, and moderate commentators noted that liberal clergymen had been just as active politically as those on the right. Voting analyses of elections in the 1980s revealed that the political clout of the televangelists and the Christian Right was less than their adversaries claimed. The most legitimate charges, some of which were made by evangelicals, were that the movement blamed others for society's ills, idealized the American past, merged God's priorities with those of the nation, and emphasized individual morality while ignoring social injustices.

Whether the influence of the Christian Right was limited or extensive is a matter of ongoing historical debate. Much more significant is how its rise revealed a vast pool of Protestant, Catholic, and Jewish Americans whose deeply held values put them at odds with the direction society and public policy was moving. Though not necessarily in full agreement with the Christian Right's positions, these citizens comprised a social movement heretofore not adequately recognized in domestic politics or by the secular media. The coalescing of white religious conservatives with free-market businessmen and politicians reshaped the Republican Party and paved the way for the election of George W. Bush in November 2000, a person whose evangelical sympathies became increasingly evident when he took office.

At the same time, it would be wrong to assume the political uniformity of conservative Christians or that evangelicals desire to undermine pluralism and institute a theocratic Christian America. Studies such as Christian Smith's *Christian America? What Do Evangelicals Really Want?* (2000) reveal that religious conservatives are much more ambivalent about politics than commentators realize and that most evangelicals do not fully endorse the tactics of the Christian Right. Furthermore, the political loyalties of African-American and other minority Christians remain tied to the Democratic Party and its social programs, a position also embraced by most mainline denominational leaders.

Denominational Dynamics

By the 1980s, a diversified, or some would say fragmented, Christianity ministered in an increasingly pluralistic society. Among the Protestant denominations existed several "families" that derived from specific traditions. Analyses of religious and church bodies in the United States and Canada during the 1990s identified 19 Presbyterian, 32 Lutheran, 36 Methodist, 60 Baptist, 37 Episcopalian/Anglican, and 241 Pentecostal fellowships of various types. There were also 22 Eastern Orthodox communions and a host of independent, sectarian groupings such as the Seventh-day Adventists.[4] The single largest Christian communion was the Roman Catholic Church, which in the new century would number over 70 million and be the largest nongovernmental organization in the country.

4. See Mark A. Noll, *The Old Religion in a New World: The History of North American Christianity* (Grand Rapids: Eerdmans, 2002), 162.

In the 1970s and 1980s, the greatest numerical growth occurred among evangelical Protestants and other religious bodies that were conservative in some way or made high demands on their adherents. Among these were Eastern Orthodox churches, the Church of Jesus Christ of Latter-day Saints (Mormons), the Seventh-day Adventists, and the Jehovah's Witnesses. An increase of parishioners took place among confessional Protestants such as the conservative wing of Lutheranism—the Wisconsin Evangelical Lutheran Synod and the Lutheran Church-Missouri Synod—and some Reformed and Presbyterian communions. America's largest Protestant denomination, the Southern Baptist Convention, inched upward in numbers in spite of a bitter struggle for control of the denomination that centered on the issue of biblical inerrancy. As a result of the debate, the denominational seminaries and program boards moved in a more conservative direction, and the losing side slowly coalesced into another Baptist denomination. The charismatic and Pentecostal groups grew rapidly as their people became more upwardly mobile, and their constituencies reached across class, racial, ethnic, and international boundaries. The historic black denominations experienced modest growth, the largest being the National Baptist Convention, U.S.A., Inc. (with its membership of 5.5 million, it was the fourth largest denomination in the country), while the most rapidly growing African-American Pentecostal body was the Church of God in Christ.

In contrast, the more liberal and pluralistic mainline denominations experienced membership declines during the last decades of the century, and some of them ended up heavily populated by older persons and women. Given the kinds of issues that buffeted the traditional churches, the remarkable fact was that so many remained loyal to their congregations. From the viewpoint of denominational leaders, the decline marked a winnowing process whereby only the most loyal members remained. In spite of the falloffs in membership, the totals in the older denominations remained substantial and numbered in the millions. However, if present trends continue, Anglican Alister McGrath suggests that the mainline denominations are unlikely to last another century.[5] In contrast, Robert Wuthnow argues that denominational bodies will last indefinitely both as sources of identity for members as well as credentialing vehicles for clergy and agencies for offering social and religious programs.[6]

Yet counting members did not sufficiently capture the complexity of late-twentieth-century church life. Among Protestant denominations, old institutional loyalties eroded, and family needs more than denominational identity often defined which local congregations prospered. For many, participation in parachurch Bible study groups or similar organizations replaced involvement in denominational programs. Moreover, ethnically or racially oriented parishes added diversity to the older churches. The vitality of the many Asian-American

5. Alister E. McGrath, *The Future of Christianity* (Oxford: Blackwell, 2002).
6. Robert Wuthnow, *Christianity in the Twenty-First Century: Reflections on the Challenges Ahead* (New York: Oxford University Press, 1993).

churches, especially those in large Chinese and Korean communities, was impressive. Mainline bodies became a hotbed of strife as gay, feminist, and minority caucuses sought to determine policy, and evangelical fellowships struggled to redirect their churches toward more orthodox channels.

A wide spectrum of worship styles was practiced, reflecting the grassroots nature of American popular religion. From high church liturgy with elegantly attired clergy, bells, and incense to the extreme informality of religious rock bands, casually attired clergy, and drama groups, many options were available that appealed to different people. Several million even found nurture on the Internet, an indicator of the resurgent search for spirituality. Another phenomenon was the growth of seeker-friendly megachurches such as Willow Creek Church in Illinois. Flexibility in worship and creative programming combined to present a message that was often therapeutic, one that emphasized self-realization and finding meaning in this world as much as rescue from sin and the hope of a new life in the next. Some church growth experts predicted that by the new century a majority of church attendees would be in the very large congregations with multiple programs, but this has not yet come to pass. Some observers, such as theologian David Wells, cautioned that an overemphasis on marketing strategies and therapeutic recovery approaches to gospel presentation could dilute Christian truth by shying away from a profound sense of sin and divine redemption in favor of human peace of mind.[7] Churches can be marketed, but the gospel in all its depth and the call for sacrificial discipleship cannot be marketed.

The situation in the African-American churches was somewhat different. There, neighborhood congregations continued to be centers of black community life together with the local self-help organizations. Yet as blacks gained access to opportunities in the larger society, the churches became less central. The number of youths preparing for the ministry declined as other avenues to leadership became available. Nevertheless, African-American clerics such as Jesse Jackson, Andrew Young, E. V. Hill, T. D. Jakes, and others remained prominent, as did theologian Cornel West. The key roles minority clergy played in the cities were reminders of their significance. Boston's Ten Point Coalition, originally led by Eugene Rivers and later by Ray Hammond, was an example. Another was the extensive ministry of Floyd Flake in New York City, who also served in the U.S. House of Representatives. John Perkins's (1930–) ministry in Mississippi and later in Pasadena, California, was a landmark of black evangelical work, while Tom Skinner and William Pannell endeavored to sensitize white evangelical churchgoers to black concerns. The most creative aspect of African-American congregational life was the combination of joyous musical forms, biblical preaching, and vigorous application of the gospel to issues of social justice.

7. David F. Wells, *God in the Wasteland: The Reality of Truth in a World of Fading Dreams* (Grand Rapids: Eerdmans, 1994).

John Perkins (1930–).
Courtesy of the Archives
of the Billy Graham
Center, Wheaton, Illinois.

Gender and Sexuality Issues

Rising feminist consciousness and the movement of women into all areas of professional life, even positions customarily held only by males, deeply affected churches. As women entered the workforce in increasing numbers, they had to rethink their positions on gender and family relationships. The stereotypical nuclear family, with the father as the breadwinner and the mother as the stay-at-home child rearer, was rapidly changing. No-fault divorce laws made the termination of marriages easy. Most married couples chose to limit family size, some couples entered into partnerships outside the bonds of marriage, and many single women raised children alone. While liberal and moderate churches accepted the changing gender roles and ministered as best they could to people in new situations, many conservative churches resisted change by supporting a variety of actions they defined as "pro-family." Such actions included discouraging abortion and advocating adoption, discouraging mothers from taking employment outside the home, and asserting male headship in marriage. A vast outpouring of literature by feminist theologians (as well as black "womanist" and Hispanic "mujerist" theologians) debated these issues, while evangelicals divided along egalitarian and complementarian lines, the latter being an affirmation of male headship.

Women's roles in the church also became an issue. From the earliest days of the nation, women had outnumbered men in church membership, and committed women had sustained the programs of the church, especially the Sunday schools and foreign missions efforts. In fact, thousands of single women served overseas as missionaries. Yet with the exception of Pentecostal and Holiness groups, few denominations permitted women to be ordained and have ministerial standing. Several of the mainline denominations, including Methodist, Presbyterian, Lutheran, American Baptist, Congregationalist, Episcopalian, and United Church of Christ, today affirm that God calls and gifts women to minister in the church and therefore ordain them for service. This did not happen, however, without considerable controversy. In fact, differences led to the formation of new denominations such as the Presbyterian Church in America and the Anglican Orthodox Church, while the Southern Baptist Convention modified its doctrinal statement to exclude women from ordained ministry.

Even more controversial was the question of homosexuality. While only the most extreme churches would deny civil rights to gays, whether to allow membership and clergy status to practicing homosexuals was a matter of intense debate. Conservatives insisted that homosexual behavior deviated from biblical norms and thus was unacceptable. This was the stance of Roman Catholics, Eastern Orthodox, and nearly all evangelical denominations. Although some churches and denominational officials ordained homosexuals, most mainline Protestant denominations declined to endorse committee reports recommending such action. (The main exception was the United Church of Christ.) Because of the controversy, the National Council of Churches was reticent to accept as an affiliate the Fellowship of Metropolitan Community Churches, a group of gay congregations that was largely evangelical in orientation. Concern with how churches should or could respond to the gay community was elevated with the emergence of AIDS, which first appeared among the homosexual community. It has since spread to heterosexuals, and globally it has reached epidemic proportions. This condition, which transcends all boundaries, calls churches to acts of mercy and compassion, not only at home but also abroad, especially in Africa.

Roman Catholic Concerns

Theological conservatism in Roman Catholicism was reaffirmed with the election of the Polish Cardinal Karol Wojtyla to the papal chair in 1978. As his biographer George Weigel points out, Wojtyla is a heroic figure who spent his entire adulthood living under authoritarian dictatorships, first the Nazis and then the communists. As Pope John Paul II (1920–), he has been creative, erudite, quick-witted, and unpredictable as he has reached out to the world's hundreds of millions of Catholics and to non-Catholics as well. His globe-straddling tours to tend his scattered flock have brought him in contact with a myriad of peoples and cultures, and he has been seen personally by more people than any other figure in history. He is a staunch defender of human rights, and his moral and spiritual leadership contributed to the peaceful end of communism in Eastern Europe.

Pope John Paul II (1920–). Courtesy of the Archives of the Archdiocese of Boston.

Despite the outward appearance of unity and control by the hierarchy, Roman Catholicism in America is deeply divided, and a great variety of viewpoints and subgroups exists. This situation is partially a result of the long-standing differences among ethnic Catholic communities, but it is also fueled by the calls of American Catholic intellectuals for revisions in the church's theology and practice. This indicates how far the Neo-Thomist theological underpinning of mid-century Catholic thought has eroded. Voices were raised questioning John Paul II's unwillingness to consider female ordination or to relax the requirement for priestly celibacy. The increasing shortage of clergy has put intense pressure on the hierarchy to consider reforms. Although Catholics remain adamantly opposed to abortion, they are less committed to upholding the church's policy on birth control. There are also demands for more lay input in church decisions.

Some Catholics today are animated by the spirit of Dorothy Day and liberation theology and call for greater concern for and service to the marginalized at home and abroad. Others seek to engage modernity by drawing on insights from theological liberalism. Considerable emphasis is placed on renewal through worship, ranging from seeking the charismatic blessing to a heightened veneration of the Virgin Mary. The increasing number of Hispanic parishes further adds to the need for creative responses to current concerns. Paramount among these concerns is the cascading accusations of sexual abuse by priests and the charges of inadequate response to the problem by bishops, which have created one of the greatest crises ever faced in American Roman Catholicism. The resignation of a leading American prelate, Cardinal Bernard Law of Boston, highlights how serious the crisis is. The result is a church in transition, grappling with daunting forces within and without. John Paul II did much to reshape the papacy and drew on the wisdom and insights of clergy from the third world, where the church's largest growth is taking place. His successor will face even greater challenges.

Ethnic Congregations

Destined to become the largest minority in America, the Spanish-speaking community had already reached 10 percent of the population by the end of the twentieth century. Four-fifths of these people were originally baptized as Catholics, and dioceses continue to labor to meet the needs of a highly diverse constituency comprised of Cuban-Americans, Mexican-Americans, Puerto Ricans, and people from every nation in the world with a Spanish heritage. Some maintain that Hispanics hold to a more flexible Catholicism than parishioners from a European background. Yet Hispanic Catholics have been recognized for their family centeredness, enthusiastic participation in religious festivals, and concern for helping those in need. It is not surprising that they are seeking and gaining greater representation among the clerical leadership.

Hispanic Protestant congregations have made dramatic advances. Some of the new churches, particularly Methodist, Presbyterian, and Baptist, drew from immigrants who had been evangelized by Protestant missions in Latin America. Likewise, an explosive growth of Pentecostalism began among Puerto Rican immigrants who already had an inclination toward the charismatic approach, and it rapidly spread to other Spanish-speaking populations. The challenge facing the Hispanic congregations, who lived astride two cultural heritages, the Anglo and the Latino, was to incorporate the best of both.

One of the most prominent evangelists in the Hispanic community is the Argentina native Luis Palau (1934–). Educated in the United States, he began preaching throughout the Americas in the 1960s. He founded his own evangelistic association in 1971 with its headquarters in Portland, Oregon, and now conducts revival campaigns in many countries.

Luis Palau (1934–).
Courtesy of the Archives of
the Billy Graham Center,
Wheaton, Illinois.

Remarkable growth has also taken place among Asian congregations. Churches comprised of Chinese, Koreans, Japanese, Vietnamese, and numerous other Asian peoples have mushroomed in number and size, and they have aggressively evangelized among their ethnic communities. The Koreans have even launched their own foreign missions program.

Ecumenical Cooperation

As mentioned earlier, the quest for greater Protestant unity continued unabated in the final decades of the twentieth century. In addition to denominational mergers, informal ecumenicity took place in the various consultations for inter-ecclesiastical understanding. The need to share resources and a shortage of pastors encouraged these exchanges. Representing one-fourth of all Protestants, the Christian Church–Disciples of Christ, Episcopal Church, Evangelical Lutheran Church in America, Moravian Church, Presbyterian Church in the U.S.A., Reformed Church in America, and United Church of Christ agreed to recognize one another's ordination, allow transfer of clergy across the communions, and accept member switches without rebaptism. This cooperation required compromises by the Episcopalians because of their belief in apostolic succession. The Second Vatican Council encouraged Catholics to engage in ecumenical dialogues, and the long-running Lutheran-Roman Catholic discussions on the nature of salvation by faith resulted in greater understanding between these traditions. Other Catholic-Protestant conversations also occurred. The "Evangelicals and Catholics Together" dialogues organized by Richard John Neuhaus and Charles Colson produced important although controversial statements in 1994 and 1997. In addition, a variety of Christian-Jewish exchanges took place, often centering on ways to counter anti-Semitism. Marvin Wilson of Gordon College orchestrated a productive series of such dialogues that began in the 1970s and continued into the 1990s.

The National Association of Evangelicals, whose membership includes denominations, parachurch agencies, and individual congregations, has tried to fulfill a unifying role for this community, but the results have been limited due to evangelical diversity and individualism. The World Relief Commission is undoubtedly its most effective effort. The competing separatist fundamentalist organization, the American Council of Christian Churches, continues to exist, but it has little influence. Ecumenical ecclesiastical structures have never flourished among evangelicals. More typical is the informal ecumenicity of cooperative evangelization, service, and fellowship. For instance, the national Bible study movement, organized by and for women and led by volunteers, gathers thousands of women weekly for Scripture classes and fellowship across denominational boundaries. Likewise, the Alpha program, imported from Britain, has done much to instruct and draw in the unchurched.

Most exemplary is the sixty-year ministry of Billy Graham and the broad base of support for his ministries. For years, polls have rated him as America's most admired religious leader, and his influence on church life has been extraordinary. His proclamation of a core gospel message, reflecting the affirmations of the Apostles' Creed, has reached across class and racial divides to moderates in mainline denominations, ethnic congregations, and even Eastern Orthodox and Roman Catholic believers. Graham has been heard by more people worldwide than any other Protestant evangelist, and it is difficult to conceive that his achievement as an evangelical leader will be replicated in the future.

On the international scene, the World Council of Churches continues to assemble every few years. As membership of third world churches grew and liberation consciousness increased, the body turned more leftward in its position on social, economic, and political questions. In the 1975 Nairobi meeting, the WCC voted to support "nonmilitary guerilla programs," a reflection of the liberation theology sentiments of many council members, and numerous churches in the United States and Europe expressed their disapproval. The WCC's Program to Combat Racism was heavily criticized in the West for its one-sidedness. The council's political stances led to a significant decline in financial support, requiring deep cuts in its personnel and programming.

The WCC sponsored mission-oriented conferences around the world in an effort to affirm the church in non-Western cultural contexts. The meeting in Bangkok in 1973 made a highly controversial recommendation calling for a moratorium on further mission activity, but many churches largely ignored the policy. A more positive move during these decades involved conversations among Roman Catholics, Eastern Orthodox, the World Council of Churches, and evangelicals on matters of global mission concern.

The most significant international gathering of evangelicals took place in Lausanne in 1974, where both evangelism and societal action were declared to be essential aspects of the ministry of the church. Aided by insights provided by Anglican John Stott and third world delegates such as René Padilla (1932–) and Orlando Costas, evangelicals were challenged to consider social justice integral to the full proclamation of the gospel, and the conference resolutions included such an affirmation. This emphasis of the "Whole Gospel to the Whole World" was forcefully restated at the Lausanne II conference in Manila in 1989.

Lausanne Conference on World Evangelism, René Padilla (1932–) speaking, 1974. Courtesy of the Archives of the Billy Graham Center, Wheaton, Illinois.

Another avenue for global cooperation by conservative groups is the loosely structured World Evangelical Alliance (formerly the World Evangelical Fellowship), which was founded in 1951 to renew the vision of the original Evangelical Alliance of 1846. The world mission efforts by evangelical boards and agencies, many of which are nondenominational in nature, offer striking examples of the collective commitment of personnel and resources to the global Christian advance. By 1990, according to the most reliable estimates, more than thirty-five thousand North American career missionaries, mainly under evangelical or Roman Catholic sponsorship, were serving overseas in a wide variety of assignments.

As the indigenous churches put down roots, the role of the missionaries changed. They became supportive co-laborers with local national leaders, learning from them as much as they were contributing to the maturing of the church in non-Western settings. In the late twentieth century, the demographic center of Christianity shifted southward to the developing nations. As a result, the majority of Christians in the world no longer live in Western countries. Christianity is now genuinely a world religion and is gaining adherents in non-Western countries even as it steadily declines in the West.

The End of the Cold War

The Cold War was still a defining reality in the 1970s and 1980s, and both sides possessed enough nuclear weapons to destroy the world. But change was in the air. The United States established relations with the People's Republic of China, a normalization of relations between the two German states defused the Berlin problem, the United States extricated itself from Vietnam, and the Soviets found themselves trapped in an unwinnable war in Afghanistan. Baptist President Jimmy Carter (the recipient of the Nobel Peace Prize in 2002) arranged the establishment of diplomatic relations between Israel and Egypt. Serious arms limitations talks began between the United States and the Soviet Union, and pressures mounted in church circles to halt the production of nuclear weapons. As both sides in the Cold War recognized its detrimental character and the Soviets approached economic meltdown, President Ronald Reagan and Mikhail Gorbachev opened talks to ease tensions. The Soviet empire in Eastern Europe began to disintegrate after democracy movements broke out in Poland and Hungary and eventually collapsed between 1989 and 1990 as a result of nonviolent revolutions in which Christians played key roles. With Germany reunified and the former satellites under new democratic regimes, the Soviet Union itself fell apart as national groups created their own independent states. Even communist China moved toward more openness and private enterprise. Christian believers the world over took heart that the Marxist-Leninist effort to create an atheistic world society had failed and that the faith had persisted in the face of bitter persecution.

America emerged as the world's lone superpower, and the world was seemingly entering a new era. The odious system of apartheid was dismantled in South Africa, and progress was made at home in improving minority rights. In the early 1990s, President George H. W. Bush spoke optimistically about a "new world order," one of harmony and peace, but this was not to last.

The United States that emerged from the Cold War was a far different society from what it had been in 1945. As a result of dramatic technological, social, and cultural shifts, secularism dominated the public realm, while religion continued to flourish in a more privatized manner. Though a majority of the populace maintained church associations, America was becoming one of the most religiously diverse countries in the world. As immigration barriers were relaxed, an influx of people who adhered to Islam, Buddhism, Hinduism, and other non-Western religions entered the country. These new religions and an increase in those who claimed no religious belief created a pluralism that exceeded past national experience. The religious and cultural custodianship that had been the province of churches and synagogues was severely eroded, and a cultural conflict among the adherents of contrasting worldviews seemed to divide society. One group reflected individualistic human autonomy and confidence in rationality and progress and paid little attention to religious authority beyond human experience. The other was guided by values drawn from the wisdom of past generations and based on moral and religious teachings considered divinely inspired.

In the midst of this diversity stood the churches, which in all their humanness and division still aspired to be the salt of the earth and a light to all peoples. In the first post–Cold War decade, Christians, like all Americans, experienced unparalleled prosperity, opportunity, and freedom from foreign threats. With great confidence, believers looked forward to the third millennium since Christ's birth and the founding of his church, one that was now global in membership and rich in cultural diversity.

Epilogue

As Americans celebrated the dawn of a new millennium, it seemed as if the country had taken a holiday from the common human experience of history. Never before had a society enjoyed such vast wealth and a sense of national security. American popular culture had worldwide influence. Revolutions in computer information technology and the medical sciences had brought about breathtaking advances in the quality and longevity of life. Confident of their prospects, Americans immersed themselves in a consumer- and entertainment-saturated culture. Yet in this secularized social order, tens of millions remained amazingly religious.

Scholars have suggested several factors that contributed to this persistence of faith among the populace, even if it was not shared by intellectual elites. Foremost was the separation of church and state, which provided social space for religious institutions, freeing them from political entanglement, bureaucratic stultification, and economic dependence on government. Second, the spirit of lay volunteerism, ardent evangelization, creative adaptability, and experimentation that animated American faith and practice from the earliest days of the republic continued unabated. Rather than withdrawing to the margins in an age of government innovation, Christians engaged in public policy debates and often were in the vanguard of social reform. Third, economic growth enabled parishioners to give large church offerings, while tax exemption for religious property and charitable donations assisted in building nonprofit institutional structures (e.g., congregations, schools, colleges, seminaries, and missionary agencies). These undergirded the effectiveness of the churches, especially in the task of nurturing their youth. Finally, the faith of numerous immigrant groups added diversity and devotion to the mix. In short, a sense of mission empowered millions of Christians to invest personal effort and financial resources in spreading the gospel and performing good works. The vitality of American Christianity never depended primarily on the professional clergy or an ecclesiastical establishment.

Beyond North America, churches in the Southern Hemisphere were experiencing explosive growth. This was especially the case among Roman Catholic, Pentecostal, and evangelically oriented congregations in which creative worship fostered a sense of community and adapted a vibrant New Testament faith to indigenous needs. As Philip Jenkins observed in 2002, the "typical" Christian believer in the world was not a white, middle-class male of European ancestry but a very poor woman of color living in a Latin American or African village or on the edge of a third world megacity.[1] A major challenge for American churches today is how to learn from, relate to, and share with the burgeoning third world Christian movement, which may be the primary shaper of the future of Christianity. In their religious viewpoints, Americans, with their pervasive faith loyalties, in certain respects have more in common with people in the developing nations than with Europeans according to the forty-four-nation Pew Global Attitudes Project conducted in 2003.[2]

Despite the assumption of secular analysts in the West that global economic and political modernization was inevitable and would lead to the demise of traditional and indigenous religions, quite the opposite has happened. In his widely discussed *Clash of Civilizations and the Remaking of World Order,* political scientist Samuel Huntington maintains that the resurgence of traditional faiths is a reaction "against secularism, moral relativism, and self-indulgence, and a reaffirmation of the values of order, discipline, work, mutual help, and human solidarity."[3] This is especially true of Islam, the second largest religion in the world after Christianity. Great variety exists among the Muslim nations, which the radical extremist elements want to unite into an integrated political and religious bloc following a strict adherence to the Qur'an. Blaming the West, particularly the United States, for the arrested development of the Islamic world, support for the state of Israel, and the media-led threat to Islamic values, these radical groups launched a campaign of terror on September 11, 2001, against those perceived to be the forces of evil. The assaults on the World Trade Center and the Pentagon, the symbolic centers of American economic and military power, marked a turning point in the national experience. Some commentators suggested that the twenty-first century actually began on September 11, 2001, just as the conflict-stained twentieth century really commenced in August 1914 with the outbreak of the First World War.

1. Philip Jenkins, *The Next Christendom: The Coming of Global Christianity* (New York: Oxford University Press, 2002), 2.

2. *Southern California Christian Times,* March 2003, 4.

3. Samuel P. Huntington, *The Clash of Civilizations and the Remaking of World Order* (New York: Simon & Schuster, 1996), 98.

In the aftermath of the terrorist attacks, the country struggled to place these tragic events in perspective. No unanimity of interpretation emerged, even among those who claimed to speak for the churches. Several observations seem evident, however. America's innocence and sense of invulnerability were shattered; the nation is no longer immune to the fears and devastation from which most of humankind suffers. The glib optimism that colored the thinking of the 1990s confronted the human capacity for radical evil, a term not frequently employed in postmodern vocabulary but now a part of public discourse. The attacks revealed the tentative quality of the country's highly vaunted economic prosperity and called the society back to a more realistic assessment of its financial future in the context of a problematic world economy. Above all, the sudden loss of so many lives and the intense emotional outpouring reminded people of the proper priorities for a meaningful existence: family, community, fulfilling one's daily responsibilities with integrity, and hope for the future.

Indeed, the initiative ordinary citizens took to meet the needs of others, even giving their lives in the effort, was truly inspiring. As Anglican Archbishop Rowan Williams stated, "Heroism may be more remote in a postwar world, but it has not disappeared."[4] Charitable giving greatly increased, and volunteers, both individuals and religious organizations such as the Salvation Army, sought every means to minister. The contributions by young people were especially noteworthy. The widespread display of American flags symbolized the wave of patriotic loyalty that swept across the nation, and the expression of religious sentiment and affirmation of a transcendent spiritual and moral order reached a height not seen in decades. Community prayer services occurred both in public places and religious centers alike, while "God Bless America" and "America the Beautiful" virtually became national anthems. The participation of Islamic clergy along with Jewish, Protestant, and Roman Catholic leaders at memorial services, including the National Day of Prayer and Remembrance on Friday, September 14, 2001, reflected the religious pluralism that had become obligatory in American civil religion.

In the next few weeks, church attendance increased by 25 percent, and those seeking comfort and meaning in the midst of an unthinkable national calamity were challenged to practice their faith more openly. Scripture sales doubled, and greater interest was shown in books on Bible prophecy and Islam. On a more theological level, parishioners, especially those suffering personal losses, grappled with how a loving God could allow evil to thrive and the innocent to suffer. Clergy attempted as best they could to provide answers.

4. Rowan Williams, *Writing in the Dust: After September 11* (Grand Rapids: Eerdmans, 2002), 44.

Also of concern to thoughtful Christians was the proper national response to the criminal acts of September 11. As the president declared an all-out war on terrorism, many turned to the traditional Christian just-war theory for help in determining how to protect America without killing innocents elsewhere. Others questioned whether calling for a war was the proper response and whether a violent response would breed only more violence. They looked to the historic peace church tradition for ideas. The burning question facing all thoughtful Christians was how they could be loyal, patriotic citizens without becoming blind nationalists who ignore international obligations and equate American national interest with the kingdom of God.

As the months passed, life appeared to return to normal. The surge of church attendance trailed off, and some suggested that the revived interest in faith had been greatly exaggerated. Yet an awareness of evil, the banality of materialism, and the limits of secularism persisted. Then the *Columbia* space shuttle disaster in early 2003 once more focused people's attention on the transitory nature of life and evoked an outpouring of national grief. Again, as in the days following September 11, President Bush assumed the role of a national spiritual leader, and he continued to do so during the war in Iraq that followed a few weeks later. Churches wrestled with the religious and moral issues of the conflict, and people were much more willing to discuss their faith in public and in the media.

As a result, churches have begun making greater efforts to build supportive communities and to find ways to participate effectively in public religious life in a pluralistic social order. Churches face the task of contributing without undermining the integrity of the Christian gospel by falling into the trap of a formless civil religion that equates Christian discipleship with patriotic senti-ments. Above all, they must eschew all forms of self-righteous triumphalism. The challenge facing churches is to speak and demonstrate the truth with love and to walk the path of faithfulness in an uncertain age, confident of the final outcome at the end of time.

Bibliography

Because the literature dealing with American Christianity has reached such vast proportions, this bibliography mainly emphasizes more recent works in the field.

General

Ahlstrom, Sydney E. *A Religious History of the American People.* New Haven: Yale University Press, 1972.

Balmer, Randall H., and Lauren F. Winner. *Protestantism in America.* New York: Columbia University Press, 2002.

Butler, Jon, Grant Wacker, and Randall Balmer. *A Short History of Religion in America.* New York: Oxford University Press, 2002.

Chinnici, Joseph P. *Living Stones: The History and Structure of Catholic Spiritual Thought in the United States.* Maryknoll, N.Y.: Orbis, 1996.

Dolan, Jay P. *The American Catholic Experience: A History from Colonial Times to the Present.* New York: Doubleday, 1985.

———, ed. *The Notre Dame History of Hispanic Catholics in the United States.* 3 vols. Notre Dame, Ind.: University of Notre Dame Press, 1994.

Dries, Angelyn. *The Missionary Movement in American Catholic History.* Maryknoll, N.Y.: Orbis, 1998.

Finke, Roger, and Rodney Stark. *The Churching of America, 1776–1990.* New Brunswick, N.J.: Rutgers University Press, 1992.

Fischer, Louis. *Religious Liberty in America: Political Safeguards.* Lawrence, Kans.: University Press of Kansas, 1992.

Fulop, Timothy E., and Albert J. Raboteau, eds. *African-American Religion: Interpretive Essays in History and Culture.* New York: Routledge, 1997.

241

Gaustad, Edwin. *Proclaim Liberty throughout All the Land: A History of Church and State in America*. New York: Oxford University Press, 2003.

Gaustad, Edwin, and Leigh Schmidt. *The Religious History of America: The Heart of the American Story from Colonial Times to Today*. San Francisco: HarperSanFrancisco, 2002.

Hall, David D., ed. *Lived Religion in America: Toward a History of Practice*. Princeton, N.J.: Princeton University Press, 1997.

Handy, Robert T. *A Christian America: Protestant Hopes and Historical Realities*. 2d ed. New York: Oxford University Press, 1984.

———. *A History of the Churches in the United States and Canada*. New York: Oxford University Press, 1977.

Hennesey, James J. *American Catholics: A History of the Roman Community in the United States*. New York: Oxford University Press, 1982.

Hudson, Winthrop. *American Protestantism*. Chicago: University of Chicago Press, 1961.

Hutchison, William R. *Religious Pluralism in America: The Contentious History of a Founding Ideal*. New Haven: Yale University Press, 2003.

Johnson, Paul E., ed. *African-American Christianity: Essays in History*. Berkeley: University of California Press, 1994.

Juhnke, James C., and Carol M. Hunter. *The Missing Peace: The Search for Nonviolent Alternatives in United States History*. Scottdale, Pa.: Herald, 2001.

Juster, Susan, and Lisa MacFarlane, eds. *A Mighty Baptism: Race, Gender, and the Creation of American Protestantism*. Ithaca, N.Y.: Cornell University Press, 1996.

Keillor, Steven J. *This Rebellious House: American History and the Truth of Christianity*. Downers Grove, Ill.: InterVarsity, 1996.

Leonard, Bill J. *Baptist Ways: A History*. Valley Forge, Pa.: Judson, 2003.

Lincoln, C. Eric, and Lawrence H. Mamiya. *The Black Church in the American Experience*. Durham, N.C.: Duke University Press, 1990.

Lindley, Susan. *You Have Stepped Out of Your Place: A History of Women and Religion in America*. Louisville: Westminster John Knox, 1996.

Lippy, Charles H. *Pluralism Comes of Age: American Religious Culture in the Twentieth Century*. Armonk, N.Y.: M. C. Sharpe, 2000.

Loveland, Anne C., and Otis B. Wheeler. *From Meetinghouses to Megachurch: A Material and Cultural History*. Columbia, Mo.: University of Missouri Press, 2003.

Maldonado, David, ed. *Protestantes/Protestants: Hispanic Christianity within Mainline Traditions*. Nashville: Abingdon, 1999.

Marini, Stephen A. *Sacred Song in America: Religion, Music, and Public Culture*. Urbana, Ill.: University of Illinois Press, 2003.

Marty, Martin E. *Pilgrims in Their Own Land: Five Hundred Years of Religion in America*. Boston: Little, Brown, 1984.

———. *Righteous Empire: Protestantism in the United States*. New York: Scribners, 1986.

McDonnell, Colleen. *Material Christianity: Religion and Popular Culture in America*. New Haven: Yale University Press, 1995.

Mead, Sidney E. *The Lively Experiment: The Shaping of Christianity in America.* New York: Harper & Row, 1963.

Morone, James A. *Hellfire Nation: The Politics of Sin in American History.* New Haven: Yale University Press, 2003.

Noll, Mark A. *American Evangelical Christianity: An Introduction.* Oxford: Blackwell, 2001.

———. *A History of Christianity in the United States and Canada.* Grand Rapids: Eerdmans, 1992.

———. *The Old Religion in a New World: The History of North American Christianity.* Grand Rapids: Eerdmans, 2002.

Rawlyk, George A., ed. *The Canadian Protestant Experience.* Toronto: Welch, 1990.

Sarna, Jonathan, ed. *Minority Faiths and the Protestant Mainstream.* Urbana, Ill.: University of Illinois Press, 1998.

Stout, Harry S., and D. G. Hart. *New Directions in American Religious History.* New York: Oxford University Press, 1997.

Synan, Vincent, ed. *Century of the Holy Spirit: One Hundred Years of Pentecostal and Charismatic Renewal, 1901–2001.* Nashville: Nelson, 2001.

Walls, Andrew F. *The Cross-Cultural Process in Christian History: Studies in the Transmission and Appropriation of Faith.* Maryknoll, N.Y.: Orbis, 2002.

———. *The Missionary Movement in Christian History: Studies in the Transmission of Faith.* Maryknoll, N.Y.: Orbis, 1996.

Wells, David F., et al., eds. *Christianity in America: A Handbook.* Grand Rapids: Eerdmans, 1983.

———, ed. *Reformed Theology in America: A History of Its Modern Development.* Grand Rapids: Baker, 2000.

Wells, Ronald A., ed. *The Wars of America.* 2d ed. Macon, Ga.: Mercer University Press, 1991.

Williams, Peter W. *America's Religions: Traditions and Cultures.* 2d ed. Urbana, Ill.: University of Illinois Press, 1998.

Reference and Documents

Anderson, Gerald, ed. *Biographical Dictionary of Christian Missions.* New York: Simon & Schuster, 1998.

Balmer, Randall. *Encyclopedia of Evangelicalism.* Louisville: Westminster John Knox, 2002.

Barrett, David B., George T. Kurian, and Todd M. Johnson, eds. *World Christian Encyclopedia: A Comparative Survey of Churches and Religions in the Modern World.* 2d ed. New York: Oxford University Press, 2001.

Brackney, William H. *Historical Dictionary of the Baptists.* Lanham, Md.: Scarecrow Press, 1999.

Burgess, Stanley M., and Eduard van der Maas, eds. *The New International Dictionary of Pentecostal and Charismatic Movements*. Grand Rapids: Zondervan, 2002.

Butler, Jon, and Harry S. Stout, eds. *Religion in American History: A Reader*. New York: Oxford University Press, 1998.

Cherry, Conrad. *God's New Israel: Religious Interpretations of American Culture*. 2d ed. Chapel Hill: University of North Carolina Press, 1998.

Gaustad, Edwin S., ed. *A Documentary History of Religion in America*. 2 vols. Grand Rapids: Eerdmans, 1993.

Gaustad, Edwin S., and Philip L. Barlow. *The New Historical Atlas of Religion in America*. New York: Oxford University Press, 2000.

Hill, Samuel S., ed. *Encyclopedia of Religion in the South*. Macon, Ga.: Mercer University Press, 1984.

Keller, Rosemary S., and Rosemary R. Reuther, eds. *In Our Voices: Four Centuries of American Women Religious Writers*. San Francisco: HarperSanFrancisco, 1996.

Krapohl, Robert H. *The Evangelicals: A Historical, Thematic, and Biographical Guide*. Westport, Conn.: Greenwood, 1999.

Larsen, Timothy, ed. *Biographical Dictionary of Evangelicals*. Downers Grove, Ill.: InterVarsity, 2003.

Lippy, Charles H., and Peter W. Williams, eds. *Encyclopedia of the American Religious Tradition*. 3 vols. New York: Scribners, 1988.

Lundin, Roger, and Mark A. Noll, eds. *Voices from the Heart: Four Centuries of American Piety*. Grand Rapids: Eerdmans, 1987.

Mathisen, Robert R., ed. *Critical Issues in American Religious History: A Reader*. Waco: Baylor University Press, 2001.

Mead, Frank S. *Handbook of Denominations in the United States*. 11th ed. Nashville: Abingdon, 2001.

Melton, Gordon J., ed. *Encyclopedia of American Religions*. 5th ed. Detroit: Gale, 1996.

Moreau, A. Scott, ed. *Evangelical Dictionary of World Missions*. Grand Rapids: Baker, 2000.

Mulder, John M., and John F. Wilson, eds. *Religion in American History: Interpretive Essays*. Englewood Cliffs, N.J.: Prentice-Hall, 1978.

New Catholic Encyclopedia. 15 vols. New York: McGraw-Hill, 1967, with supplementary volumes, 1974, 1979, 1989, 1996.

Newman, William M., and Peter L. Halvorson. *Atlas of American Religion: The Denominational Era*. Blue Ridge Summit, Pa.: AltaMira, 2000.

Piepkorn, Arthur C. *Profiles in Belief: The Religious Bodies of the United States and Canada*. 4 vols. New York: Harper & Row, 1977–79.

Reid, Daniel G., et al., eds. *Dictionary of Christianity in America*. Downers Grove, Ill.: InterVarsity, 1990.

Reuther, Rosemary Radford, and Rosemary Skinner Keller, eds. *Women and Religion in America*. 3 vols. New York: Harper & Row, 1981–86.

Sarna, Jonathan D., ed. *The American Jewish Experience*. 2d ed. New York: Holmes and Meier, 1997.

Smith, Shelton H., et al., eds. *American Christianity: An Historical Interpretation with Representative Documents.* 2 vols. New York: Scribners, 1960–63.

Toulouse, Mark G., and James O. Duke. *Sources of Christian Theology in America.* Nashville: Abingdon, 1999.

Tweed, Thomas A., ed. *Retelling U.S. Religious History.* Berkeley: University of California Press, 1998.

Chapter 1: Christianity as a World Faith

Bainton, Roland H. *Here I Stand: A Life of Martin Luther.* Nashville: Abingdon, 1950.

Bireley, Robert. *The Counter-Reformation Prince: Anti-Machiavellianism or Catholic Statecraft in Early Modern Europe.* Chapel Hill: University of North Carolina Press, 1990.

Bouwsma, William J. *John Calvin: A Sixteenth Century Portrait.* New York: Oxford University Press, 1988.

Cohn, Norman. *The Pursuit of the Millennium: Revolutionary Messianism in Medieval and Reformation Europe.* New York: Harper, 1961.

Estep, William R. *The Anabaptist Story.* Grand Rapids: Eerdmans, 1975.

———. *Renaissance and Reformation.* Grand Rapids: Eerdmans, 1986.

George, Timothy. *Theology of the Reformers.* Nashville: Broadman, 1988.

Gregory, Brad. *Salvation at Stake: Christian Martyrdom in Early Modern Europe.* Cambridge: Harvard University Press, 1999.

Gritsch, Eric W. *A History of Lutheranism.* Minneapolis: Fortress, 2002.

Kenny, Anthony, ed. *Wyclif in His Times.* Oxford: Clarendon, 1997.

Kittelson, James M. *Luther the Reformer: The Story of the Man and His Career.* Minneapolis: Augsburg, 1986.

Kolb, Robert. *Martin Luther as Prophet, Teacher, and Hero: Image of the Reformer, 1520–1620.* Grand Rapids: Baker, 1999.

Lindberg, Carter. *The European Reformation.* Oxford: Blackwell, 1996.

McGrath, Alister E. *A Life of John Calvin: A Study in the Shaping of Western Culture.* Oxford: Blackwell, 1990.

Muller, Richard A. *The Unaccommodated Calvin: Studies in the Foundation of a Theological Tradition.* New York: Oxford University Press, 2000.

Oberman, Heiko A. *Luther: Man between God and the Devil.* Garden City, N.Y.: Doubleday, 1992.

———. *The Two Reformations: The Journey from the Last Days to the New World.* New Haven: Yale University Press, 2003.

Olin, John C. *Catholic Reform: From Cardinal Ximenes to the Council of Trent.* New York: Fordham University Press, 1990.

Reid, W. Stanford, ed. *John Calvin: His Influence in the Western World.* Grand Rapids: Zondervan, 1982.

Spinka, Matthew. *John Hus: A Biography.* Princeton, N.J.: Princeton University Press, 1968.

Spitz, Lewis W. *The Religious Renaissance of the German Humanists.* Cambridge: Harvard University Press, 1963.

Steinmetz, David C. *Luther in Context.* 2d ed. Grand Rapids: Baker, 2002.

Walzer, Michael. *The Revolution of the Saints: A Study in the Origins of Radical Politics.* Cambridge: Harvard University Press, 1982.

Chapter 2: The English Reformation

Barbour, Hugh. *The Quakers in Puritan England.* New Haven: Yale University Press, 1964.

Bremer, Francis J., ed. *Puritanism: Transatlantic Perspectives on a Seventeenth-Century Anglo-American Faith.* Boston: Northeastern University Press, 1993.

Champion, J. A. I. *The Pillars of Priestcraft Shaken: The Church of England and Its Enemies, 1660–1730.* New York: Cambridge University Press, 1992.

Collinson, Patrick. *The Religion of Protestants: The Church in English Society, 1559–1625.* New York: Oxford University Press, 1984.

Doran, Susan, and Christopher Durston. *Prince, Pastors, and People: The Church and Religion in England, 1529–1689.* New York: Routledge, 1991.

Duffy, Eamon. *The Stripping of the Altars: Traditional Religion in England, 1400–1580.* New Haven: Yale University Press, 1992.

Elton, G. R. *Reform and Reformation: England, 1509–1558.* Cambridge: Harvard University Press, 1979.

Foster, Stephen. *The Long Argument: English Puritanism and the Shaping of New England Culture, 1570–1700.* Chapel Hill: University of North Carolina Press, 1991.

Hibbert, Christopher. *Cavaliers and Roundheads: The English Civil War, 1642–1649.* London: Robert Stewart, 1993.

Hill, Christopher. *Antichrist in Seventeenth-Century England.* New York: Verso, 1991.

———. *The World Turned Upside Down: Radical Ideas during the English Revolution.* New York: Penguin, 1975.

Lake, Peter. *Moderate Puritans and the Elizabethan Church.* Cambridge: Cambridge University Press, 1982.

Lamont, William. *Puritanism and Historical Controversy.* Montreal: McGill-Queens University Press, 1996.

MacCulloch, Diamaid. *Thomas Cranmer: A Life.* New Haven: Yale University Press, 1996.

Marsh, Christopher. *Popular Religion in Sixteenth-Century England: Holding Their Peace.* New York: St. Martin's, 1998.

Poole, Kristen. *Radical Religion from Shakespeare to Milton.* Cambridge: Cambridge University Press, 2000.

Russell, Conrad. *The Causes of the English Civil War.* Oxford: Oxford University Press, 1990.

Ryken, Leland. *Worldly Saints: The Puritans as They Really Were.* Grand Rapids: Zondervan, 1986.

Smith, Lacey Baldwin. *Henry VIII: The Mask of Royalty.* Boston: Houghton Mifflin, 1971.

Solt, Leo F. *Church and State in Early Modern England, 1509–1640.* New York: Oxford University Press, 1990.

Sommerville, C. John. *The Secularization of Early Modern England: From Religious Culture to Religious Faith.* New York: Oxford University Press, 1992.

Trevor-Roper, Hugh. *Catholics, Anglicans, and Puritans: Seventeenth-Century Essays.* Chicago: University of Chicago Press, 1988.

Underwood, Ted Leroy. *Primitivism, Radicalism, and the Lamb's War: The Baptist-Quaker Conflict in Seventeenth-Century England.* New York: Oxford University Press, 1997.

Weddle, Meredith Baldwin. *Walking the Way of Peace: Quaker Pacifism in the Seventeenth Century.* New York: Oxford University Press, 2001.

Zahl, Paul F. M. *Five Women of the English Reformation.* Grand Rapids: Eerdmans, 2001.

Chapter 3: Church Planting on the Atlantic Seaboard

Axtell, James. *Natives and Newcomers: The Cultural Origins of North America.* New York: Oxford University Press, 2001.

Balmer, Randall H. *A Perfect Babel of Confusion: Dutch Religion and English Culture in the Middle Colonies.* New York: Oxford University Press, 1989.

Bond, Edward L. *Damned Souls in a Tobacco Colony: Religion in Seventeenth-Century Virginia.* Macon, Ga.: Mercer University Press, 2000.

Bonomi, Patricia U. *Under the Cope of Heaven: Religion, Society, and Politics in Colonial America.* New York: Oxford University Press, 1986.

Boyer, Paul, and Stephen Nissenbaum. *Salem Possessed: The Social Origins of Witchcraft.* Cambridge: Harvard University Press, 1974.

Breen, Louis A. *Transgressing the Bounds: Subversive Enterprises among the Puritan Elite in Massachusetts.* New York: Oxford University Press, 2001.

Bushman, Richard L. *From Puritan to Yankee: Character and the Social Order in Connecticut, 1690–1765.* Cambridge: Harvard University Press, 1967.

Butler, Jon. *Religion in Colonial America.* New York: Oxford University Press, 2000.

Carlson, Laurie Winn. *A Fever in Salem: A New Interpretation of the New England Witch Trials.* Chicago: Ivan R. Dee, 1999.

Cohen, Charles L. *God's Caress: The Psychology of Puritan Religious Experience.* New York: Oxford University Press, 1986.

Cooper, James F. *Tenacious of Their Liberties: The Congregationalists in Colonial Massachusetts.* New York: Oxford University Press, 2002.

Gaustad, Edwin S. *Liberty of Conscience: Roger Williams in America.* Grand Rapids: Eerdmans, 1991.

Gildrie, Richard P. *The Profane, the Civil, and the Godly: The Reformation of Manners in Orthodox New England, 1679–1749.* University Park, Pa.: Pennsylvania State University Press, 1994.

Hall, David D. *Worlds of Wonders, Days of Judgment: Popular Religious Belief in Early New England.* New York: Knopf, 1989.

Hall, Michael G. *The Last American Puritan: The Life of Increase Mather.* Middletown, Conn.: Wesleyan University Press, 1988.

Hall, Timothy L. *Separating Church and State: Roger Williams and Religious Liberty.* Urbana, Ill.: University of Illinois Press, 1998.

Hambrick-Stowe, Charles E. *The Practice of Piety: Puritan Devotional Discipline in Seventeenth-Century New England.* Chapel Hill: University of North Carolina Press, 1982.

Holifield, E. Brooks. *Era of Persuasion: American Thought and Culture, 1521–1680.* New York: Twayne, 1989.

Knight, Janice. *Orthodoxies in Massachusetts: Rereading American Puritanism.* Cambridge: Harvard University Press, 1997.

Lindenauer, Leslie J. *Piety and Power: Gender and Religious Culture in the American Colonies, 1630–1700.* New York: Routledge, 2002.

Longenecker, Stephen L. *Piety and Tolerance: Pennsylvania German Religion, 1700–1850.* Blue Ridge Summit, Pa.: Scarecrow, 1994.

Marietta, Jack D. *The Reformation of American Quakerism, 1748–1783.* Philadelphia: University of Pennsylvania Press, 1984.

Middlekauff, Robert. *The Mathers: Three Generations of Puritan Intellectuals, 1596–1728.* New York: Oxford University Press, 1971.

Miller, Perry G. *Errand into the Wilderness.* Cambridge: Harvard University Press, 1956.

Morgan, Edmund S. *The Puritan Dilemma: The Story of John Winthrop.* Boston: Little, Brown, 1958.

———. *Visible Saints: The History of a Puritan Idea.* New York: New York University Press, 1963.

Nelson, John K. *A Blessed Company: Parishes, Parsons, and Parishioners in Anglican Virginia, 1690–1775.* Chapel Hill: University of North Carolina Press, 2002.

Norton, Mary Beth. *In the Devil's Snare: The Salem Witchcraft Crisis of 1692.* New York: Knopf, 2002.

Pestana, Carla Gardina. *Quakers and Baptists in Colonial Massachusetts.* New York: Cambridge University Press, 1991.

Pointer, Richard W. *Protestant Pluralism and the New York Experience.* Bloomington, Ind.: Indiana University Press, 1988.

Porterfield, Amanda. *Female Piety in Puritan New England.* New York: Oxford University Press, 1992.

Roeber, A. G. *Palatines, Liberty, and Property: German Lutherans in Colonial British America.* Baltimore: Johns Hopkins University Press, 1993.

Scherer, Lester B. *Slavery and the Churches in Early America, 1619–1819.* Grand Rapids: Eerdmans, 1975.

Schwartz, Sally. *"A Mixed Multitude": The Struggle for Toleration in Colonial Pennsylvania.* New York: New York University Press, 1987.

Stout, Harry S. *The New England Soul: Preaching and Religious Culture in Colonial New England.* New York: Oxford University Press, 1986.

Winship, Michael F. *Making Heretics: Militant Protestantism and Free Grace in Massachusetts, 1636–1641.* Princeton, N.J.: Princeton University Press, 2002.

Chapter 4: Rekindling the Spiritual Vision

Bushman, Richard L., ed. *The Great Awakening: Documents on the Revival of Religion, 1740–1745.* New York: Atheneum, 1969.

Butler, Jon. *Awash in a Sea of Faith: Christianizing the American People.* Cambridge: Harvard University Press, 1992.

Cairns, Earle E. *An Endless Line of Splendor: Revivals and Their Leaders from the Great Awakening to the Present.* Wheaton: Tyndale, 1986.

Conforti, Joseph A. *Jonathan Edwards, Religious Tradition, and American Culture.* Chapel Hill: University of North Carolina Press, 1995.

Crawford, Michael. *Seasons of Grace: Colonial New England's Revival Tradition in Its British Context.* New York: Oxford University Press, 1991.

Gaustad, Edwin S. *The Great Awakening in New England.* Chicago: Quadrangle, 1968.

Goen, Clarence C. *Revivalism and Separatism in New England: Strict Congregationalists and Separate Baptists in the Great Awakening.* New York: Yale University Press, 1962.

Hall, Timothy D. *Contested Boundaries: Itinerancy and the Reshaping of the Colonial American Religious World.* Durham, N.C.: Duke University Press, 1994.

Hatch, Nathan O., and Harry S. Stout, eds. *Jonathan Edwards and the American Experience.* New York: Oxford University Press, 1988.

Heimert, Alan E. *Religion and the American Mind from the Great Awakening to the Revolution.* Cambridge: Harvard University Press, 1966.

Lambert, Frank. *Inventing the "Great Awakening."* Princeton, N.J.: Princeton University Press, 1999.

———. *"Pedlar in Divinity": George Whitefield and the Transatlantic Revivals, 1737–1770.* Princeton, N.J.: Princeton University Press, 1994.

Lovelace, Richard F. *The American Pietism of Cotton Mather: Origins of American Evangelicalism.* Grand Rapids: Eerdmans, 1979.

Marsden, George M. *Jonathan Edwards: A Life.* New Haven: Yale University Press, 2003.

McDermott, Gerald. *Jonathan Edwards Confronts the Gods: Christian Theology, Enlightenment Religion, and Non-Christian Faiths.* New York: Oxford University Press, 2000.

———. *One Holy and Happy Society: The Public Theology of Jonathan Edwards.* University Park, Pa.: Penn State University Press, 1994.

Payne, Rodger. *The Self and the Sacred: Conversion and Autobiography in Early American Protestantism.* Knoxville: University of Tennessee Press, 1998.

Schmidt, Leigh Eric. *Hearing Things: Religion, Illusion, and the American Enlightenment.* Cambridge: Harvard University Press, 2000.

———. *Holy Fairs: Scottish Communions and American Revivals in the Early Modern Period.* Princeton, N.J.: Princeton University Press, 1989.

Seeman, Erik. *Pious Persuasions: Laity and Clergy in Eighteenth-Century New England.* Baltimore: Johns Hopkins University Press, 1999.

Stout, Harry S. *The Divine Dramatist: George Whitefield and the Rise of Modern Evangelicalism.* Grand Rapids: Eerdmans, 1991.

Tanis, James R. *Dutch Calvinistic Pietism in the Middle Colonies: A Study in the Life of Theodorus Jacobus Frelinghuysen.* Leiden: Martinus Nijhof, 1967.

Tomkins, Stephen. *John Wesley: A Biography.* Grand Rapids: Eerdmans, 2003.

Westerkamp, Marilyn J. *Triumph of the Laity: Scots-Irish Piety and the Great Awakening, 1625–1760.* New York: Oxford University Press, 1988.

Wilson, Renate. *Pious Traders in Medicine: A German Pharmaceutical Network in Eighteenth-Century North America.* University Park, Pa.: Pennsylvania State University Press, 2000.

Wilson, Robert J., III. *The Benevolent Deity: Ebenezer Gay and the Rise of Rational Religion in New England, 1696–1787.* Philadelphia: University of Pennsylvania Press, 1984.

Zakai, Avihu. *Jonathan Edward's Philosophy of History: The Reenchantment of the World in the Age of Enlightenment.* Princeton, N.J.: Princeton University Press, 2003.

Chapter 5: The Church in the Midst of Revolution

Aldridge, Owen. *Benjamin Franklin and Nature's God.* Durham, N.C.: Duke University Press, 1967.

Bailyn, Bernard. *The Ideological Origins of the American Revolution.* Cambridge: Harvard University Press, 1967.

Baldwin, Alice M. *The New England Clergy and the American Revolution.* Durham, N.C.: Duke University Press, 1988.

Bradley, James E., and Dale K. Van Kley. *Religion and Politics in Enlightenment Europe.* Notre Dame, Ind.: University of Notre Dame Press, 2002.

Davis, David Brion. *The Problem of Slavery in the Age of Revolution, 1770–1823.* Ithaca, N.Y.: Cornell University Press, 1975.

Davis, Derek H. *Religion and the Continental Congress, 1774–1789: Contributions to Original Intent.* New York: Oxford University Press, 2000.

Doll, Peter M. *Revolution, Religion, and National Identity: Imperial Anglicanism in British North America, 1745–1795.* Madison, N.J.: Fairleigh-Dickinson, 2000.

Gaustad, Edwin J. *Sworn on the Altar of God: A Religious Biography of Thomas Jefferson.* Grand Rapids: Eerdmans, 2001.

Griffin, Keith. *Revolution and Religion: The American Revolutionary War and the Reformed Clergy.* New York: Paragon House, 1994.

Hanson, Charles B. *Necessary Virtue: The Pragmatic Origins of Religious Liberty in New England.* Charlottesville, Va.: University of Virginia Press, 1998.

Hatch, Nathan O. *The Sacred Cause of Liberty: Republican Thought and the Millennium in Revolutionary New England.* New Haven: Yale University Press, 1977.

Hoffman, Ronald, ed. *Religion in a Revolutionary Age.* Charlottesville, Va.: University of Virginia Press, 1994.

Hutson, James H., ed. *Religion and the New Republic: Faith in the Founding of America.* New York: Rowman & Littlefield, 2000.

Juster, Susan. *Disorderly Women: Sexual Politics and Evangelicalism in Revolutionary New England.* Ithaca, N.Y.: Cornell University Press, 1994.

MacMaster, Richard K., ed. *Conscience in Crisis: Mennonites and Other Peace Churches in America, 1739–1789.* Scottdale, Pa.: Herald, 1979.

Marini, Stephen A. *Radical Sects in Revolutionary New England.* Cambridge: Harvard University Press, 1982.

May, Henry F. *The Enlightenment in America.* New York: Oxford University Press, 1976.

McLoughlin, William G. *Isaac Backus and the American Pietistic Tradition.* Boston: Little, Brown, 1967.

Noll, Mark A. *Christians in the American Revolution.* Grand Rapids: Eerdmans, 1976.

Rhoden, Nancy L. *Revolutionary Anglicanism: The Colonial Church of England during the American Revolution.* New York: New York University Press, 1999.

Smith, Page. *Religious Origins of the American Revolution.* Missoula, Mont.: Scholars Press, 1976.

Sommer, Elizabeth. *Serving Two Masters: Moravian Brethren in Germany and North Carolina, 1727–1801.* Lexington: University Press of Kentucky, 2000.

Valeri, Mark. *Law and Providence in Joseph Bellamy's New England: The Origins of the New Divinity in Revolutionary America.* New York: Oxford University Press, 1994.

Chapter 6: New Churches for a New Society

Andrews, Dee E. *The Methodists and Revolutionary America, 1760–1800: The Shaping of an Evangelical Culture.* Princeton, N.J.: Princeton University Press, 2000.

Curry, Thomas J. *The First Freedoms: Church and State in America to the Passage of the First Amendment.* New York: Oxford University Press, 1986.

Dreisbach, Daniel L., ed. *Religion and Politics in the Early Republic: Jasper Adams and the Church-State Debate.* Lexington: University Press of Kentucky, 1996.

George, Carol V. R. *Segregated Sabbaths: Richard Allen and the Rise of Independent Black Churches, 1760–1840.* New York: Oxford University Press, 1973.

Hatch, Nathan. *The Democratization of American Christianity.* New Haven: Yale University Press, 1989.

Howe, Daniel Walker. *Making the American Self: Jonathan Edwards to Abraham Lincoln.* Cambridge: Harvard University Press, 1997.

Kling, David. *A Field of Divine Wonders: The New Divinity and Village Revivals in North-western Connecticut, 1792–1822.* University Park, Pa.: Pennsylvania State University Press, 1993.

Kuehne, Dale S. *Massachusetts Congregationalist Political Thought, 1760–1790: The Design of Heaven.* Columbia, Mo.: University of Missouri Press, 1996.

Lambert, Frank. *The Founding Fathers and the Place of Religion in America.* Princeton, N.J.: Princeton University Press, 2003.

Longenecker, Stephen L. *Shenandoah Religion: Outsiders and the Mainstream, 1716–1865.* Waco: Baylor University Press, 2002.

Lyerly, Cynthia Lyn. *Methodism and the Southern Mind.* New York: Oxford University Press, 1998.

Miller, Perry. *The Life of the Mind in America: From the Revolution to the Civil War.* New York: Harcourt, Brace and World, 1965.

Moore, R. Laurence. *Selling God: American Religion in the Marketplace of Culture.* New York: Oxford University Press, 1994.

Nagel, Paul C. *This Sacred Trust: American Nationality, 1798–1898.* New York: Oxford University Press, 1971.

Niebuhr, H. Richard. *The Social Sources of Denominationalism.* New York: Henry Holt, 1929.

Noll, Mark A. *America's God: From Jonathan Edwards to Abraham Lincoln.* New York: Oxford University Press, 2002.

———. *Princeton and the Republic, 1768–1822: The Search for a Christian Enlightenment in the Era of Samuel Stanhope Smith.* Princeton, N.J.: Princeton University Press, 1989.

Raboteau, Albert J. *Slave Religion: The "Invisible Institution" in the Antebellum South.* New York: Oxford University Press, 1978.

Reid-Maroney, Nina. *Philadelphia's Enlightenment, 1740–1800: Kingdom of Christ, Empire of Reason.* Westport, Conn.: Greenwood, 2001.

Rohrer, James R. *Keepers of the Covenant: Frontier Missions and the Decline of Congregational-ism, 1774–1818.* New York: Oxford University Press, 1995.

Sailant, John. *Black Puritan, Black Republican: The Life and Thought of Lemuel Haynes, 1753–1833.* New York: Oxford University Press, 2002.

Sassi, Jonathan D. *A Republic of Righteousness: The Public Christianity of the Post-Revolutionary New England Clergy.* New York: Oxford University Press, 2001.

Stokes, Anson Phelps. *Church and State in the United States.* New York: Harper, 1950.

Sutton, William R. *Journeymen for Jesus: Evangelical Artisans Confront Capitalism in Jacksonian Baltimore.* University Park, Pa.: Pennsylvania State University Press, 1998.

West, John G. *The Politics of Revelation and Reason: Religion and Civic Life in the New Nation.* Lawrence, Kans.: University of Kansas Press, 1996.

Wiebe, Robert. *The Opening of American Society: From the Adoption of the Constitution to the Era of Disunion.* New York: Knopf, 1984.

Witte, John. *Religion and the American Constitutional Experiment: Essential Rights and Liberties.* Boulder, Colo.: Westview, 2000.

Chapter 7: The Second Awakening

Barkun, Michael. *Crucible of the Millennium: The Burned-Over District of New York in the 1840s.* Syracuse: Syracuse University Press, 1986.

Bilhartz, Terry D. *Urban Religion and the Second Great Awakening: Church and Society in Early National Baltimore.* Madison, N.J.: Fairleigh-Dickinson, 1986.

Boles, John B. *The Great Revival: Beginnings of the Bible Belt.* Lexington: University Press of Kentucky, 1996.

Brekus, Catherine. *Strangers and Pilgrims: Female Preaching in America, 1740–1845.* Chapel Hill: University of North Carolina Press, 1998.

Bruce, Dickson D. *And They All Sang Hallelujah: Plain-Folk Camp-Meeting Religion, 1800–1845.* Knoxville: University of Tennessee Press, 1981.

Carwardine, Richard. *Transatlantic Revivalism: Popular Evangelicalism in Britain and America, 1790–1865.* Westport, Conn.: Greenwood, 1978.

Conkin, Paul V. *Cane Ridge: America's Pentecost.* Madison: University of Wisconsin Press, 1990.

Cross, Whitney R. *The Burned-Over District: The Social and Intellectual History of Enthusiastic Religion in Western New York: 1800–1850.* Ithaca, N.Y.: Cornell University Press, 1950.

Eslinger, Ellen. *Citizens of Zion: The Social Origins of Camp Meeting Revivalism.* Knoxville: University of Tennessee Press, 1999.

Hambrick-Stowe, Charles E. *Charles G. Finney and the Spirit of American Evangelicalism.* Grand Rapids: Eerdmans, 1996.

Hardman, Keith J. *Charles Grandison Finney, 1792–1875.* Syracuse: Syracuse University Press, 1987.

———. *Seasons of Refreshing: Evangelism and Revivals in America.* Grand Rapids: Baker, 1994.

Hyerman, Christine Leigh. *Southern Cross: The Beginnings of the Bible Belt.* New York: Knopf, 1997.

Johnson, Charles A. *The Frontier Camp Meeting: Religion's Harvest Time.* Dallas: Southern Methodist University Press, 1955.

Johnson, Curtis. *Islands of Holiness: Rural Religion in Upstate New York, 1790–1860.* Ithaca, N.Y.: Cornell University Press, 1989.

Long, Kathryn Teresa. *The Revival of 1857–58: Interpreting an American Religious Awakening.* New York: Oxford University Press, 1998.

McLoughlin, William G. *Modern Revivalism: Charles Grandison Finney to Billy Graham.* New York: Ronald, 1959.

Miyakawa, T. Scott. *Protestants and Pioneers: Individualism and Conformity on the American Frontier.* Chicago: University of Chicago Press, 1964.

Mulder, Philip N. *A Controversial Spirit: Evangelical Awakenings in the South.* New York: Oxford University Press, 2002.

Posey, Walter B. *Frontier Mission: A History of Religion West of the Southern Appalachians to 1861.* Lexington: University Press of Kentucky, 1966.

Richey, Russell E. *Early American Methodism.* Bloomington, Ind.: Indiana University Press, 1991.

Rosell, Garth M., and Richard A. G. Dupuis, eds. *The Original Memoirs of Charles G. Finney.* Grand Rapids: Zondervan, 2002.

Sweeney, Douglas A. *Nathaniel Taylor, New Haven Theology, and the Legacy of Jonathan Edwards.* New York: Oxford University Press, 2002.

Weisberger, Bernard A. *They Gathered at the River: The Story of the Great Revivalists and Their Impact upon Religion in America.* Boston: Little, Brown, 1958.

Wigger, John N. *Taking Heaven by Storm: Methodism and the Rise of Popular Christianity in America.* New York: Oxford University Press, 1997.

Chapter 8: Envisioning a Christian Social Order

Andrews, John A. *From Revivals to Removal: Jeremiah Evarts, the Cherokee Nation, and the Search for the American Soul.* Athens, Ga.: University of Georgia Press, 1992.

Bodo, John R. *The Protestant Clergy and Public Issues, 1812–1845.* Princeton, N.J.: Princeton University Press, 1954.

Bowden, Henry Warner. *American Indians and Christian Missions.* Chicago: University of Chicago Press, 1981.

Caskey, Marie. *Chariot of Fire: Religion and the Beecher Family.* New Haven: Yale University Press, 1978.

Cott, Nancy R. *The Bonds of Womanhood: "Women's Sphere" in New England, 1780–1835.* 2d ed. New Haven: Yale University Press, 1997.

Dayton, Donald W. *Discovering an Evangelical Heritage.* New York: Harper, 1976.

Douglas, Ann. *The Feminization of American Culture.* New York: Knopf, 1977.

Essig, James D. *The Bonds of Wickedness: American Evangelicals against Slavery.* Philadelphia: Temple University Press, 1982.

Foster, Charles I. *An Errand of Mercy: The Evangelical United Front, 1790–1837.* Chapel Hill: University of North Carolina Press, 1954.

Frey, Sylvia R., and Betty Wood. *Come Shouting to Zion: African-American Protestantism in the American South and British Caribbean to 1830.* Chapel Hill: University of North Carolina Press, 1998.

Hanley, Mark Y. *Beyond a Christian Commonwealth: The Protestant Quarrel with the American Republic, 1830–1860.* Chapel Hill: University of North Carolina Press, 1994.

Hardesty, Nancy A. *Women Called to Witness: Evangelical Feminism in the Nineteenth Century.* 2d ed. Knoxville: University of Tennessee Press, 1999.

Hirrel, Leo P. *Children of Wrath: New School Calvinism and Antebellum Reform.* Lexington: University Press of Kentucky, 1998.

Kraditor, Aileen. *Means and Ends in American Abolitionism: Garrison and His Critics on Strategy and Facts, 1834–1850.* New York: Pantheon, 1969.

Lazerow, Jama. *Religion and the Working Class in Antebellum America.* Washington, D.C.: Smithsonian Institution Press, 1995.

Lesick, Lawrence T. *The Lane Rebels: Evangelicalism and Antislavery in Antebellum America.* Metuchen, N.J.: Scarecrow, 1980.

Loveland, Anne C. *Southern Evangelicals and the Social Order, 1800–1860.* Baton Rouge: Louisiana State University Press, 1980.

Mathews, Donald G. *Slavery and Methodism: A Chapter in American Morality, 1780–1845.* Princeton, N.J.: Princeton University Press, 1965.

McKivigan, John R., and Mitchell Snay, eds. *Religion and the Antebellum Debate Over Slavery.* Athens, Ga.: University of Georgia Press, 1998.

McLoughlin, William G. *Champions of the Cherokees: Evan and John B. Jones.* Princeton, N.J.: Princeton University Press, 1989.

———. *Revivals, Awakenings, and Reform, 1607–1977.* Chicago: University of Chicago Press, 1978.

Noll, Mark A., ed. *God and Mammon: Protestants, Money, and the Market.* New York: Oxford University Press, 2002.

Smith, Timothy L. *Revivalism and Social Reform: American Protestantism in Mid-Nineteenth-Century America.* Baltimore: Johns Hopkins University Press, 1980.

Speicher, Anna M. *The Religious World of Antislavery Women: Spirituality in the Lives of Five Abolitionist Lecturers.* Syracuse: Syracuse University Press, 2000.

Strong, Douglas M. *Perfectionist Politics: Abolitionism and the Religious Tensions of American Democracy.* Syracuse: Syracuse University Press, 1999.

Van Broekhoven, Deborah B. *The Devotion of These Women: Rhode Island in the Antislavery Network.* Amherst: University of Massachusetts Press, 2002.

Whelchel, Love Henry, Jr. *Hell without Fire: Conversion in Slave Religion and the Founding of the C.M.E. Church.* Nashville: Abingdon, 2002.

Yellin, Jean Fagan, and John C. Van Horne. *The Abolitionist Sisterhood: Women's Political Culture in Antebellum America.* Ithaca, N.Y.: Cornell University Press, 1994.

Young, Jeffrey Robert. *Domesticating Slavery: The Master Class in Georgia and South Carolina, 1670–1837.* Chapel Hill: University of North Carolina Press, 1999.

Chapter 9: Diversity in Religious Life

Barlow, Philip L. *Mormons and the Bible: The Place of the Latter-day Saints in American Religion.* New York: Oxford University Press, 1991.

Barnes, Howard A. *Horace Bushnell and the Virtuous Republic.* Metuchen, N.J.: Scarecrow, 1991.

Bozeman, T. D. *Protestants and the Age of Science: The Baconian Ideal and Antebellum American Religious Thought.* Chapel Hill: University of North Carolina Press, 1977.

Bratt, James D. *Dutch Calvinism in Modern America: A History of a Conservative Subculture.* Grand Rapids: Eerdmans, 1984.

Bressler, Ann Lee. *The Universalist Movement in America, 1770–1880.* New York: Oxford University Press, 2001.

Butler, Diana Hochstedt. *Standing against the Whirlwind: Evangelical Episcopalians in Nineteenth-Century America.* New York: Oxford University Press, 1994.

Conklin, Paul K. *The Uneasy Center: Reformed Christianity in Antebellum America.* Chapel Hill: University of North Carolina Press, 1994.

Doan, Ruth Alden. *The Miller Heresy, Millennialism, and American Culture.* Philadelphia: Temple University Press, 1987.

Dolan, Jay P. *The Immigrant Church: New York's Irish and German Catholics, 1815–1865.* Baltimore: Johns Hopkins University Press, 1975.

Franchot, Jenny. *Roads to Rome: The Antebellum Protestant Encounter with Catholicism.* Berkeley: University of California Press, 1994.

Givens, Terry L. *By the Hand of Mormon: The American Scripture That Launched a New World Religion.* New York: Oxford University Press, 2002.

Hamm, Thomas. *The Transformation of American Quakerism: Orthodox Friends, 1800–1907.* Bloomington, Ind.: Indiana University Press, 1992.

Hughes, Richard T. *Reviving the Ancient Faith: The Story of Churches of Christ in America.* Grand Rapids: Eerdmans, 1996.

Hughes, Richard T., and C. Leonard Allen. *Illusions of Innocence: Protestant Primitivism in America, 1630–1875.* Chicago: University of Chicago Press, 1985.

Hutchison, William R. *The Transcendentalist Ministers: Church Reform in the New England Renaissance.* New Haven: Yale University Press, 1959.

Land, Gary, ed. *Adventism in America: A History.* Grand Rapids: Eerdmans, 1986.

Marsden, George. *The Evangelical Mind and the New School Presbyterian Experience: A Case Study of Thought and Theology in Nineteenth-Century America.* New Haven: Yale University Press, 1970.

Moore, R. Laurence. *Religious Outsiders and the Making of Americans.* New York: Oxford University Press, 1986.

Morgan, David. *Adventism and the American Republic.* Knoxville: University of Tennessee Press, 2001.

Mullin, Robert Bruce. *The Puritan as Yankee: A Life of Horace Bushnell.* Grand Rapids: Eerdmans, 2002.

Numbers, Ronald. *Prophetess of Health: Ellen G. White and the Origins of Seventh-day Adventist Health Reform.* 2d ed. Knoxville: University of Tennessee Press, 1992.

Rankin, Richard. *Ambivalent Churches and Evangelical Churchmen: The Religion of the Episcopal Elite in North Carolina, 1800–1860.* Columbia, S.C.: University of South Carolina Press, 1993.

Shipps, Jan. *Mormonism: The Story of a New Religious Tradition.* Urbana, Ill.: University of Illinois Press, 1985.

Stein, Stephen. *The Shaker Experience in America: A History of the United Society of Believers.* New Haven: Yale University Press, 1992.

Swierenga, Robert P., and Elton J. Bruins. *Family Quarrels in the Dutch Reformed Church of the Nineteenth Century.* Grand Rapids: Eerdmans, 2000.

Winn, Kenneth H. *Exiles in a Land of Liberty: Mormons in America, 1830–1846.* Chapel Hill: University of North Carolina Press, 1989.

Wright, Conrad. *The Beginnings of Unitarianism in America.* Boston: Beacon, 1955.

Chapter 10: Following the Faith in a Divided Nation

Aamodt, Terrie. *Righteous Armies, Holy Cause: Apocalyptic Imagery and the Civil War.* Macon, Ga.: Mercer University Press, 2002.

Boles, John B. *Masters and Slaves in the House of the Lord: Race and Religion in the American South, 1740–1870.* Lexington: University Press of Kentucky, 1988.

Carwardine, Richard. *Evangelicals and Politics in Antebellum America.* New Haven: Yale University Press, 1993.

Davis, David Brion. *In the Image of God: Religion, Moral Values, and Our Heritage of Slavery.* New Haven: Yale University Press, 2002.

Diggins, John Patrick. *On Hallowed Ground: Abraham Lincoln and the Foundations of American History.* New Haven: Yale University Press, 2000.

Douglass-Chin, Richard J. *Preacher Woman Sings the Blues: The Autobiographies of Nineteenth-Century African-American Evangelists.* Columbia, Mo.: University of Missouri Press, 2001.

Fredrickson, George M. *The Inner Civil War: Northern Intellectuals and the Crisis of the Union.* New York: Harper, 1965.

Fuller, A. James. *Chaplain to the Confederacy: Basil Manly and Baptist Life in the Old South.* Baton Rouge: University of Louisiana Press, 2000.

Genovese, Eugene D. *A Consuming Fire: The Fall of the Confederacy in the Mind of the White Christian South.* Athens, Ga.: University of Georgia Press, 1999.

Goen, Clarence C. *Broken Churches, Broken Nation: Denominational Schisms and the Coming of the Civil War.* Macon, Ga.: Mercer University Press, 1985.

Guelzo, Allen C. *Abraham Lincoln: Redeemer President.* Grand Rapids: Eerdmans, 1999.

Harvey, Paul. *Redeeming the South: Religious Cultures and Racial Identities among Southern Baptists, 1865–1925.* Chapel Hill: University of North Carolina Press, 1997.

Haynes, Stephen R. *Noah's Curse: The Biblical Justification of Slavery.* New York: Oxford University Press, 2001.

Hildebrand, Reginald. *The Times Were Strange and Stirring: Methodist Preachers and the Crisis of Emancipation.* Durham, N.C.: Duke University Press, 1995.

Jacobs, Donald M. *Courage and Conscience: Black and White Abolitionists in Boston.* Bloomington, Ind.: Indiana University Press, 1992.

Johnson, Curtis. *Redeeming America: Evangelicals and the Road to the Civil War.* Chicago: I. R. Dee, 1993.

Mathews, Donald G. *Religion in the Old South.* Chicago: University of Chicago Press, 1979.

McMillen, Sally G. *To Raise Up the South: Sunday Schools in Black and White Churches, 1865–1915.* Baton Rouge: Louisiana State University Press, 2001.

Miller, Randall M., Harry S. Stout, and Charles Reagan Wilson, eds. *Religion and the American Civil War.* New York: Oxford University Press, 1998.

Montgomery, William E. *Under Their Own Vine and Fig Tree: The African-American Church in the South, 1865–1900.* Baton Rouge: Louisiana State University Press, 1993.

Moorhead, James. *American Apocalypse: Yankee Protestants and the Civil War.* New Haven: Yale University Press, 1978.

Neely, Mark E., Jr. *The Last Best Hope of Earth: Abraham Lincoln and the Promise of America.* Cambridge: Harvard University Press, 1993.

Shattuck, Gardiner H., Jr. *Episcopalians and Race: Civil War to Civil Rights.* Lexington: University of Kentucky Press, 2000.

———. *A Shield and Hiding Place: The Religious Life of the Civil War Armies.* Macon, Ga.: Mercer University Press, 1987.

Snay, Mitchell. *Gospel of Disunion: Religion and Separatism in the Antebellum South.* New York: Cambridge University Press, 1993.

Stowell, Daniel W. *Rebuilding Zion: The Religious Reconstruction of the South, 1863–1877.* New York: Oxford University Press, 1998.

White, Ronald C. *Lincoln's Greatest Speech: The Second Inaugural.* New York: Simon & Schuster, 2002.

Wilson, Charles Reagan. *Baptized in Blood: The Religion of the Lost Cause, 1865–1920.* Athens, Ga.: University of Georgia Press, 1980.

Woodworth, Steven E. *While God Is Marching On: The Religious World of Civil War Soldiers.* Lawrence, Kans.: University of Kansas Press, 2001.

Yee, Shirley J. *Black Women Abolitionists: A Study in Activism, 1828–1860.* Knoxville: University of Tennessee Press, 1992.

Chapter 11: Evangelical Initiatives

Abell, Tony D. *Better Felt Than Said: The Holiness-Pentecostal Experience in Southern Appalachia.* Waco: Baylor University Press, 1998.

Dayton, Donald W. *Theological Roots of Pentecostalism.* Peabody, Mass.: Hendrickson, 1987.

Dieter, Melvin E. *The Holiness Revival of the Nineteenth Century.* Metuchen, N.J.: Scarecrow, 1980.

Dorsett, Lyle W. *A Passion for Souls: The Life of D. L. Moody.* Chicago: Moody, 1997.

Eason, Andrew M. *Women in God's Army: Gender and Equality in the Early Salvation Army.* Waterloo, Ont.: Wilfrid Laurier University Press, 2003.

Evensen, Bruce J. *God's Man for the Gilded Age: D. L. Moody and the Rise of Modern Evangelism.* New York: Oxford University Press, 2003.

Findlay, James F. *Dwight L. Moody: American Evangelist, 1837–1899.* Chicago: University of Chicago Press, 1969.

Frank, Douglas W. *Less Than Conquerors: How Evangelicals Entered the Twentieth Century.* Grand Rapids: Eerdmans, 1986.

Grammer, Elizabeth Elkin. *Some Wild Visions: Autobiographies by Female Itinerant Evangelists in Nineteenth-Century America.* New York: Oxford University Press, 2002.

Green, Roger J. *Catherine Booth.* Grand Rapids: Baker, 1996.

Handy, Robert T. *We Witness Together: A History of Cooperative Home Missions.* New York: Friendship, 1956.

Harrell, David Edwin. *All Things Are Possible: The Healing and Charismatic Revivals in Modern America.* Bloomington, Ind.: Indiana University Press, 1975.

Hobbs, June Hadden. *"I Sing for I Cannot Be Silent": The Feminization of American Hymnody, 1870–1920.* Pittsburgh: University of Pittsburgh Press, 1997.

Kraybill, Donald B., and Carl D. Bowman. *On the Backroad to Heaven: Old Order Hutterites, Mennonites, Amish, and Brethren.* Baltimore: Johns Hopkins University Press, 2001.

Leonard, Bill J., ed. *Christianity in Appalachia: Profiles in Regional Pluralism.* Knoxville: University of Tennessee Press, 1995.

McKinley, Edward H. *Marching to Glory: The History of the Salvation Army in the United States, 1880–1992.* 2d ed. Grand Rapids: Eerdmans, 1995.

McLoughlin, William G. *Modern Revivalism: Charles Grandison Finney to Billy Graham.* New York: Ronald, 1959.

Minnix, Kathleen. *Laughter in the Amen Corner: The Life of Evangelist Sam Jones.* Athens, Ga.: University of Georgia Press, 1993.

Ostrander, Richard. *The Life of Prayer in a World of Science: Protestants, Prayer, and American Culture, 1870–1930.* New York: Oxford University Press, 2000.

Rosell, Garth M., ed. *Communicating the Faith: The Preaching of D. L. Moody.* Peabody, Mass.: Hendrickson, 1999.

Schneider, A. Gregory. *The Way of the Cross Leads Home: The Domestication of American Methodism.* Bloomington, Ind.: Indiana University Press, 1993.

Sizer, Sandra S. *Gospel Hymns and Social Religion: The Rhetoric of Nineteenth-Century Revivalism.* Philadelphia: Temple University Press, 1978.

Smith, Timothy L. *Called unto Holiness; The Story of the Nazarenes: The Formative Years.* Kansas City: Nazarene Publishing House, 1962.

Stanley, Susie Cunningham. *Feminist Pillar of Fire: The Life of Alma White.* Cleveland: Pilgrim Press, 1993.

Taiz, Lillian. *Hallelujah Lads and Lasses: Remaking the Salvation Army in America, 1880–1930.* Chapel Hill: University of North Carolina Press, 2001.

White, Charles E. *The Beauty of Holiness: Phoebe Palmer as Theologian Revivalist and Humanitarian.* Grand Rapids: Zondervan, 1986.

Winston, Diane. *Red-Hot and Righteous: The Urban Religion of the Salvation Army.* Cambridge: Harvard University Press, 1999.

Chapter 12: The Old Religion Reacts to New Ideas

Bannister, Robert C. *Social Darwinism: Science and Myth in Anglo-American Social Thought.* Philadelphia: Temple University Press, 1979.

Bendroth, Margaret. *Fundamentalism and Gender, 1875–Present.* New Haven: Yale University Press, 1995.

Berkhofer, Robert F., Jr. *Salvation and the Savage: An Analysis of Protestant Missions and American Indian Response, 1787–1862.* Westport, Conn.: Greenwood, 1977.

Blumhofer, Edith L. *Restoring the Faith: The Assemblies of God, Pentecostalism, and American Culture.* Urbana, Ill.: University of Illinois Press, 1993.

Blumhofer, Edith, Russell Spittler, and Grant Wacker, eds. *Pentecostal Currents in American Protestantism.* Urbana, Ill.: University of Illinois Press, 1999.

Clark, Michael D. *Worldly Theologians: The Persistence of Religion in Nineteenth-Century American Thought.* Lanham, Md.: University Press of America, 1982.

Dorrien, Gary. *The Making of American Liberal Theology: Imagining Progressive Religion, 1805–1900.* Louisville: Westminster John Knox, 2001.

Goff, James R., Jr. *Fields White unto Harvest: Charles F. Parham and the Missionary Origin of Pentecostalism.* Fayetteville, Ark.: University of Arkansas Press, 1988.

Goff, James R., Jr., and Grant Wacker, eds. *Portraits of a Generation: Early Pentecostal Leaders.* Fayetteville, Ark.: University of Arkansas Press, 2002.

Goldberg, Steven. *Seduced by Science: How American Religion Has Lost Its Way.* New York: New York University Press, 1999.

Graham, Stephen R. *Cosmos in the Chaos: Philip Schaff's Interpretation of Nineteenth-Century American Religion.* Grand Rapids: Eerdmans, 1995.

Hutchison, William R. *The Modernist Impulse in American Protestantism.* Cambridge: Harvard University Press, 1976.

Jodock, Darrell, ed. *Catholicism Contending with Modernity: Roman Catholic Modernism and Anti-Modernism in Historical Context.* New York: Cambridge University Press, 2000.

Kennedy, Rick, ed. *Aristotelian and Cartesian Logic at Harvard.* Charlottesville, Va.: University of Virginia Press, 1995.

Livingstone, David N. *Darwin's Forgotten Defenders: The Encounter between Evangelical Theology and Evolutionary Thought.* Grand Rapids: Eerdmans, 1987.

Marsden, George M. *Fundamentalism and American Culture: The Shaping of Twentieth-Century Evangelicalism, 1870–1925.* New York: Oxford University Press, 1980.

———. *The Soul of the American University: From Protestant Establishment to Established Nonbelief.* New York: Oxford University Press, 1994.

Massa, Mark S. *Charles Augustus Briggs and the Crisis of Historical Criticism.* Minneapolis: Fortress, 1990.

Moore, James R. *The Post-Darwinian Controversies: A Study of the Protestant Struggle to Come to Terms with Darwin in Great Britain and America, 1870–1900.* Cambridge: Cambridge University Press, 1979.

Moorhead, James H. *World without End: Mainstream American Protestant Visions of the Last Things, 1880–1925.* Bloomington, Ind.: Indiana University Press, 1999.

Numbers, Ronald L. *Darwinism Comes to America.* Cambridge: Harvard University Press, 1998.

Numbers, Ronald L., and John Stenhouse, eds. *Disseminating Darwinism: The Role of Place, Race, Religion, and Gender.* Cambridge: Cambridge University Press, 1999.

Roberts, Jon H. *Darwinism and the Divine in America: Protestant Intellectuals and Organic Evolution, 1859–1900.* Madison: University of Wisconsin Press, 1988.

Sandeen, Ernest R. *The Roots of Fundamentalism: British and American Millenarianism, 1800–1930.* Chicago: University of Chicago Press, 1970.

Schultz, Jack M. *The Seminole Baptist Churches of Oklahoma: Maintaining a Traditional Community.* Norman, Okla.: University of Oklahoma Press, 1999.

Smith, Gary S. *The Seeds of Secularization: Calvinism, Culture, and Pluralism in America, 1870–1915.* Grand Rapids: Eerdmans, 1985.

Wacker, Grant. *Augustus H. Strong and the Dilemma of Historical Consciousness.* Macon, Ga.: Mercer University Press, 1985.

———. *Heaven Below: Early Pentecostals and American Culture.* Cambridge: Harvard University Press, 2001.

Watts, Jill. *God, Harlem U.S.A.: The Father Divine Story.* Berkeley: University of California Press, 1991.

Chapter 13: Churches in the Gilded Age

Carter, Paul A. *The Spiritual Crisis of the Gilded Age.* DeKalb, Ill.: Northern Illinois University Press, 1971.

Coletta, Paolo E. *William Jennings Bryan.* 3 vols. Lincoln: University of Nebraska Press, 1964–1969.

Cross, Robert D., ed. *The Church and the City, 1865–1910.* Indianapolis: Bobbs-Merrill, 1967.

Dorn, Jacob H. *Washington Gladden: Prophet of the Social Gospel.* Columbus: Ohio State University Press, 1967.

———, ed. *Socialism and Christianity in Early Twentieth-Century America.* Westport, Conn.: Greenwood, 1998.

Dorrien, Gary J. *Soul in Society: The Making and Renewal of Social Christianity.* Minneapolis: Fortress, 1995.

Gibson, Scott. *A. J. Gordon: American Premillennialist.* Lanham, Md.: University Press of America, 2001.

Handy, Robert T., ed. *The Social Gospel in America, 1870–1920.* New York: Oxford University Press, 1966.

———. *Undermined Establishment: Church-State Relations in America, 1880–1920.* Princeton, N.J.: Princeton University Press, 1991.

Harper, Keith. *A Quality of Mercy: Southern Baptists and Social Christianity, 1890–1920.* Tuscaloosa, Ala.: University of Alabama Press, 1996.

Kilde, Jeanne H. *When Church Became Theatre: The Transformation of Evangelical Architecture and Worship in Nineteenth-Century America.* New York: Oxford University Press, 2002.

Luker, Ralph. *The Social Gospel in Black and White: American Racial Reform, 1885–1912.* Chapel Hill: North Carolina University Press, 1991.

Magnuson, Norris. *Salvation in the Slums: Evangelical Social Welfare Work, 1865–1920.* Metuchen, N.J.: Scarecrow, 1977.

May, Henry F. *Protestant Churches and Industrial America.* New York: Harper, 1949.

Miller, Randall M., and Thomas D. Marzik, eds. *Immigrants and Religion in Urban America.* Philadelphia: Temple University Press, 1977.

Miller, Timothy. *Following in His Steps: A Biography of Charles M. Sheldon.* Knoxville: University of Tennessee Press, 1987.

Minus, Paul N. *Walter Rauschenbusch: American Reformer.* New York: Macmillan, 1988.

Oberdeck, Kathryn J. *The Evangelist and the Impresario: Religion, Entertainment, and Cultural Politics in America, 1884–1914.* Baltimore: Johns Hopkins University Press, 1999.

Orsi, Robert A. *The Madonna of 115th Street: Faith and Community in Italian Harlem, 1880–1950.* 2d ed. New Haven: Yale University Press, 2002.

Putney, Clifford. *Muscular Christianity: Manhood and Sports in Protestant America, 1880–1920.* Cambridge: Harvard University Press, 2002.

Schenkel, Albert F. *The Rich Man and the Kingdom: John D. Rockefeller, Jr. and the Protestant Establishment.* Minneapolis: Augsburg Fortress, 1994.

Schweiger, Beth Barton. *The Gospel Working Up: Progress and the Pulpit in Nineteenth-Century Virginia.* New York: Oxford University Press, 2000.

Thomas, George M. *Revivalism and Cultural Change: Christianity, Nation Building, and the Market in the Nineteenth-Century United States.* Chicago: University of Chicago Press, 1989.

Wellman, James K. *The Gold Coast Church and the Ghetto: Christ and Culture in Mainline Protestantism.* Urbana, Ill.: University of Illinois Press, 1999.

White, Ronald C., Jr., and C. Howard Hopkins. *The Social Gospel: Religion and Reform in Changing America.* Philadelphia: Temple University Press, 1978.

Chapter 14: International Engagement and Mission

Ariel, Yaakov. *Evangelizing the Chosen People: Missions to the Jews in America, 1880–2000.* Chapel Hill: University of North Carolina Press, 2000.

Askew, Thomas A. "The New York Ecumenical Missionary Conference: A Centennial Reflection." *International Bulletin of Missionary Research* 24, no. 4 (October 2000): 146–54.

Bays, Daniel H., and Grant Wacker, eds. *The Foreign Missionary Enterprise at Home: Explorations in North American Cultural History.* Tuscaloosa, Ala.: University of Alabama Press, 2003.

Beaver, R. Pierce. *American Protestant Women in World Mission: A History of the First Feminist Movement in North America.* Grand Rapids: Eerdmans, 1980.

———. *Envoys of Peace: The Peace Witness in the Christian Mission.* Grand Rapids: Eerdmans, 1964.

Brackney, William H. "Helen B. Montgomery, 1861–1934; Lucy W. Peabody, 1861–1949." In *Mission Legacies,* edited by Gerald H. Anderson et al. Maryknoll, N.Y.: Orbis, 1994.

Brereton, Virginia Lieson. *Training God's Army: The American Bible School, 1880–1940.* Bloomington, Ind.: Indiana University Press, 1990.

Brown, G. Thompson. *Earthen Vessels and Transcendent Power: American Presbyterians in China, 1837–1952.* Maryknoll, N.Y.: Orbis, 1997.

Brumberg, Joan J. *Mission for Life: The Story of the Family of Adoniram Judson, the Dramatic Events of the First American Foreign Mission, and the Course of Evangelical Religion in the Nineteenth Century.* New York: Free Press, 1980.

Bush, Perry. *Two Kingdoms, Two Loyalties: Mennonite Pacifism in Modern America.* Baltimore: Johns Hopkins University Press, 1999.

Cavert, Samuel McCrea. *The American Churches in the Ecumenical Movement, 1900–1968.* New York: Association, 1968.

Clymer, Kenton J. *Protestant Missionaries in the Philippines, 1898–1916: An Inquiry into the American Colonial Mentality.* Urbana, Ill.: University of Illinois Press, 1986.

Harris, Paul. *Nothing but Christ: Rufus Anderson and the Ideology of Protestant Foreign Missions.* New York: Oxford University Press, 1999.

Hill, Patricia. *The World Their Household: The American Women's Foreign Mission Movement and Cultural Transformation, 1870–1922.* Ann Arbor, Mich.: University of Michigan Press, 1985.

Hopkins, C. Howard. *John R. Mott, 1865–1955: A Biography.* Grand Rapids: Eerdmans, 1979.

Hunter, Jane. *The Gospel of Gentility: American Women Missionaries in Turn-of-the-Century China.* New Haven: Yale University Press, 1984.

Hutchison, William R. *Errand to the World: American Protestant Thought and Foreign Missions.* Chicago: University of Chicago Press, 1987.

———. "A Moral Equivalent for Imperialism: Americans and Promotion of Christian Civilization, 1880–1910." In *Missionary Ideologies in the Imperialist Era: 1880–1920,* edited by Torben Christiansen and William R. Hutchison. Aarhaus, Denmark: Forlaget Aros, 1982.

Mackenzie, Kenneth M. *The Robe and the Sword: The Methodist Church and the Rise of American Imperialism.* Washington, D.C.: Public Affairs Press, 1961.

Martin, Sandy D. *Black Baptists and African Missions: The Origins of a Movement, 1880–1915.* Macon, Ga.: Mercer University Press, 1998.

Parker, Michael. *The Kingdom of Character: The Student Volunteer Movement for Foreign Missions, 1886–1926.* Lanham, Md.: University Press of America, 1998.

Porterfield, Amanda. *Mary Lyon and the Mount Holyoke Missionaries.* New York: Oxford University Press, 1997.

Robert, Dana Lee. *American Women in Mission*. Macon, Ga.: Mercer University Press, 1996.

———. *Occupy until I Come: A. T. Pierson and the Evangelization of the World*. Grand Rapids: Eerdmans, 2003.

Rouse, Ruth, and Stephen C. Neill, eds. *A History of the Ecumenical Movement, 1517–1948*. Philadelphia: Westminster, 1967.

Showalter, Nathan D. *The End of a Crusade: The Student Volunteer Movement for Foreign Missions and the Great War*. Lanham, Md.: Scarecrow, 1997.

Varg, Paul A. *Missionaries, Chinese, and Diplomats: The American Protestant Missionary Movement in China, 1890–1952*. Princeton, N.J.: Princeton University Press, 1958.

Yaremko, Jason M. *U.S. Protestant Missions in Cuba: From Independence to Castro*. Gainesville, Fla.: University Press of Florida, 2000.

Ziegler, Valerie H. *The Advocates of Peace in Antebellum America*. Bloomingon, Ind.: Indiana University Press, 1992.

Chapter 15: War, Prosperity, and Depression

Abrams, Douglas C. *Selling the Old-Time Religion: American Fundamentalism and Mass Culture, 1920–1940*. Athens, Ga.: University of Georgia Press, 2001.

Abrams, Ray H. *Preachers Present Arms*. Wellesley: Roundtable Press, 1933.

Blumhofer, Edith L. *Aimee Semple McPherson: Everybody's Sister*. Grand Rapids: Eerdmans, 1993.

Bruns, Roger A. *Billy Sunday and Big-Time American Evangelism*. Urbana, Ill.: University of Illinois Press, 2002.

Chatfield, Charles. *For Peace and Justice: Pacifism in America, 1914–1941*. Knoxville: University of Tennessee Press, 1971.

Cohen, Daniel. *Prohibition: America Makes Alcohol Illegal*. Brookfield, Conn.: Millbrook, 1995.

Conkin, Paul K. *When All the Gods Trembled: Darwinism, Scopes, and American Intellectuals*. Lanham, Md.: Rowman & Littlefield, 1998.

DeBerg, Betty. *Ungodly Women: Gender and the First Wave of American Fundamentalism*. Memphis: Fortress, 1990.

Dorsett, Lyle W. *Billy Sunday and the Redemption of Urban America*. Grand Rapids: Eerdmans, 1991.

Ernst, Eldon G. *Moment of Truth for Protestant America: Interchurch Campaigns Following World War I*. Missoula, Mont.: Scholars Press, 1974.

Glass, William R. *Strangers in Zion: Fundamentalists in the South, 1900–1950*. Macon, Ga.: Mercer University Press, 2001.

Handy, Robert T. *The American Religious Depression, 1925–1935*. Philadelphia: Fortress, 1968.

Hankins, Barry. *God's Rascal: J. Frank Norris and the Beginnings of Southern Fundamentalism*. Lexington: University Press of Kentucky, 1996.

Hart, D. G. *Defending the Faith: J. Gresham Machen and the Crisis of Conservative Protestantism in Modern America*. Baltimore: Johns Hopkins University Press, 1994.

Jacobsen, Douglas, and William Vance Trollinger Jr., eds. *Re-Forming the Center: American Protestantism 1990 to the Present*. Grand Rapids: Eerdmans, 1998.

Juhnke, James C. *Vision, Doctrine, War: Mennonite Identity and Organization in America, 1890–1930*. Scottdale, Pa.: Herald, 1989.

Kerr, K. Austin. *Organized for Prohibition: A New History of the Anti-Saloon League*. New Haven: Yale University Press, 1985.

Larson, Edward J. *Summer for the Gods: The Scopes Trial and America's Continuing Debate over Science and Religion*. New York: Basic Books, 1997.

Longfield, Bradley R. *The Presbyterian Controversy: Fundamentalists, Modernists, and Moderates*. New York: Oxford University Press, 1991.

Linkh, Richard M. *American Catholicism and European Immigration, 1900–1924*. Staten Island, N.Y.: Center for Migration Studies, 1975.

Machen, J. Gresham. *Christianity and Liberalism*. New York: Macmillan, 1923.

Miller, Robert M. *American Protestantism and Social Issues, 1919–1939*. Chapel Hill: University of North Carolina Press, 1958.

———. *Harry Emerson Fosdick: Preacher, Pastor, Prophet*. New York: Oxford University Press, 1985.

Piper, John F., Jr. *The American Churches in World War I*. Athens, Ohio: Ohio University Press, 1985.

———. *Robert E. Speer: Prophet of the American Church*. Louisville: Geneva Press, 2000.

Robert, Dana L. "The First Globalization: The Internationalization of the Protestant Missionary Movement between the World Wars." *International Bulletin of Missionary Research* 26, no. 2 (April 2002): 50–66.

Trollinger, William. *God's Empire: William Bell Riley and Midwestern Fundamentalism*. Madison: University of Wisconsin Press, 1990.

Tyrell, Ian R. *Women's World/Women's Empire: The Women's Christian Temperance Union in International Perspective, 1880–1930*. Chapel Hill: University of North Carolina Press, 1991.

Chapter 16: World War II and Religious Change

Berger, Peter L. *The Noise of Solemn Assemblies: Christian Commitment and the Religious Establishment in America*. Garden City, N.Y.: Doubleday, 1961.

Carpenter, Joel A. *Revive Us Again: The Awakening of American Fundamentalism*. New York: Oxford University Press, 1997.

Chadwick, Owen. *The Christian Church in the Cold War*. London: Penguin, 1993.

Dalhouse, Mark T. *An Island in the Lake of Fire: Bob Jones University, Fundamentalism, and the Separatist Movement*. Athens, Ga.: University of Georgia Press, 1996.

Dayton, Donald W., and Robert K. Johnson, eds. *The Variety of American Evangelicalism*. Knoxville: University of Tennessee Press, 1991.

Fox, Richard Wightman. *Reinhold Niebuhr.* New York: Harper, 1985.

George, Carol V. R. *God's Salesman: Norman Vincent Peale and the Power of Positive Thinking.* New York: Oxford University Press, 1993.

Herberg, Will. *Protestant, Catholic, Jew: An Essay in American Religious Sociology.* Garden City, N.Y.: Doubleday, 1955.

Loveland, Anne C. *American Evangelicals and the U.S. Military, 1942–1993.* Baton Rouge: Louisiana State University Press, 1997.

Lovin, Robin. *Reinhold Niebuhr and Christian Realism.* New York: Cambridge University Press, 1995.

Lynch, Christopher O. *Selling Catholicism: Bishop Sheen and the Power of Television.* Lexington: University Press of Kentucky, 1998.

Marsden, George. *Reforming Fundamentalism: Fuller Seminary and the New Evangelicalism.* Grand Rapids: Eerdmans, 1987.

Martin, William. *A Prophet with Honor: The Billy Graham Story.* New York: Morrow, 1991.

Meyer, Donald B. *The Protestant Search for Political Realism, 1919–1941.* Berkeley: University of California Press, 1961.

Nelson, Rudolph *The Making and Unmaking of an Evangelical Mind: The Case of Edward Carnell.* New York: Cambridge University Press, 1987

Niebuhr, Reinhold. *The Irony of American History.* New York: Scribners, 1952.

Ribuffo, Leo P. *The Old Christian Right: The Protestant Far Right from the Depression to the Cold War.* Philadelphia: Temple University Press, 1983.

Sittser, Gerald L. *A Cautious Patriotism: The American Churches and the Second World War.* Chapel Hill: University of North Carolina Press, 1997.

Stone, Jon R. *On the Boundaries of American Evangelicalism: The Postwar Evangelical Coalition.* New York: St. Martin's, 1997.

Synan, Vincent. *The Holiness-Pentecostal Tradition: Charismatic Movements in the Twentieth Century.* 2d ed. Grand Rapids: Eerdmans, 1997.

Warren, Heather A. *Theologians of a New World Order: Reinhold Niebuhr and the Christian Realists, 1920–1948.* New York: Oxford University Press, 1997.

Chapter 17: Unity and Service at Home and Abroad

Barrett, David B., George T. Kurian, and Todd M. Johnson, eds. *World Christian Encyclopedia: A Comparative Survey of Churches and Religions in the Modern World.* 2d ed. New York: Oxford University Press, 2001.

Bilheimer, Robert. *Breakthrough: The Emergence of the Ecumenical Tradition.* Geneva: World Council of Churches, 1989.

Carpenter, Joel A., and Wilbur R. Shenk, eds. *Earthen Vessels: American Evangelicals and Foreign Missions, 1880–1980.* Grand Rapids: Eerdmans, 1990.

Ellwood, Robert. *The Fifties: Spiritual Marketplace: American Religion in a Decade of Conflict.* New Brunswick, N.J.: Rutgers University Press, 1997.

Fey, Harold E., ed. *The Ecumenical Advance: A History of the Ecumenical Movement.* Vol. 2, 1948–1968. 3d ed. Geneva: World Council of Churches, 1993.

Hogg, William Richey. *Ecumenical Foundations: A History of the International Missionary Council and Its Nineteenth-Century Background.* New York: Harper, 1952.

Holifield, E. Brooks. *A History of Pastoral Care in America: From Salvation to Self-Realization.* Nashville: Abingdon, 1983.

Holmes, David L. *A Brief History of the Episcopalian Church.* Harrisburg, Pa.: Trinity Press, 1993.

Kane, J. Herbert. *A Concise History of the Christian World Mission: A Panoramic View of Missions from Pentecost to the Present.* Grand Rapids: Baker, 1978.

Lotz, David W., ed. *Altered Landscapes: Christianity in America, 1935–1985.* Grand Rapids: Eerdmans, 1989.

Neill, Stephen C. *Colonialism and Christian Missions.* New York: McGraw-Hill, 1966.

———. *A History of Christian Missions.* New York: Penguin, 1964.

Neils, Patricia, ed. *United States Attitudes toward China: The Impact of American Missionaries.* Armonk, N.Y.: M. E. Sharpe, 1990.

Nelson, E. Clifford, ed. *The Lutherans in North America.* Minneapolis: Fortress, 1980.

Reeves, Thomas C. *The Empty Church: The Suicide of Liberal Christianity.* New York: Free Press, 1996.

Rudnick, Milton L. *Fundamentalism and the Missouri Synod.* St. Louis: Concordia, 1966.

Sanneh, Lamin. *Translating the Message: The Missionary Impact on Cultures.* Maryknoll, N.Y.: Orbis, 1995.

Tucker, Ruth. *From Jerusalem to Irian Jaya: A Biographical History of Christian Missions.* Grand Rapids: Zondervan, 1983.

Verstraelen, F. J., et al., eds. *Missiology: An Ecumenical Introduction: Texts and Contexts of Global Christianity.* Grand Rapids: Eerdmans, 1995.

Yates, Timothy. *Christian Mission in the Twentieth Century.* New York: Cambridge University Press, 1994.

Young, J. William T. *The Congregationalists.* Westport, Conn.: Greenwood, 1998.

Chapter 18: Tradition under Fire

Ainzer, Thomas J. J., and William Hamilton. *Radical Theology and the Death of God.* Indianapolis: Bobbs-Merrill, 1966.

Bellah, Robert N., and Phillip E. Hammond. *Varieties of Civil Religion.* San Francisco: Harper, 1980.

Bendroth, Margaret L., and Virginia L. Brereton. *Women and Twentieth-Century Protestantism.* Urbana, Ill.: University of Illinois Press, 2002.

Cobb, John B., Jr., ed. *Christian Faith and Religious Diversity.* Minneapolis: Fortress, 2002.

Cox, Harvey. *The Secular City: Secularization and Urbanization in Theological Perspective.* New York: Macmillan, 1965.

Deedy, John, ed. *The Catholic Church in the Twentieth Century: Renewing and Reimaging the City of God.* Collegeville, Minn.: Liturgical Press, 2000.

Erickson, John A. *Orthodox Christians in America.* New York: Oxford University Press, 1999.

Fowler, Robert Booth. *A New Engagement: Evangelical Political Thought, 1966–1976.* Grand Rapids: Eerdmans, 1982.

———. *Unconventional Partners: Religion and Liberal Culture in the United States.* Grand Rapids: Eerdmans, 1989.

Gleason, Philip. *Keeping the Faith: American Catholicism Past and Present.* Notre Dame, Ind.: University of Notre Dame Press, 1987.

Greeley, Andrew M. *The Catholic Myth: The Behavior and Beliefs of American Catholics.* New York: Scribners, 1990.

Hughes, Thomas. *The Believer as Citizen: John Courtney Murray in a New Context.* Mahwah, N.J.: Paulist Press, 1993.

Hunter, James Davison. *American Evangelicalism: Conservative Religion and the Quandary of Modernity.* New Brunswick, N.J.: Rutgers University Press, 1983.

Klejment, Anne, and Nancy Roberts, eds. *American Catholic Pacifism: The Influence of Dorothy Day and the Catholic Worker Movement.* Westport, Conn.: Praeger, 1996.

Meyer, Donald B. *The Positive Thinkers: Popular Religious Psychology from Mary Baker Eddy to Norman Vincent Peale and Ronald Reagan.* Middletown, Conn.: Wesleyan University Press, 1988.

Miller, William D. *Dorothy Day: A Biography.* New York: Harper & Row, 1982.

Murray, John Courtney. *We Hold These Truths: Catholic Reflections on the American Proposition.* New York: Sheed and Ward, 1960.

Noll, Mark A., George M. Marsden, and Nathan O. Hatch. *The Search for Christian America.* 2d ed. Colorado Springs: Helmers and Howard, 1989.

Ogletree, Thomas W. *The Death of God Controversy.* Nashville: Abingdon, 1966.

Pierard, Richard V., and Robert D. Linder. *Civil Religion and the Presidency.* Grand Rapids: Zondervan, 1988.

Richey, Russell E., and Donald G. Jones, eds. *American Civil Religion.* New York: Harper, 1974.

Robbins, Thomas, and Dick Anthony, eds. *In Gods We Trust: New Patterns of Religious Pluralism in America.* New Brunswick, N.J.: Transaction Publications, 1991.

Roszak, Theodore. *The Making of a Counter-Culture.* Garden City, N.Y.: Doubleday, 1969.

Whitten, Marsha G. *All Is Forgiven: The Secular Message in American Protestantism.* Princeton, N.J.: Princeton University Press, 1993.

Wuthnow, Robert. *The Restructuring of American Religion: Society and Faith since World War II.* Princeton, N.J.: Princeton University Press, 1988.

Chapter 19: Urban Migration and Civil Rights

Angell, Stephen W., and Anthony B. Pinn, eds. *Social Protest Thought in the African Methodist Episcopal Church, 1862–1939.* Knoxville: University of Tennessee Press, 2001.

Avant, Albert. *The Social Teaching of the Progressive National Baptist Convention, Inc. since 1961: A Critical Analysis of the Least, the Less, and the Left-Out.* New York: Routledge, 2003.

Baer, Hans, and Merrill Singer. *African-American Religion in the Twentieth Century: Varieties of Protest and Accommodation.* Knoxville: University of Tennessee Press, 1992.

Bass, S. Jonathan. *Blessed Are the Peacemakers: Martin Luther King, Jr., Eight White Religious Leaders, and the "Letter from Birmingham Jail."* Baton Rouge: Louisiana State University Press, 2001.

Berman, William C. *The Politics of Civil Rights in the Truman Administration.* Columbus: Ohio State University Press, 1970.

Billingsley, Andrew. *Mighty like a River: The Black Church and Social Reform.* New York: Oxford University Press, 2002.

Branch, Taylor. *America in the King Years.* Vol. 1, *Parting of the Waters, 1954–1963;* Vol. 2, *Pillars of Fire, 1963–1965.* New York: Simon & Schuster, 1988, 1998.

Cone, James H. *Black Theology and Black Power.* New York: Seabury, 1969.

Emerson, Michael O., and Christian Smith. *Divided by Faith: Evangelical Religion and the Problem of Race in America.* New York: Oxford University Press, 2000.

Findlay, James F. *Church People in the Struggle: The National Council of Churches and the Black Freedom Movement, 1950–1970.* New York: Oxford University Press, 1993.

Frazier, E. Franklin. *The Negro Church in America.* New York: Schocken, 1964.

Garrow, David J. *Bearing the Cross: Martin Luther King, Jr. and the Southern Christian Leadership Conference.* New York: Morrow, 1986.

Gregg, Robert. *Sparks from the Anvil of Oppression: Philadelphia's African Methodists and Southern Migrants, 1890–1940.* Philadelphia: Temple University Press, 1993.

Hamilton, Charles V. *The Black Preacher in America.* New York: Morrow, 1972.

Harris, Michael W. *The Rise of Gospel Blues: The Music of Thomas A. Dorsey in the Urban Church.* New York: Oxford University Press, 1992.

Higginbotham, Evelyn Brooks. *Righteous Discontent: The Women's Movement in the Black Baptist Church, 1880–1920.* Cambridge: Harvard University Press, 1993.

Hopkins, Dwight N. *Down, Up, and Over: Slave Religion and Black Theology.* Minneapolis: Fortress, 2000.

King, Martin Luther, Jr. *The Papers of Martin Luther King, Jr.* Edited by Ralph Luker et al. Berkeley: University of California Press, 1992.

Ling, Peter J. *Martin Luther King, Jr.* New York: Routledge, 2002.

Lischer, Richard. *Preacher King: Martin Luther King, Jr. and the Word That Moved America.* New York: Oxford University Press, 1997.

Manis, Andrew M. *Southern Civil Religion in Conflict: Black and White Baptists and Civil Rights, 1947–1957.* Athens, Ga.: University of Georgia Press, 1987.

McGreevy, John. *Parish Boundaries: The Catholic Encounter with Race in the Twentieth-Century Urban North.* Chicago: University of Chicago Press, 1997.

Newman, Mark. *Getting Right with God: Southern Baptists and Desegregation, 1945–1995.* Tuscaloosa, Ala.: University of Alabama Press, 2001.

Paris, Arthur. *Black Pentecostalism: A Southern Religion in a Northern Urban World.* Amherst, Mass.: University of Massachusetts Press, 1982.

Pinn, Anthony B. *The Black Church in the Post-Civil Rights Era.* Maryknoll, N.Y.: Orbis, 2002.

Raboteau, Albert J. *African-American Religion.* New York: Oxford University Press, 1999.

Sanders, Cheryl. *Saints in Exile: The Holiness Pentecostal Experience in African-American Religion and Culture.* New York: Oxford University Press, 1996.

Turner, Richard B. *Islam in the African-American Experience.* Bloomington, Ind.: Indiana University Press, 1997.

Washington, Joseph R. *Black Religion: The Negro and Christianity in the United States.* Boston: Beacon, 1964.

West, Cornel. *Race Matters.* Boston: Beacon, 1993.

Chapter 20: From the Bicentennial to the New Millennium

Bellah, Robert, et al. *Habits of the Heart: Individualism and Commitment in American Life.* Berkeley: University of California Press, 1985.

Boyer, Paul S. *When Time Shall Be No More: Prophecy Belief in Modern America.* Cambridge: Harvard University Press, 1994.

Casanova, Jose. *Public Religions in the Modern World.* Chicago: University of Chicago Press, 1994.

Ellingsen, Mark. *The Evangelical Movement: Growth, Impact, Controversy, Dialog.* Minneapolis: Augsburg, 1998.

Eskridge, Larry, and Mark A. Noll, eds. *More Money, More Ministry: Money and Evangelicals in Recent North American History.* Grand Rapids: Eerdmans, 2000.

Green, John, James Guth, Corwin Smidt, and Lyman Kellstedt. *Religion and the Culture Wars.* Lanham, Md.: Rowman & Littlefield, 1996.

Green, John C., Mark J. Rozell, and Clyde Wilcox, eds. *The Christian Right in American Politics: Marching to the Millennium.* Washington, D.C.: Georgetown University Press, 2003.

Hangan, Tona J. *Redeeming the Dial: Radio, Religion, and Popular Culture in America.* Chapel Hill: University of North Carolina Press, 2002.

Hankins, Barry. *Uneasy in Babylon: Southern Baptist Conservatives and American Culture.* Tuscaloosa, Ala.: University of Alabama Press, 2002.

Harding, Susan Friend. *The Book of Jerry Falwell: Fundamentalist Language and Politics.* Princeton, N.J.: Princeton University Press, 2000.

Harper, Nile. *Urban Churches, Vital Signs: Beyond Charity toward Justice.* Grand Rapids: Eerdmans, 1997.

Harvey, Paul. *Redeeming the South: Religious Identities among Southern Baptists.* Chapel Hill: University of North Carolina Press, 2000.

Heclo, Hugh, and Wilfred McClay, eds. *Religion Returns to the Public Square: Faith and Policy in America.* Baltimore: Johns Hopkins University Press, 2003.

Housden, Roger. *Sacred America: The Emerging Spirit of the People.* New York: Simon & Schuster, 1999.

Ho-Youn Kwon, Kwang Chung Kim, and R. Stephen Warner. *Korean Americans and Their Religions: Pilgrims and Missionaries from a Different Shore.* University Park, Pa.: Penn State University Press, 2001.

Hunter, James Davison. *Culture Wars: The Struggle to Define America.* New York: Basic Books, 1991.

Lienesch, Michael. *Redeeming America: Piety and Politics in the New Christian Right.* Chapel Hill: University of North Carolina Press, 1993.

Marty, Martin E., and R. Scott Appleby, eds. *Fundamentalism Observed.* Chicago: University of Chicago Press, 1991.

McGirr, Lisa. *Suburban Warriors: The Origins of the New American Right.* Princeton, N.J.: Princeton University Press, 2001.

McGrath, Alister E. *Evangelicalism and the Future of Christianity.* Downers Grove, Ill.: InterVarsity, 1995.

———. *The Future of Christianity.* Oxford: Blackwell, 2002.

Murray Brown, Ruth. *For a Christian America: A History of the Religious Right.* New York: Prometheus Books, 2002.

Numbers, Ronald L. *The Creationists.* New York: Knopf, 1992.

Porterfield, Amanda. *The Transformation of American Religion: The Story of Late-Twentieth-Century Awakening.* New York: Oxford University Press, 2001.

Shibley, Mark A. *Resurgent Evangelicalism in the United States: Mapping Cultural Change since 1970.* Columbia, S.C.: University of South Carolina Press, 1997.

Smith, Christian. *American Evangelicalism: Embattled and Thriving.* Chicago: University of Chicago Press, 1998.

———. *Christian America? What Evangelicals Really Want.* Berkeley: University of California Press, 2000.

Szasz, Ferenc Morton. *Religion in the Modern American West.* Phoenix: University of Arizona Press, 2000.

Watt, David H. *A Transforming Faith: Explorations of Twentieth-Century American Evangelicalism.* New Brunswick, N.J.: Rutgers University Press, 1991.

Weigel, George. *Witness to Hope: The Biography of Pope John Paul II.* New York: Harper, 1999.

Wells, David F. *God in the Wasteland: The Reality of Truth in a World of Fading Dreams.* Grand Rapids: Eerdmans, 1994.

Wuthnow, Robert. *After Heaven: Spirituality in America since the 1950s.* Berkeley: University of California Press, 1998.

Wuthnow, Robert, and John H. Evans, eds. *The Quiet Hand of God: Faith-Based Activism and the Public Role of Mainline Protestantism*. Berkeley: University of California Press, 2002.

Zoller, Michael. *Washington and Rome: Catholicism in American Culture*. Notre Dame, Ind.: University of Notre Dame Press, 1999.

Epilogue

Barkun, Michael. *A Culture of Conspiracy: Apocalyptic Visions in Contemporary America*. Berkeley: University of California Press, 2003.

Clapp, Rodney. *Border Crossings: Christian Trespasses on Popular Culture and Public Affairs*. Grand Rapids: Brazos Press, 2000.

Clouse, Robert G., Robert N. Hosack, and Richard V. Pierard. *The New Millennium Manual: A Once and Future Guide*. Grand Rapids: Baker, 1999.

Gallup, George, Jr. *The Next American Spirituality: Finding God in the Twenty-First Century*. Colorado Springs: Cook Communications, 2001.

Jenkins, Philip. *The Next Christendom: The Coming of Global Christianity*. New York: Oxford University Press, 2002.

Kew, Richard. *Brave New Church: What the Future Holds*. Harrisburg, Pa.: Morehouse, 2001.

Marty, Martin E. *Politics, Religion, and the Common Good*. Somerset, N.J.: Jossey-Bass, 2002.

Miller, Donald E. *Reinventing American Protestantism: Christianity in the New Millennium*. Berkeley: University of California Press, 1997.

Noonan, John T., Jr. *The Lustre of Our Country: The American Experience of Religious Freedom*. Berkeley: University of California Press, 1998.

Penning, James M., and Corwin Smidt. *Evangelicalism: The Next Generation*. Grand Rapids: Baker, 2002.

Sanneh, Lamin. *Whose Religion Is Christianity? The Gospel beyond the West*. Grand Rapids: Eerdmans, 2003.

Stackhouse, John G., Jr. *Evangelical Landscapes: Facing Critical Issues of the Day*. Grand Rapids: Baker, 2002.

Webber, Robert E. *The Younger Evangelicals: Facing the Challenges of the New World*. Grand Rapids: Baker, 2002.

Williams, Rowan. *Writing in the Dust: After September 11*. Grand Rapids: Eerdmans, 2002.

Wolfe, Alan. *The Transformation of American Religion: How We Actually Live Our Faith*. New York: Free Press, 2003.

Index